Tackling Disadvantage and Underachievement in Schools

This practical resource shows what teachers can do to combat disadvantage and underachievement in schools and from early years to secondary education. Written by an experienced teacher, teacher educator and chartered psychologist, the book highlights effective teaching and learning methods that can be used to overcome barriers to learning, satisfy different learning needs and help students achieve their full potential.

Packed with up-to-date research, useful guidance and examples, the book explores what schools have done and what they can do without need for extra resourcing. It includes case studies that examine the types of underachievement patterns that are found across age ranges and, by detailing approaches in subject teaching, defines the nature of effective learning and shows what strategies can be used to meet these criteria. Moreover, the chapters provide:

- An exploration into the central needs of underachieving and disadvantaged learners across the ability range
- Information about how to audit the provision and the needs
- Accessible resources for the classroom changes that need to be made to the education and training of teachers

Tackling Disadvantage and Underachievement in Schools is essential reading for teachers in early years education and primary and secondary schools, teachers in training and their educators, as well as leaders, policymakers, researchers and anyone interested in improving performance in schools.

Diane Montgomery is professor emerita in education at Middlesex University, London, UK. She is a qualified and experienced teacher, teacher educator and chartered psychologist. She was recently awarded the 'Above and Beyond' Lifetime Achievement Award for her contribution to work with the more able and DME.

Tackling Disadvantage and Underachievement in Schools

A Practical Guide for Teachers

Diane Montgomery

Routledge
Taylor & Francis Group

LONDON AND NEW YORK

First published 2020
by Routledge
2 Park Square, Milton Park, Abingdon, Oxon, OX14 4RN

and by Routledge
52 Vanderbilt Avenue, New York, NY 10017

Routledge is an imprint of the Taylor & Francis Group, an informa business.

British Library Cataloguing-in-Publication Data
A catalogue record for this book is available from the British Library.

Library of Congress Cataloging-in-Publication Data
A catalog record for this book has been requested

ISBN: 978-0-367-42156-4 (hbk)
ISBN: 978-0-367-42158-8 (pbk)
ISBN: 978-0-367-82226-2 (ebk)

Typeset in Optima
by Apex CoVantage, LLC

Visit the eResource: www.routledge.com/9780367421588

Contents

Author biography

Diane Montgomery is professor emerita in education at Middlesex University, London, where she was formerly dean of faculty and head of the School of Education. She is a qualified and experienced teacher, teacher educator and chartered psychologist. Her PhD was on improving teaching and learning in schools and teacher education and training. At college, she won the Elsie Haydon-Carrier prize for teaching.

She was recently awarded the 'Above and Beyond' Lifetime Achievement Award for her contribution to work with the more able and DME. She has lectured widely internationally on these subjects and on positive appraisal and teaching methods.

She has written and tutored distance learning MA programmes in SEN, SpLD, SEBD, Gifted Education and Management Education for the university. The modules have now been converted to free study guides (www.ldrp.org.uk).

She has authored more than 35 books and many articles and runs the Learning Difficulties Research Project from her home, where she currently researches dyslexia and handwriting problems, dual and multiple exceptionality (DME), giftedness and underachievement.

Introduction

Disadvantage and underachievement are very broad ranging topics in social, educational, psychological, political and cultural terms. In the area of disadvantage, poverty, class and social perspectives form the main areas of concern and investigation. In research terms, these topics are frequently narrowed down in the UK to poverty defined as those children who are eligible for free school meals or school premium payments.

Most texts on underachievement (UAch) deal with it from the perspective of the needs of gifted children, those with high learning potential, when in fact children across the ability range are underachieving. This is perhaps because UAch is easier to identify in the more able. But in a series of over 1,250 classroom observation sessions across the age and ability ranges, it was estimated that 80 per cent of pupils in mainstream education were underachieving much of the time.

The perspective in this book is that the major area for intervention to raise the achievement of all pupils is to be found in the teaching and learning methods used by individual teachers.

Disadvantaged learners are particularly susceptible to become disruptive in didactic and coercive teaching and learning environments. Thus education needs to become more therapeutic and constructivist to promote their talents. The methods to be described and exemplified have been shown to be effective through teacher research in classrooms and belong to the constructivist rather than the didactic approach to teaching and learning.

In extensive meta-analyses of teaching and learning, Hattie (2018, 21) also concluded that, 'Teachers are among the most powerful influences in learning' and, 'Quality of teaching had the highest effect size of 0.77. 0.3 to 0.6 is a medium sized effect 0.4 is the average effect from a year's schooling' (p. 20). Other effect sizes he found were:

Student 0.39, Home 0.31, School 0.23, Teacher 0.47, Curricula 0.43, Teaching 0.43

> Visible learning occurs when there is deliberate practice aimed at mastery of obtaining a goal, when there is feedback given and sought, and when there are active, passionate and engaging people participating in the act of learning.
>
> (p. 21)

His data indicate that whilst ordinary teaching produces an uplift of one year per year of teaching, high quality teaching can almost double this. The disadvantaged and underachieving are those most in need of quality in teaching, and the following chapters seek to define and exemplify this.

Frequently schools are blamed for pupil underachievement because they do not hold high enough expectations for them. This book shows what teachers already do to combat underachievement and disadvantage and what more needs to be done that can enable them to do this through their teaching and learning strategies whilst not making their workload heavier. In essence, the headline banner is that 'the teacher is the key' to lifting both disadvantage and achievement. It is a phrase that is often used but not always borne out in practice.

This is not to ignore other important practices by schools, such as breakfast clubs, counselling and mentoring, pastoral care, monitoring, homework clubs and parent liaison. What this text will show is the powerful significance of the daily, hourly and minute-by-minute interactions between teachers and pupils in lifting underachievement from whatever cause. It can also provide opportunities for identifying a variety of other needs and designing appropriate interventions.

An example of a school's early intervention is the case of Ryan. Late in the reception year, Ryan was discovered stealing other children's lunches. He was generally overactive and inattentive and showed behavioural difficulties. The family had a history of low-achieving children coming through the school, and Social Services were frequently involved. Ryan was their fifth and most difficult child from the family so far. The class teacher asked about how to manage the problem behaviour. One brief classroom observation session was enough to identify his real problem. He had Kwashiorkor – he was starving. He had thin, stick-like arms and legs; swollen ankles; a pot-belly; dry, lank, and thinning hair; and scaly skin. No wonder he was taking and eating other children's food. He was on survival watch for food. The rest was irrelevant to him. The danger was that with the labels of 'thief' and 'behaviour problem', he would be set upon a career in disruption and criminality if he survived.

Immediately, the school ensured that he had some breakfast as soon as he arrived, and they gave him double helpings at lunchtime to tide him over until the next day. A pack of biscuits and some fruit were always discreetly available for him to dip into. Social Services found out that at home he was the youngest and least favoured. Meals were not provided, but food was left out on a shelf too high for him to reach, so the older children had to help him to it and did not always choose to do so, as they were also hungry. His was a clear example of child abuse by neglect. Once properly fed, his problem behaviours and his tense overactivity disappeared, and he began to learn and became a charming and quite clever boy to work with.

Teaching is about more than subject knowledge. At all levels of schooling, behavioural issues can be the overt signs of inner distress and conflict.

Chapter 1 presents an analysis of the internal and external factors involved in underachievement, the models of analysis and intervention and related research. By teasing out the different barriers to and gaps in learning, it is possible to establish a foundation for the development of more appropriate and effective teaching methods that satisfy different learning needs. These can then foster inclusion and personalisation. Practices used worldwide for lifting achievement are identified as well as the nature of effective schools according to official documents and reports.

Three major areas of concern are identified in this consideration of the origins of underachievement. They are socio-cultural, personal and school factors. These factors can conspire to provoke underachievement or prevent an individual's achievement at an appropriate level.

The chapter ends with a consideration of research on behaviour management and how this links with effective teaching provision and the development of social and self-management skills and autonomous or self-regulated learning and social skills.

Chapter 2 gives an analysis of the nature of disadvantage and its consequences for learners. It examines poverty from economic, social, cultural and subcultural perspectives. It shows the importance of language, gender, ethnicity, culture and behavioural interventions in overcoming disaffection and disadvantage. It suggests that education can compensate for society once the appropriate identification and intervention procedures are undertaken. The needs of 'interrupted learners' are examined as a special group that has been overlooked for too long.

In addition, the contribution of the 'school effect' is explored for the ways in which it can put some pupils at risk and how the needs of all pupils can be met, including black, Asian and minority ethnicity (BAME); refugee and immigrant children. The conclusion is that the education and training of teachers is not fit for purpose in the majority of cases and needs to be changed.

Chapter 3 presents a discussion of research and recommendations for overcoming UAch and disadvantage by schools, showing the underlying themes and results. Early years gaps, the reasons for them and remedial strategies that can close them are discussed. The reasons and concerns about boys' and girls' underachievement are addressed, and two example case studies are detailed, showing the needs and how teachers might have intervened.

Five audit steps are discussed, showing how the school provision can be assessed for basic skills needs and provision, teaching provision, motivation and communication, behaviour management and ways in which the audit results may be used to improve performance and support underachievers and all learners in a gender-equal context. It concludes with ways of auditing and reframing teaching and learning to personalise learning development and foster social constructivism and constructivist teachers.

Chapter 4 addresses the profiles and needs of three underachieving boys as they enter secondary schools and compares their capabilities and needs with cohorts of other pupils. The profiles show the main problem area was difficulty with writing skills, in particular, spelling and handwriting. The second section details the profiles of five referred underachieving girls from years 2 to 8. They too were all found to have writing difficulties of some kind, and the interventions they needed are detailed.

The final section analyses the mock examination answers of two referred BAME girls in year 11 to help the teacher and head understand why they have not performed as well as expected.

Chapter 5 deals with the early years gaps and how to address them so that disadvantaged children are not left a year behind by the end of their reception year. It involves changing the early years curriculum and general teaching methods, reverting to former best practice. It shows how and why the literacy gaps of disadvantaged groups arise and what needs to be done to close them in reading, spelling and handwriting. A similar investigation is made in relation to number, and girls' fear of maths is explained to show how it too can be overcome.

In Chapter 6, the literacy gap in older pupils is addressed by attention to higher-order compositional skills. Emphasis is placed on looking and learning, oracy practices, creative and problem-based activities that stimulate curiosity and motivate learning and writing across the curriculum.

Five projects are exemplified that were devised to improve boys' writing. These were from an educational consultant, the Primary National Strategy for Boy's Writing, the Oxfordshire Writing Project and the Kent 'Writing in the Air' project. The strategies can obviously be used or adapted to help all pupils.

The next section deals with strategies and examples that promote higher order reflective reading, critical comprehension and different levels of study skills. Seventeen different strategies are exemplified with curriculum materials and show how to foster collaborative work and self-regulated learning.

The final section details thinking skills models, and seven different programmes are exemplified and discussed.

In the final chapter, motivation to learn is identified as the key construct in changing the teaching of disadvantaged, underachieving and disaffected learners who engage in disruptive and attention-seeking behaviours. As didactic formal or transmission methods have not addressed these problems, other methods are reviewed. The research and practice shows that the most effective are problem-based strategies.

The model developed is one that is intrinsic to the teachers' daily provision to become a way of life in classrooms. This type of provision was termed 'brain engage' Cognitive Process Strategies, and they are inclusive and permit developmental differentiation. These were shown to be constructivist and to front-load learning. Ten strategies that form the cognitive and talking curricula are discussed and exemplified. They were developed to meet the criteria established in wider research on effective teaching and learning.

The postscript suggests forward directions in school development. Each chapter is supported by a CPD plan and resources for use by schools.

DfE research by Cullen et al. (2018, 57) on *Research to Understand Successful Approaches to Supporting the Most Academically Able Disadvantaged Pupils* found the following problems or barriers:

- Pupils' fear of failure
- Pupils' and parents' fear of the costs of higher education
- Pupils not knowing what they are really interested in academically
- Lack of awareness on the part of pupils and their parents of the wider world, leading to low aspirations
- Pupils' fear of leaving home and mixing with people not like them
- Lower aspirations at home and not working hard at home after school
- The difficulties schools face in trying to raise the aspirations of parents and pupils
- Difficulties in getting parental support
- Problems with engaging parents
- Hard to reach parents with low aspirations for their children
- Bright pupils hiding the fact as a strategy to avoid being isolated
- Lack of self-confidence
- Attendance issues
- Pupils refusing to accept help because they feel a stigma attached to the help

One interviewee summed all this up saying that it was 'aspirations at home – that's where the attitude to education comes from – schools can't change this,' (School 29 Interviewee 17).

What we observe in this report is what is actually going on in schools, not necessarily what should be going on, especially in terms of teaching quality. This is what the following chapters will try to address.

What should be going on was set out in education department documents, e.g. there are five interlinked aspects for development and which form the Institutional Quality Standards (DfES 2005):

- Assessment for learning (AfL)
- Effective teaching and learning
- A flexible curriculum – extension and enrichment
- Organising the school for a pupil focus
- Beyond the classroom – community involvement, partnerships

It was the DfES concepts of effective teaching and learning that were found to be most problematic and will be the subject of much of this book.

The identification of underachievement

Introduction

Underachievement is widely defined as the failure of individuals to live up to or meet their potential. Potential is usually estimated in relation to IQ, and IQ itself is usually defined as a general problem solving ability, the result of what has been learned in the environment without necessarily having been specifically taught. A rich experiential environment will provide greater opportunities for learning than a poor one. Thus, the home environment in addition to what schools offer can facilitate learning or diminish it. The 'home' effect, according to Ofsted (2006), is around 10 per cent and stronger than school effects. However what Ofsted can measure is somewhat limited. About half the home effect is created by parents taking their children to museums, galleries and other cultural experiences (Sutton Trust, 2010).

Figure 1.1 represents the major internal and external factors that have been identified as contributing to underachievement across the ability and age

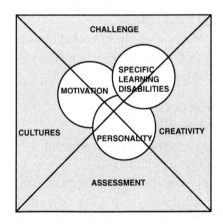

Figure 1.1 Internal and external barriers creating underachievement

ranges. The degree and pattern of the effects of each varies according to the individual.

Models used in analysis and intervention

The following models represent different approaches to analysis and intervention:

- **'Within child' model** – the pupil is a problem pupil, and all the reasons are to be found in his or her character and makeup. It is a defective personality-type model.
- **Social model** – all the difficulties observed are ascribed to the influences of poor housing, social disadvantage and poverty. If these were set right, then the child's behaviour would automatically improve.
- **Ecological model** – this is the newest approach in the field and argues that the interaction of personal, social and contextual factors all contribute to create or remove the 'problem' and difficulties or increase/reduce the challenging behaviour. This is an interactionist model.
- **Pedagogical model** – this is the approach that argues that teachers, teaching method, school ethos and style all interact to create the UAch and any behaviour difficulties observed. Improvements in these can change the behaviour of even the most disaffected pupils over a period of time. It can be regarded perhaps as a more focused interactive model.

Sometimes behaviour difficulties are the only sign that a pupil is underachieving, especially if the work set is completed and only at the same standard as that of peers.

High learning potential

Another way of looking at the problem of UAch is to think of an individual's potential for learning. IQ may be one indication of this, but in the presence of a more modest IQ, some children may nevertheless have high learning potential (HLP). It may be this that enables them to succeed in life if not in school. They may display what we recognise as wisdom as young as five years old, seeming much more mature than peers.

Particular types of learning disability, such as in language, literacy, visuo-spatial and coordination difficulties may lower IQ subtest scores just as a poor socio-cultural environment can. This may not affect the learning potential in other spheres. If the learning disabilities can be overcome, the true learning potential may be revealed and achieved. These are regarded in the UK as learners with 'additional needs', formerly termed 'special educational needs and disabilities' (SEND).

An IQ is difficult to establish with accuracy in pre-school, and the tests are time-consuming to administer. Early years teachers are often reluctant to engage with such measures. But it is evident that there is a need for some early and easily accessible indicator(s) that will alert educators to high potential and also potential problems. It will enable them to organise additional support, compensation or intervention. Even later when some stability is established, IQ may not be the best predictor of later achievement with a correlation of +0.6 or a 36 per cent predictive capacity (Labon, 1973, McCoach et al., 2017).

The English Foundation Year assessments (DfE, 2014a) failed to identify 'gifted' children in reception, much less their potential underachievement. The baseline assessments for 4–5-year-olds in England and Wales asked teachers to assess if each child could do the following:

- Recognise and write numbers 1–10
- Write his or her own name and recognise letters by shape and sound (all?)
- Concentrate without supervision for 10 minutes (on what?)

Not surprisingly, the results failed to identify gifted pupils at the start of school, given the nature of the questions and lack of relevant criteria.

Sutton Trust Research (2010) identified 'Early Years Gaps' in children growing up in the UK and found that children of the poorest fifth of families were already nearly a year (11.1 months) behind those children from middle-income families in vocabulary tests by age 5, when most children start school. In later Sutton Trust research, Jerrim (2013) found that disadvantaged learners were 11 months behind peers in reading by the end of the foundation year (reception) and never managed to catch up. It means that using early reading as an indicator of potential achievement as some teachers do will miss the disadvantaged learners and learners with dyslexia with high potential.

A longitudinal study of intellectual ability and academic achievement (McCoach et al., 2017) was the Fullerton Study. It examined the relationship between intelligence and school achievement from elementary through secondary school in the US. The findings showed that the students' achievement was highly stable across the school years. The researchers found that after seven years intelligence was not predictive of either reading or mathematics achievement when prior achievement was accounted for.

> Students who enter school with strong academic skills tend to maintain their academic advantage throughout their elementary and secondary school careers.
>
> (p. 7)

They concluded that students who enter school at a disadvantage are likely to lag behind their peers throughout elementary and secondary school. Thus, high-quality learning experiences are essential for all children, especially in the foundation year, to gain academic success and if we wish to narrow the achievement gaps among sub-groups.

Even when IQs are established later, a year 7 pupil with an IQ score of 115 but with dyslexia, spelling and/or handwriting difficulties or from a disadvantaged environment will be likely to have a learning potential 10 points higher. A threshold level of only 120 IQ points was found to be necessary for great creative achievements (Torrance, 1963; Silverman, 2002).

Threshold levels are however suspect. This is because of the built-in errors of measurement in the tests. In the best constructed, individually administered tests, this standard error (SE) is between plus and minus 3 and 4 points. It means that a measured IQ of 120 can be between 115 and 124 points. Group tests have higher SEs and at the best this is plus or minus 5 points.

The policy (DfEE, 1999) that schools should identify the top 5 per cent by ability in each school and have a reserve or shadow register also proved problematic. This was because the cognitive abilities tests that are used by many schools will miss many of the more able because of the SE and because literacy skills are involved in reading and responding to the test items. Primary schools use SATs levels to identify the more able. The mean level of achievement expected in year 6 is level 4, and the more able are expected to achieve level 5 and the most able level 6 or more. These levels are vulnerable to error because literacy skills are intimately involved in English, maths and science, although maths maybe less susceptible until problems are set in words. Research on high ability (Tannenbaum, 1993) recommended that for gifted programmes the top 15 per cent by ability plus the top 15 per cent by school achievements should be selected, and even then, many of the most able would be missed. Gagne's (1995) research showed that 40 per cent of pupils in schools would qualify as potentially gifted and talented. The fact that many still regard a figure of 1 or 2 per cent of pupils as potentially gifted shows a large gap in our expectations.

Lower attainment

After the introduction of the comprehensive system of education in the 1970s, it became impossible to lecture about giftedness and talent and in a series of in-service training courses in Surrey at their Teacher's Centres, for example, the courses could not be called 'gifted education,' 'education for the more able,' or even 'mixed-ability teaching.' They had to be termed 'study skills' courses. Even publishers would not accept 'gifted' in their titles. Underachieving more able pupils were gathered up in provision for 'lower attainers' (Montgomery, 1998). This term includes the widest range of pupils, the slower learners, the average, and the gifted, all of whom may be underachieving or just not meeting the targets set for them.

The Nebraska Starry Night (NSN) Project (Griffin et al., 1995) was an example of authentic assessment by teachers in the early identification of more able/creative children from non-traditional backgrounds. It is a general screening device expected to identify 12 to 15 per cent of children functioning at above grade level. There is no precise score or label. After factor analyses, four profiles or types emerged:

- Type One: The knowing, verbal, independent child
- Type Two: The curious, moving, and doing explorer child
- Type Three: The quiet, focused, unexpectedly humorous child
- Type Four: The socially interactive, engaging, 'on stage' child

A second result from the three-year research was that teachers with a directive, behaviour-based approach (traditional non-constructivist) could identify children showing early signs of able/creative behaviour. Teachers in child-centred, constructivist classrooms had more opportunities to identify able/creative behaviours and therefore found more children with these abilities.

NSN takes skill and training to use and is an assessment that can require considerable observation time to achieve with accuracy. In our current objectives-based assessment climate in the UK, it would not be feasible to use NSN, but the profiles are worth keeping in mind. Authentic assessment is an important consideration, and it matters greatly that an open cognitive- and problem-based curriculum is on offer so that high ability as well as creativity can be identified. There are now many examples of these types of initiatives in the gifted education field, such as Maker's DISCOVER and REAP projects (2013), Wallace's TASC project (2009), Warwick's (2009) REAL project initially with BAME groups and McCluskey et al.'s (2000) 'Lost Prizes' for disadvantaged groups. What is needed is a strategy that will reveal HLP or some aspect of it for the regular classroom teacher. It needs to be one that does not require a special training programme or materials other than normal classroom activities.

Intrinsic factors

Motivation and personality factors

In a longitudinal study of a gifted cohort of 1500 pupils with a mean IQ of 154, Terman (1925) estimated that only 1 of them would be remembered in 100 years and perhaps 6 might become national figures (Terman, 1954). Freeman (1991, 2010) found a similar lack of very high achievement in her longitudinal study of a gifted cohort of children in England.

The most successful achievers did however share some common attributes, according to Terman. They were emotionally stable; had high degrees of motivation, interest and persistence; and were self-confident enough to pursue their ideas when others did not agree with them. Lower achievement was associated with a lack of these factors and family disruption. In both the UK and the US, the ability to pay for private education and private personal tuition appears to be a significant factor in achieving high-status jobs whatever the level of ability.

Analysis by Cropley (1994) found that there was no true giftedness without creativity. Creativity however is difficult to measure as potential but is evident in productive problem solving. It is both an intrinsic and an extrinsic factor in that it includes an individual's creative potential and abilities and the opportunities for its development and facilitation in the home, school and environment.

Learning disability

This intrinsic factor generally termed 'learning difficulties' in the UK would appear to be particularly problematic to identify in the literacy area before the age of 7 years. This is when failure to learn to read at the expected level becomes evident despite normal teaching methods and additional support. This is a traditional view established in the UK for Early Years education in the Bullock Report (DES, 1975) and endorsed since by dyslexia researchers and tutors. This will need to be reviewed in subsequent chapters.

Children with HLP and dyslexia are regarded as twice exceptional (2E). Up to 50 per cent of children with a special need, such as dyslexia, may also have another co-occurring learning difficulty/disability, such as handwriting problems (including developmental coordination disorder, or DCD), or attention deficit hyperactivity disorder (ADHD) and autism spectrum disorders (ASD) (co-occurring at 30 per cent) making their condition dual and multiply exceptional (DME).

Dyslexia is a severe literacy problem in reading *and* spelling found across the ability range. In the UK, it makes up 10 per cent of the school population with 4 per cent being severe cases (BDA, 2019a). Higher numbers can be found in disadvantaged populations. Other co-occurring disabilities can be Asperger syndrome and ADHD, but their incidence is much smaller in the order of 1 and 3 per cent of the school population respectively. Their impact is more social and behavioural, whereas literacy difficulties and handwriting problems can have a more profound effect on school achievement. Literacy and developmental coordination skills will need further consideration in later chapters.

Writing problems

Silverman (2004) showed that the most common factor in underachievement of the gifted worldwide was a problem with writing. This is illustrated in the following checklist that a variety of researchers have validated. The general characteristics of underachieving gifted students were found to be

- Large gap between oral and written work
- Failure to complete schoolwork
- Poor execution of work and avoidance of tasks
- Negativism and lack of motivation
- Lack of concentration especially in didactic sessions
- Difficulties with peers and group work
- Low self-image and unrealistic goals
- Poor attitudes to school and dissatisfaction with it
- Only satisfactory work in most areas in the presence of high ability

(Whitmore, 1982; Butler-Por, 1987, 1993;
Montgomery, 2000, 2019; Wallace, 2000; Silverman, 2004)

These students did not have a diagnosis of dyslexia. Writing problems however appear to be a hidden barrier to achievement in schools across the age and ability ranges (Montgomery, 1998, 2009, 2017a), and it is the poorly developed lower order (basic) skills of handwriting and spelling that are the key contributors (Berninger, 2008, 2015). These poor basic skills lower the level and quality of compositional or higher order skills and achievement. This occurs throughout school Key Stages 1 to 4 and into degree-level programmes (Montgomery, 2000; Berninger, 2008; Connelly et al., 2005).

For example, at year 7 (age 12 years), it was found that over 30 per cent of children showed spelling and/or handwriting difficulties in three disadvantaged area schools (Montgomery, 2008a, N=531). Boys' handwriting skills were significantly poorer than those of girls. In SATs, at Key Stage 2 boys' (Year 6) writing has always been found to be significantly poorer than girls' (DfE, 2018). Thus by investigating writing in Key Stages 1 and 2, it may be possible to find indicators for later UAch.

Extrinsic factors – teachers and teaching

Traditionally it is taught that the teacher is

1   In authority, in a legal sense, and must preserve the safety of the pupils and take charge of them

2   An authority, that she or he should be an expert in the knowledge and skills required by the pupils and has the ability to transmit these

3   Charismatic, that she or he should have those qualities that will inspire and cause children to want to learn

In practice, to succeed, a teacher needs to demonstrate each of them. The designation of 'teacher' no longer confers authority and respect. The pupils, paradoxically, although sometimes hostile still hold these expectations of the teacher's role but make each new teacher undergo the '*rites des passages*' of earning what in the past was ascribed to them.

Coming to terms with the different demands of individuals, small groups and class groups in relation to role and style is an important stage in the teacher's development. Learning to identify and deal successfully with the 'pack instinct' and the development of dominance hierarchies and maladaptive behaviours is now part of many teachers' daily tasks. It can create high levels of stress and induce fatigue in addition to that created by preparation and the teaching itself.

Although charisma is a very helpful attribute, it has inherent dangers for pupils. A 45-minute English lesson was observed when a group of Year 8s were entranced and hung upon the teacher's every word as he went over an examination paper. We were totally entertained but learned not one thing. We should have protested but were beguiled. At a later stage, pupils may make option choices on the basis of the charismatic qualities of their teachers. Their lives from that point may be directed to specific goals not necessarily related to need or suitability. It seems that to motivate pupils to learn, charisma is still paramount but has dangers that teachers should protect pupils by discussing the issue with them referring to 'likes', models and suitable career pathways.

In addition, pupils also have high expectations of their teachers, and even though they behave badly, they despise the teachers who cannot manage them and then behave worse to provoke them. Once this downward spiral has begun, it can take months to recover the ground even though one has learned from the initial mistakes. In terms of teacher training, for this reason, it is helpful to have teaching practices in different schools to gain a fresh start.

What we know about pedagogy and the more able is that whatever they learn, the opportunities for cognitive challenge and stretch are essential, as they also are for creativity and independent study (Renzulli and Reis, 2008; Montgomery, 2008b; Wallace et al., 2009), for example. Interestingly, the same is true of all learners, including slower learners (Montgomery, 1990). If the pedagogy is not effective in offering these opportunities, pupils can become disaffected and vulnerable to underachievement. The underachievement may cause the behaviour to deteriorate into 'acting out' or 'acting in' patterns. Thus, pedagogy can be a major component in arresting and lifting underachievement and improving behaviour. One major component in the teacher-pupil interaction is that the teacher should hold high expectations of the pupils and believe in them so that achievement should become the self-fulfilling prophesy (Rosenthal and Jacobsen, 1968; Good and Brophy, 1986).

Practices identified for lifting UAch worldwide

In a critical review of the literature on able underachievers, Reis and McCoach (2000) came to the conclusion (as had Passow (1990) a decade earlier) that underachievement was a complex area about which there had been a dearth of research. A review by Delisle and Berger (2009) confirmed four major effective strategies for intervention in underachievement from Whitmore (1982), Rimm (1986) and Silverman (1989). These were as follows:

- **Supportive strategies** – represented in flexible, respectful, non-authoritarian, questioning environments
- **Intrinsic strategies** – those that are motivating, raise self-esteem, and are intellectually stimulating
- **Remedial strategies** – responsive to pupils' needs and difficulties and so help them to overcome them and bring them up to grade level
- **Compensatory strategies** – using areas of strength to circumvent weaknesses

Now we can add to this group **assistive technologies**

What these reflect is that the basic provision is deemed correct and appropriate, and it is the individual underachiever who must be helped to change or adapt to it, **'the within child'** model. I think we need to question this approach and suggest it is traditional provision itself that needs to be changed or challenged because it has permitted or even provoked underachievement. In this respect, inclusive teaching and learning require a 21st-century style of teaching rather than the 19th-century didactics that form the training basis of many teachers' experience. Twenty-first-century pupils need 21st-century methods. This will be discussed and exemplified in later chapters.

In the intervening period between the Reis and McCoach review and now, the position has begun to change in the UK. We still have a dearth of research, especially on UAch uplift, but we now understand much more about underachievement and its origins. What has been learnt is that there need to be some fundamental changes to ITT and CPD in order that schools address the problems better than they currently do. More recent case study research by Wallace et al. (2009), outlined in a later section, has shown that successful schools that use a range of appropriate strategies can address and overcome underachievement.

Effective schools – the official position, 1994 DfEE circular: pupils with problems

These build on the recommendations of the Elton Report (1989) and good practice from HMI reports. They regard good behaviour and discipline as essential to effective teaching and learning. Five key elements were identified in Pupil Behaviour and Discipline as follows:

- Whole school policies must be developed on behaviour and discipline. These must be underpinned by rules of conduct developed by staff in consultation with parents and pupils and provide pupils with clear boundaries of acceptable behaviour.
- Positive behaviour is to be encouraged, and there must be coherent and consistent policies for rule breaking.
- A moral code conducive to a respect for others must be developed through the curriculum and in social interaction between pupils and teachers.
- Students must have effective teaching that provides differentiated learning experiences according to pupils' needs and effective classroom management.
- Positive behaviour should be encouraged through the use of formal rewards and other forms of positive reinforcement. When special problems occur, such as bullying, truancy, racial harassment and sexually inappropriate behaviours, prompt action is required.

The Steer Report (DCFS, 2009) 'learning behaviour: lessons learned'

Evidence collected by a group of professionals endorsed these views and made similar recommendations to schools. This final report, the fourth in the series starting in 2005, by Sir Alan Steer was published in April 2009. It emphasised that most pupils behave well in school, and it is rare to find challenging behaviours. Those who do engage in challenging behaviour do not do so all the time.

The report found that the small minority who engage in problem behaviours were usually from difficult and disadvantaged family circumstances, and their needs were becoming increasingly complex. Their needs were to be distinguished from the general 'irritating low level nuisance behaviours' also identified by the Elton Report and account needed to be taken that childhood is a period when mistakes are made and lessons learned.

School leaders did not make sufficient use of the powers that they had, according to this report. They needed to intervene early and not permit problem pupils to disturb the learning of other pupils. They needed to make use of 'withdrawal' sooner and more frequently than they did. Every school needed a 'withdrawal room' or rooms to use as a temporary measure to stop class disruption.

The strongest recommendation among many in the report was that **schools be required to have a learning and teaching policy that underpinned the behaviour policy**. Schools had more than 70 policies but had never yet been required to have one on learning and teaching! Ofsted surveys and inspections had consistently shown that the quality of teaching and learning experienced by pupils directly affected their behaviour in schools and classrooms.

Chapter 4 of the report listed the effective policies that schools operated, and these consisted of positive behaviour management strategies, consistent and supportive discipline, quality in teaching and learning, whole school staff training, good home-school communication and co-operation and early interventions before problems grew out of proportion.

The report also suggested that PRUs and special schools catering for pupils with SEBD should become training schools. One hundred and thirty pages of the 200-page report were Appendices A to G and were useful, for they contained an example teaching and learning policy, what works in schools list and a rights and responsibilities chart.

Recommendations from the 2.1.1 Steer Report (DCFS, 2009b, 15) include:

'Schools should review their behaviour, learning and teaching policies and undertake an audit of pupil behaviour'

Section 24. 'In undertaking the audit schools should reflect on ten aspects of school practice that, when effective, contribute to the quality of pupil behaviour:

- A consistent approach to behaviour management, teaching and learning
- School leadership
- Classroom management, learning and teaching
- Rewards and sanctions
- Behaviour strategies and the teaching of good behaviour
- Staff development and support
- Pupil support systems
- Liaison with parent and other agencies
- Managing pupil transitions, and
- Organisation and facilities'

Section 35

- 'Research evidence shows that where pupils are allowed to determine where they will sit, their social interactions can inhibit teaching and create behaviour problems

- Ensure that teachers build into their lessons opportunities to receive feedback from pupils on their progress and their future learning needs
- Recognise that pupils are knowledgeable about their school experience, and have views about what helps them learn and how others' poor behaviour stops them from learning; and
- Give opportunities for class, year and school councils to discuss and make recommendations about bullying and the effectiveness of rewards and sanctions.'

Section 36

- 'We believe homework can be a major source of challenge that often results in confrontation. Planning homework carefully and setting it early in a lesson can significantly increase the number of pupils who subsequently have a clear understanding of what is expected of them. This is particularly helpful to pupils with special educational needs who can be disadvantaged by the volume of work presented.'

Section 37

- 'As experienced practitioners we know many schools have excellent systems in place to reward good work and behaviour. However we believe some schools use sanctions to enforce good behaviour but neglect the use of appropriate rewards.'

Section 38

- 'Schools should provide a range of opportunities in which pupils can excel and be rewarded. Of equal importance is a practical set of sanctions that deal appropriately with poor behaviour.'

As can be seen, this report contains a good outline of best practice, and it is backed up by research evidence and quotes from teachers. It is somewhat different in tone and content from many government reports because it was compiled by a committee of professionals knowledgeable about the field not 'placemen and women'.

In 2019, concerns are once again being raised about the number of pupils being excluded from schools, often to massage the league table examination results, and the inadequate provision available for them to be assessed and supported by their local authorities. The PRU (Pupil Referral Unit) assessment provision that was once thought to be the answer was not found to be meeting the needs. It has meant that many of these pupils were receiving only a few hours' tuition per week and could rove the area and be recruited by gangs to engage in criminal activities.

Effective schools and behaviour management strategies

Wilson and Evans' (1980) survey found that instead of psychodynamics, special schools and units for children with EBD focused on

- Reversing the child's expectancy of failure
- Counselling, both directive and Rogerian
- Help with basic literacy and numeracy
- General education as therapy

These pupils were seen to need steady routines, structure and discipline.

In *Managing Behaviour in Schools*, Charlton and David (1993) gave a list of 11 key effectiveness factors that characterised schools that successfully managed difficult behaviour as follows:

1 Effective, consultative style of leadership of head teacher and senior management team that takes into account pupil and parent opinion
2 Clear school-wide policies on education and behaviour management that are meaningful to pupils and consistently and humanely enforced
3 Differential curricula
4 High but not unreasonable academic expectations
5 Positive attitudes to pupil behaviour with more rewards than sanctions
6 High professional standards (efficient planning, setting, marking, punctuality)
7 Skilful teaching that arouses pupil interest and motivates
8 Preventative rather than reactive strategies to classroom disruption
9 Supporting and respectful relationships between all adults and pupils in the school system
10 Involvement of pupils in school's life: giving pupils responsibility
11 An effective system of pastoral care

Cole et al. (1998) analysed data from a survey of 156 EBD special schools during 1996/7 containing 7000 pupils to try to identify factors that made for good practice and effectiveness. From this text, mainstream teachers could learn much that was applicable to managing difficult behaviours. Not least in importance is the following quote:

> Our study clearly shows that good pedagogy provided by teachers, secure in their subject knowledge, well organised, matched to individual needs and based on the 'plus one principle' . . . does elicit good responses, lessening the tendencies of most pupils to engage in disruptive behaviour in class.
>
> (Cole et al., 1998, 153–154)

They go on to confirm the work of other researchers that

> Their previous disruption often appears to be a response to imperfect environments.
>
> (Cole et al., 1998, 154)

For imperfect environments, they cited a lack of differentiated and skilled teaching.
This is particularly crucial when the survey found that 50 per cent of the pupils in the special schools were 'significant underachievers' (p. 35). They found the following results in relation to ability levels of the pupils with EBD:

Significant Learning Difficulties not caused by EBD	c 18 per cent
Mild Leaning Difficulties not caused by EBD	c 25 per cent
Of average ability	c 47 per cent
Of above average ability	c 10 per cent

(Cole et al., 1998, 35)

In addition to the underachievement of the pupils, particularly in the core subjects English, maths and science, Cole et al. recorded a pattern of characteristics that make helping these pupils especially difficult, for example,

> Short attention span, low self esteem, fear of new material which might lead to more failure, mercurial temperament, distractibility, reluctance and difficulties in putting pen to paper or exploring their feelings.
>
> (p. 35)

It can be seen that these traits are also to be found in pupils with EBD in mainstream school; thus the education they are offered needs to be therapeutic (Mongon and Hart, 1989). Educational therapy is of necessity positive and supportive, builds self-esteem, reteaches basic skills where necessary and improves academic achievement, allowing pupils to catch up. It also must connect the learning experiences in the curriculum with opportunities for exploring, understanding and expressing feelings. They need to gain metacognitive insights and controls in all aspects of their mental and physical lives.

Very often, art and craft are considered to be those offering most therapeutic value (91 per cent of Cole & Vissers et al.'s study agreed with this, p. 101) with PE (53 per cent), English/reading (42 per cent) and music (41 per cent). However, we need to regard all subjects as offering and providing significant opportunities for such therapy. It is surprising to find drama, PSHE design and technology and IT were in the 32 to 21 per cent band with maths 12 per cent and science 9 per cent.

The high therapeutic value of art is significant, and there is a combination of likely reasons that include the opportunities for self-expression, quiet reflection and individual discussions with teacher and peers and the lack of need for reading and writing, time to complete work at one's own speed and so on.

A number of other studies have shown how boys can be helped (Kent Co. Co., 2003; Wilson, 2019), but a major concern still is how to help the disadvantaged. The Ofsted (1996) reports on Traveller children and helping minority/ethnic groups (1999) and the research of Jordan (2001) are relevant as is research by Wallace et al. (2008) on *Raising the Achievement of Able, Gifted and Talented Pupils within an Inclusive School Framework*. This research took place in six primary and six secondary schools identified by inspections and winning the NACE Challenge Award as successful in identifying and overcoming underachievement. The purpose of the research was to identify common factors that enabled them to lift achievement. These factors were

- Posts of special responsibility
- Delegated but shared responsibility
- Influence of lead teachers
- Close primary-secondary cluster liaison
- Continuous assessment of pupil progress
- National Quality Standards and NACE Challenge Award
- Continuous monitoring of CPD

Could it be feasible to identify a lead teacher on lower attainment? This would be someone who would do the research and help the school develop solutions in lifting achievement across the years, arrange the CPD and undertake the monitoring.

The NACE research also found there was

> Visionary, distributed leadership: Practical, hands-on leadership, shared communication, an ethos of inclusive community, strong pupil and parent/governor voice – ownership, personalised learning, an ethos of celebration of effort, transition and transfer strategies.
>
> There was regular monitoring of individual achievement, regular sharing of pupil progress, avoidance of repetition of skills and content, close communication with other phases, parents, schools.

Potential underachievement was prevented by designating staff with special responsibilities; by whole-school planning for differentiation and personalised learning; strong pupil voice and ownership; collaborative, networked e-learning; an extended range of teaching and learning strategies; emphasis on problem-solving and thinking skills; flexible grouping and a negotiated curriculum; CPD; extensive creative cross-cultural and out-of-school-hours activities; negotiated achievement targets and personal mentors; and open, regular dialogue with pupils, teachers and parents.

There was systematic recording and communication of pupil progress; careful avoidance of repetition of skills and content; curriculum assessment of pupils' questioning, problem-solving and thinking skills; attention to social and emotional aspects of development and independent learning; pupil choice, self-assessment and peer assessment; active participation in decision-making.

These attributes compare favourably with the DFES (2009c) nine key features in a practical guide to personalised learning, e.g. 1 High-quality teaching and learning, 2 Target setting and tracking, 3 Focused assessment, 4 Intervention, 5 Pupil grouping, 6 The learning environment, 7 Curriculum organisation, 8 The extended curriculum, and 9 Supporting children's wider needs.

Knowing what makes ineffective provision is also helpful, and Kerry (1983) identified some results of it. Ineffective or inadequate teaching strategies of themselves can create a series of effects that can lead to underachievement, and disadvantaged groups are particularly vulnerable in such circumstances. Kerry found five main features of such lessons:

- **Dead time** between finishing one activity and starting another, which is spent waiting for attention or distracting others. Bright pupils work very quickly and so make a lot of dead time. Slow pupils work superficially and soon finish or get stuck.
- **Boredom** sets in during dead time or in rote activities and leads to pupils finding other ways of entertaining themselves and others.
- **Lack of interest** and relevance of topics not made clear lead to more boredom.
- **Motivation**—pupils don't try properly, don't listen, and so don't follow instructions or ideas.
- **Disruption**—the unoccupied pupil most often spreads a trail of disruption or waves of disruption, annoying already working groups.

Effective teaching provision

What we know is that boredom and lack of cognitive challenge in the daily curriculum is playing a major role in causing pupils across the ability range to become more disaffected than was formerly the case. If resources permit, as an in-service training strategy, key staff, such as learning mentors, and SEN staff should be enabled to **shadow** one pupil for a day to see what he or she is subjected to and to do the curriculum audit. Senior staff can carry with them an aura that makes pupils behave better when they are present, so staff peers can gain more realistic information when they do the observations.

21

At present, it seems an overwhelming task to provide educational experiences that are, as it were, tailor-made for each individual child. With increased knowledge, both about the ways in which different children learn and the different approaches particularly suited to these ways, this task is likely to become less formidable. However, structure for learning and understanding rather than authority and control appear to represent many learners' needs in the early stages; they then can profit from freedom and a responsive environment. Underachievement, like envy, seems to feed on itself. A poor start soon snowballs into chronic failure, and the teacher's understandable disappointment in poor progress only serves to lead to further discouragement in the pupil. Both are caught in the vicious cycle of discouragement, disapproval, unresponsiveness and further failure.

What can be deduced is that the classroom setting of 20 or 30 years ago, when most teachers, parents and pundits were being taught, has changed radically. In the distant past, the teacher was a person of status approaching that of the doctor and parson, accorded respect because of that status. Today, a teacher has to **earn that respect** in an often hostile setting. The lone teacher with books and activities has to try to interest and involve pupils raised on YouTube, i-Phones, Instagram and Xbox.

In addition, pupils are required by law to put themselves in the unnatural setting of a classroom when they might be enjoying themselves elsewhere. Pupils who have a well-developed hostility to authority represented by the teacher now may openly challenge that authority, whilst others, less daring, more subtly and systematically seek to undermine the teacher, making both the competent and the less-experienced become vulnerable. The technique is continuous low-level noise and chattering.

To combat these changes in pupils' attitudes, the teacher must work systematically to make each one enjoy the educational experience. Each must feel supported and successful, whatever level of ability and potential, so that learning becomes a positive experience. It is a sad reflection that, as yet, 40 to 80 per cent of our pupils, according to various estimates, do not find their learning experiences positive. It is important to turn off-task behaviours into approximations towards on-task ones so that the number of positive reinforcements steadily outweigh the negatives or desists (Scott MacDonald, 1972). The best ratios are 5 to 1 positives to negatives, and this can change the whole classroom climate and ethos to a motivational and effortful one (Montgomery, 1989, 2002).

Traditionally, it is taught that the teacher is in authority, an authority and charismatic; to this, we need to add the following: is an expert in pedagogy or teaching and learning methods. This pedagogy needs to be explicitly taught in colleges, not assumed to be absorbed as a learner at school or by 'sitting by Nellie' as a student teacher.

Some simple first-level strategies for teachers might be

* Identify the person who is able to be the pupil's 'significant adult' or mentor. This person, preferably the class teacher, should talk with the pupil for a few minutes each day at an adult level on a one-to-one basis – positive cognitive intervention (PCI).
* Catch pupils being clever (CBC).
* Use more open questions to promote reflection and reasoning – the Socratic method and positive cognitive intervention.
* Review all worksheets, and reject those that offer only mundane and repetitive practice.
* Share examples of success with colleagues.
* Encourage creative competition with self rather than between pupils.
* Consider changing teaching methods at different times.

Developing social and self-management skills

Children who misbehave in classrooms prevent themselves as well as others from learning. Behaviour management and control skills are thus essential for all teachers if they are to be able to teach. It is not untypical that children with behavioural difficulties often have problems interacting satisfactorily with both peers and teachers, although this is not always the case. Poor social skills may well be the reason for them being seen as a challenge to teachers and to good order.

Children with learning difficulties are frequently slower to develop their social skills or more likely to remain immature in them. Pupils with specific difficulties, such as ADHD, autism and Asperger's syndrome, have particular problems in the social skills areas. However, even very able pupils can have immature social skills and may need help with them and with resilience-building. Particularly problematic are the cases where bright children have never really been challenged in school and begin to experience failure and difficulty late in their school careers. They frequently do not know how to cope with failure in school subjects or failure in social relations and need help with both. This is particularly important in the context of cyberbullying. Self-management skills and resilience become important as part of becoming independent learners.

Without support and understanding of this inability to cope with failure, perfectionism may result in similar stresses and responses when the standards pupils set themselves are too high. Case studies show that the responses can lead to problems of 'acting out' or 'acting in' but also to patterns that simulate ADHD.

According to Falvey et al. (1994), there are three main conditions for positive social interaction and the development of friendships. These are

- Opportunities to be with other children frequently enough
- Continuity – being involved with the same group over time
- Support – being helped and encouraged to make contact with other children, such as visiting with and staying at a friend's

However, children with difficulties do not always model the age-appropriate social models around them, or they may have immature development in these areas. Other children may reject or provoke them because of this difference, and teachers and other adults may not intervene to promote positive social interactions. Other children from disorganised families have few or inappropriate social models, and some model themselves on disturbing models on favourite video clips or inappropriate models in the local area.

Identifying these difficulties in the classroom can be undertaken by discreet, naturalistic observation.

Intervention strategies to help develop social interaction skills

There is a range of strategies that teachers can use to promote social interaction skills during class time and subject learning, and these are as follows:

- Collaborative group work involving real group activity
- Think–pair–share strategies in all curriculum areas
- Use of circle time activities
- Topic work – for making friends and team building
- Planned programme of work in PSE to include conflict management
- Role play and trust building work in drama and PE
- Team-building work in games, PE and other curriculum and extracurricular activities as appropriate
- Adequate and appropriate teacher and adult models
- Character analysis in relation to social skills in English and history
- Deliberate intervention, modelling and direct teaching as appropriate
- Cognitive intervention, modelling through use of videos and TV where appropriate
- Discussion and information time to create understanding of differences
- Conflict management problem-solving techniques (Bowers and Wells, 1988; Rawlings, 1996) (This contains work on 'I messages' and mediation skills.)
- Teaching children to express their anger and concerns verbally as in the preceding

- Assertiveness training to harness aggression and help children understand that they have rights to express their feelings
- Pre-teaching a special skill or information which the group needs to the problem pupil
- Peer tutoring and mentoring and the 'buddy system'
- Developing understanding of interpersonal issues, attitudes and stereotypes
- Nurture groups (Bannathan and Boxall 1998)

There are particular behaviours that help us initiate and maintain positive interactions with others and then close or terminate these when desired in appropriate ways, for example, through using eye contact, smiling, showing interest, giving social space, greeting and meeting, managing quality of voice, engaging in age-appropriate conversation, playing with others, gaining attention and asking for help, practicing personal hygiene, accepting criticism, dealing with aggression and anger in others and with one's own anger and frustration and inhibiting irritating behaviours, such as interrupting, not listening and so on.

In some instances, specific social skills may need to be taught, and the following procedure is generally used in social skills programmes:

- **Define the skill** to be taught; describe and discuss it. Illustrate it if possible with a videotape, or use simulations on puppets.
- **Model the skill.** Break it down into components or steps, and then demonstrate these or get a child to do this.
- **Imitate and rehearse.** The child tries out the skill.
- **Give feedback** on the performance in a supportive manner; coaching is required, and video recording can help.
- **Apply it.** Provide opportunities for the skill to be used and generalised to the school setting.
- **Intermittently reinforce it.** Watch for the child applying the skill on his or her own initiative, and provide praise and reward.

As social skills improve, they receive natural reinforcement from peers, who reward the progress with more and more positive interaction.

Self-regulation in the learning situation – autonomous learning

If a pupil is intrinsically motivated by something she or he will want to study for its own sake and complete the task in hand whether the teacher is present or not. The fact that pupils, especially underachievers and those with behaviour problems, spend a lot of time off-task shows that they are not fully 'brain engaged' and motivated by the task. The nature and ways of developing of SRL strategies are discussed later.

Good behaviour management, as already described, can help settle the pupil to the task. Pupils may also need help in organising themselves – self-management skills, for example, organising materials, knowing how and when to seek help from the teacher or from peers, knowing what to do when work is completed, checking work and maintaining attention and concentration without constant supervision. It also includes how to follow the established class and school routines for collecting apparatus, changing lessons, bringing PE equipment, walking (not running) in the corridors, talking quietly rather than loudly and so on. Well-organised teachers and lessons can help such pupils considerably, but there will be some who need explicit teaching of the routines and then their reinforcement.

For example, if the teacher requires pupils to stop talking and put hands up to answer the question, then pupils must be made to stop talking before anyone is allowed to answer the question. The teacher must then choose someone who has a hand up to answer and not accept called-out answers.

Learning support assistants may offer too much support and guidance rather than requiring the pupil, for example, to read the worksheet for him- or herself several times. The pupil may read it but not be able immediately to follow the instructions. Instead of the LSA reading it to the pupil and prompting step by step, the pupil should be asked to read instructions aloud sentence by sentence and implement them step by step.

Pupils should be able to be adaptive in their self-regulation skills so that they can respond to the different classroom environments established by teachers. Teachers can help the development of these skills by being explicit about classroom rules and routines and writing them up on posters or on the whiteboard. Such rules need to be discussed and agreed upon with the pupils so that they understand why they should not run about, shout or call out answers.

A piece of writing should not be accepted until it has been proofread. The point can be made by showing the simple errors that occur during writing without checking. Most work is preceded by date, name (if not writing in books) and a heading. Completed and corrected work can be signed and then put in the teacher's tray, and the pupil then proceeds to the next task. Thus the teacher must have a set of activities for 'next tasks', for example, silent reading, computer application, problem-solving tasks, preparation for the next piece of work and so on.

It is also important for the teacher to introduce 'rest periods' when the pupils can sit back from their labours legitimately and listen to a reading or further ideas. Alternatively, a pair-and-share talking interlude about an aspect of the work can give this relaxation and reduce the emotional need to engage in conversational self-expression.

Many underachievers have had so many negative school experiences that they feel that their efforts have little impact on their progress. They think what happens to them is unrelated to their own actions and are thus said to have an external locus of control. In its extreme form, it is seen as 'learned helplessness', where the learner anticipates failure in any new situation and uses avoidance and evasion strategies to avoid loss of self-esteem through failure.

They need to experience success and to relearn that persistence, and careful analysis can enable them to overcome failure. This will help them increase 'internality'. Working in pairs can help provide a behavioural and cognitive scaffold to enable aspects of the work to be completed successfully within the zone of proximal development (ZPD) (Vygotsky, 1978). The zone of proximal development is the area between what the pupil can do unaided and with structured guidance. Pupils can provide the scaffold or some teaching within this area by pairing their knowledge and discussing what to do. The teacher with a class of thirty cannot be on hand to do this microteaching every time it is required. Different working pairs opportunities need to be introduced to offer the widest experience.

In addition to this, achievements in self-control and self-regulation should be noted by the teacher and supported through recognition and quiet praise. There will always of course be lapses, but as self-regulation improves, then lapses will be more infrequent and in the end will only appear again under duress and direct fear of failure.

Conclusion

To sum up, education systems worldwide are unfair to many learners and doubly so where the learners come from disadvantaged circumstances. Pupils with dual and multiple exceptionalities from these backgrounds will thus be multiply handicapped. What is needed is high-quality education that will enable all learners to achieve their full potential. In this respect, the 'English model' proposed here is that to overcome underachievement and disadvantage, all pupils need high-quality basic education in every classroom in all schools to develop abilities and talent. This is the foundation of an inclusive education that meets the needs of all learners for motivation, interest and cognitive challenge in a developmental context.

There have been three major areas of concern in this consideration of the origins of underachievement. These are socio-cultural, personal and school factors. These factors conspire to provoke underachievement or prevent an individual's achievement at an appropriate level. It would also seem that most societies and researchers regard the underachiever as someone with a problem or problems who needs to be 'fixed'. However the alternative view here is that it is the general school system and higher education that need to be 'fixed'.

The argument is that underachievement arises in a systemic failure of schools and teachers to educate pupils appropriately and according to need. In this respect, the cry is 'differentiation', but some forms of differentiation merely perpetuate a segregated school system at the classroom level. The common thread running through many of the studies on underachievement is that the majority of these pupils may be very good orally but are poor at writing ideas or almost anything down at more than an average or even more limited level. However, there are, in addition, many undiscovered underachievers who have not been able to develop their oral skills to match their ability because of socio-cultural, behavioural and other disadvantages; they are linguistically disadvantaged. The needs of these groups will be considered in the next chapter.

After considering these factors, it is concluded that it is schools and teachers that can have the most far-reaching effects on underachievers to change their lives and lifelong achievements but not in education as we know it now. It is proposed that fundamental reframing of teaching and learning provision in most schools needs to take place to achieve change and equity for learners, and these will be discussed in a later chapter. Assessment also needs some fundamental changes. It will be shown that a system of **assessment through provision** needs to be a major component in the work in schools.

It is in more open approaches to the curriculum of all learners and in the up-skilling in the teaching of basic and cognitive skills that we can help underachieving learners reveal their potential. These measures in an inclusive context will help provide the supportive, the remedial, the compensatory and the inspirational approaches that Whitmore (1982), Rimm (1986), Baum et al. (1995) and Renzulli and Reis (2008) found successful in combating underachievement.

Following the introduction of comprehensive education in 1970, it became evident that the curriculum needed to be differentiated to cater for the needs of mixed ability classes that contained the widest range of pupil skills and abilities. This took place first in relation to pupils with special educational needs and then following the introduction of the national curriculum in 1990 to the needs of more able learners as well, in fact all learners (DfEE, 1994). In DCFS (2009c), the construct was redeveloped as 'personalised learning' provision, and nine steps to guide its implementation were published (DCFS, 2009c). These constructs will need interrogation in later chapters for their suitability to meet the needs of disadvantaged and underachieving learners, and it will be suggested that the definitions are often subject to misunderstanding and misapplication.

2 | Disadvantage and underachievement

Introduction

Disadvantage, in current research terms, is narrowly defined as applicable to those children who are eligible for free school meals. It is used as an indicator of poverty, and poverty is generally associated with disadvantage. The average annual income in the UK is said to be around £25,000. Some families however have an income of only £12,500 a year, and some pensioners have to live on less than that. Are the children of the family on the low-income side disadvantaged? Do they live in poverty? Not in comparison with those in many countries who have to live on less than two dollars a day – even £1,000 would be vast riches to them. Disadvantage therefore needs to be seen in context. It is sometimes only at school that some children begin to learn that they are disadvantaged and not at all equal. Even those in families who can afford a Facebook or Instagram account soon find that any kind of difference and even none at all can put them at a disadvantage. Stress is thus induced in addition to any other problems they meet at school and in the curriculum.

The fact that their 'trainers' are not current, their 'Gameboy' is not the latest version, and the car is an old one and not a big four by four will make many feel deprived and disadvantaged, especially when they see what others have. In fact, many children in the middle of riches can feel deprived when they do not have what their friends do. They may never gain a balanced perspective until perhaps something happens that changes the family fortunes and with it their perspective.

This kind of 'deprivation' does not usually of itself create disadvantage or loss of potential, but problems do arise when being poor or less well-off results in a lack of opportunity to go to a 'good' or high-achieving school. Fewer of these are to be found in poorer areas, such as inner-city districts. We might regard some of these areas to be 'toxic environments' and 'toxic schools' in the ways in which they lower the achievements of children. But the 'school effect', when averaged out, only approximates to 10 per cent improvement (DfE, 2016).

Poverty's serious manifestations can still be seen in the UK, especially when families become destitute and have no home or income for periods of time or when children are neglected and not fed or cared for by their parents or carers. This is particularly prevalent in dysfunctional families, where children may be exposed to a 'toxic childhood'. Even so, these families are not always poor.

Disadvantage has been commonly associated with poverty, but it has much wider implications than this. It is a relative term, for we are disadvantaged in relation to something or someone else.

Another way of looking at disadvantage is through the perspective of exclusions. If pupils are excluded from school on a fixed term or a permanent basis, this is disadvantaging – 78 per cent of permanent exclusions were issued to pupils who either had SEND, were classified as in need or were eligible for free school meals (Timpson Report, 2019). The numbers dropped significantly when pupils with SEND had an education and health-care plan (EHCP). Pupils with SEND were five times more likely to have permanent exclusion than pupils without SEND (Ofsted Report, 2018–2019). The Ofsted report found that in 2018, 27 per cent – 93,000 – of pupils with SEND had a fixed-term exclusion, and nearly 5,800 pupils with SEND left their schools between Years 10 and 11; some of those were likely to have been 'off-rolled'. Pupils with SEND account for 13 per cent of all pupils but 30 per cent of those who leave their school.

Dyslexia is the most common form of SEND found in schools, and the British Dyslexia Association (BDA, 2019b) reported on the human cost of this in emotional well-being and mental health. Dyslexics make up 10 per cent of the general population. The report showed that 88 per cent of parents reported that their dyslexic child suffered from low self-esteem, and 84 per cent observed high levels of anxiety exhibited by their children in relation to school.

Disadvantaged pupils were significantly poorer in their basic skills than the rest of the population, 65 per cent achieving the expected SATs standards, whereas 81 per cent of the rest did so. At the end of Key Stage 2 in writing, 51 per cent of the disadvantaged attained the expected standard at level 4, but 70 per cent of the better off did so.

The casework on which much of this book is based has shown that pupils with autism spectrum disorders (ASD) in mainstream education are frequently undiagnosed, and parents are desperately trying to obtain an EHCP. By the time the child is 9 or 10 years old, he or she may refuse to go to school at all or be so distressed that the parent decides to try home schooling before the child is excluded. If these children manage to stay on to enter secondary school, the constant changes in teachers, timetabled subjects and rooms can defeat them and make them ill.

SEND and this book

The strategies set out in this book apply to general learning needs and behavioural issues. They are interventions that every teacher can learn and use to lift the achievement of the widest range of pupils. Specialist and specific remedial SEN programmes for Dyslexia, ADHD, ASD and DCD are to be found in *Teaching Gifted Children with SEN, Supporting Dual and Multiple Exceptionality* (Montgomery, 2015). The most recent Ofsted report (2019) showed that significant numbers of pupils were being classified as having a special need when this was not the case. This group is disadvantaged. They have overlooked needs and would benefit from the help suggested in this book.

The whole person – our target

Maslow researched personal attributes and human needs and identified a hierarchy of needs; each level had to be satisfied before we could progress to the higher ones. For the highest level in his hierarchy, he researched people who were in robust psychological health. He found they were in the process of realising their potential. He called them self-actualising (Maslow, 1970).

They were not self-centred but had a mission in life that served the larger good, they respected all persons and had a sense of kinship with all human beings; and they had an existential sense of humour and detested laughing at the expense of others.

At the base of the hierarchy was the need to satisfy our hunger and thirst; then we needed safety and warmth. After these, we have social and emotional needs to satisfy, and then comes the need for self-fulfillment and achievement. Maslow found that the average was a stunted norm.

Although children in school cannot be expected to be self-actualised, they should be moving through the upper stages towards it. They should not become stuck in the lower stages or end up as overdomesticated chickens. Schools should be modelling and helping them towards autonomy and self-actualisation; that is the goal. Unfortunately, the rest of the chapter shows how we can become stuck in a lower phase by a range of disadvantages. If these can be removed, then healthy personal growth can be resumed. Sometimes resilience building may be necessary to resume this growth.

Giftedness, talent and disadvantage – high learning potential (HLP)

Underachievements in those with HLP are more widespread than is generally believed, but IQ tests and teacher assessments frequently fail to identify them. For example, Stamm (2005) found 50 per cent of her HLP pupils were systematically underachieving.

Three groups of more able underachievers can be defined, and it is the lack of identification that in itself becomes disadvantaging. If they also come from a disadvantaging environment, any low achievement is often assigned to this cause, and it is common for less to be expected from them.

Group 1 (usually identifiable) 'Discrepancies'

- Those who have been identified by discrepancies between high scores on ability tests and low achievement in school subjects or SATs
- Those who show discrepant scores on IQ tests between verbal and performance items (e.g. CAT scores) but may be performing in class at an average level
- Those who show an uneven pattern of high and low achievements across school subjects with only average ability test scores
- Those whose only high achievements seem to be in out-of-school or non-school activities

Group 2 (usually the disability masks their abilities) 'Disabilities'

- Those who have a specific learning difficulty – dyslexia-type or language difficulties in the presence of average ability test scores
- Those with spelling or handwriting difficulties and average ability scores
- Those with gross motor co-ordination problems or sensory impairment

Group 3 (usually not identified) 'Deceptives'

- Pupils with social and behavioural difficulties
- Daydreamers, uninterested in school, or so-called 'lazy' pupils
- Linguistically disadvantaged background

In each category, there will also be significant numbers of disadvantaged individuals who will be overlooked because of this, and it can become the reason for not intervening to encourage their learning potential. Where IQ or cognitive ability tests are not used, teachers use the SATs levels obtained to determine potential. Children know these and can set their sights at these levels, and then they feel they cannot achieve more or they have failed in comparison to peers. High SATs scores are very much dependent upon language and literacy levels, and disadvantaged children are thus vulnerable to scoring lower levels, and so their potential is underestimated. Success in SATs can be promoted by extra and private tuition and by the extraordinary motivation and persistence to work hard of some pupils and not necessarily high learning potential.

In the case of talent, there may never be the opportunity to discover it if there is only a narrow range of exposure to experiences. In the arts, theatre, and music, for example, there may be little or no active experience fostered by the home. At school, as budgets decline, a wide range of experience in the arts can also decline. League table competition can cause schools to narrow the curriculum experience to so-called academic subjects. Often, only chance factors result in the acquisition and development of a creative skill. Online access, especially to popular music, can mitigate this to some extent.

Because IQ test scores are very much the result of general experience in the environment and long- and short-term memory, disadvantage can diminish such scores by at least 10 per cent. In addition, those with learning disabilities can also require 10 points to be added to their scores to indicate the more realistic potential (Silverman, 2004). The best plan is to regard every child as capable of so much more than his or her current performance would indicate and seek ways to improve it. Evidence suggests that offering more challenging learning experiences for all learners can achieve this, and *challenge* and *stretch* are words to be increasingly found in DfE documents.

Reasons for failure to identify more able underfunctioning pupils

Group one pupils, although they have some high scores on ability tests, will have underlying learning difficulties that if not uncovered and given support lead to lower attainment. Group two, because of their dual (or multiple) exceptionalities, have patterns of depressed scores on abilities tests that mask their potential, and they need specialist support for their specific learning difficulties. Masking may lead to long-term failure. The third group underfunction for a variety of reasons, such as the need for the 'cool' image in boys so that they fear to try in case they fail, or their 'subculture' is that school is not 'cool'. Others fear the label 'boff' and the bullying that can ensue. Girls may develop similar images about what is 'cool' and 'uncool' because it is not seen as feminine to do well in subjects such as maths or be seen to work hard. For some girls, it even becomes 'childish' to do what the rest of the class is doing; they prefer to sit out and chat. Some pupils come from linguistically disadvantaged or different backgrounds that hamper their ability to express themselves adequately. Others come from subcultures in which schooling is not valued. All these factors can increase the likelihood of school failure.

Underlying all of these underachievements is a low sense of self-esteem and a range of strategies being used to defend the sense of self or prop it up. Characteristic also is the need in all these pupils to have something interesting and challenging intellectually to engage with. It helps that the teacher interacts sensitively with them to support any effort that might be forthcoming. They also need more participatory lesson structures and other forms of learning and recording that are permitted besides writing. Especially important is structuring on-task and legitimate talk between pupils about the work in hand. This helps facilitate language development and language competency.

Because in many classrooms the lessons are teacher-led and information is imparted verbally, has to be recorded in writing and then learned and recalled in writing, pupils can lose motivation as their involvement in making meaning for themselves diminishes. Most commonly they find school 'very boring', as they cannot achieve the top levels in SATs that other pupils have or they experience early failures so they feel undermined and grow disaffected as their failures and perceived failures multiply. These perceived failures and low self-esteem can lead to depressive symptoms in some vulnerable pupils. If the pressures of cyberbullying and identity dysphoria are added to this, it forms a toxic cocktail for a young person to negotiate. Such is the concern about this that all teachers and trainees are to be trained to identify early symptoms of mental illness.

Because even the term 'underachievement' arouses negative attitudes, Plucker (2015) recommended that the differences are better termed 'excellence gaps' and this has been adopted and begun to be used in both the US and the UK. He decided to focus on high-end achievement gaps to redress the lack of improvement that was observed across the ability range because it was felt it would gain more attention from the legislators. Getting the right term or label was important.

Spotting general underachievement

Year heads, gifted and talented co-ordinators and SENCos need to encourage all departments or class teachers to identify **the top 20 per cent** of pupils in their subject area in each class, for example, 5 or 6 or more pupils. This will begin the building of the patterns on a grid that shows, for example, subject grades, spelling test and CATs test scores, SEN, behaviour problems and so on. Particularly significant will be the identification of pupils who are good orally but 'cannot write it down' or only very good when there is some kind of problem to solve or who have a lot of common sense but are only an 'average' in classroom work or those who are excellent at art or PE but 'no good' at so called academic subjects; they may be leaders in every bit of mischief but not school work.

Whilst most will eventually read adequately, the spelling test will identify a significant number of underachievers across the ability range. For example, those who make more than ten misspellings per 100 words fall into the learning difficulties dyslexic category (Montgomery, 2017a). It will also show handwriting difficulties that significantly lower attainment (see Chapters 5 and 6). Another important contribution to make to developing the grids can be information from a short questionnaire to parents on 'What are your child's strengths?'

The reason for selecting the top 20 per cent is because Tannenbaum (1993), in his meta-analysis, found that selecting the top 20 per cent by IQ and the top 20 per cent by school achievement would include most of those who were the most gifted and talented. Even so, the learning disabled, many disadvantaged learners and some of the most 'gifted' will still be missed.

Table 2.1 Example Achievement Record Grid

Pupil name	Verbal IQ	Perform IQ	Reading age	Spelling age	H'writing speed
A					
B					
C					
N					

Subjects grades or levels 10 subjects or more

English	Maths	Science	Art	Music	Geography

Clubs, teams and societies in school

Football	Gym	Dance	Drama	Chess	Etc.

Clubs and societies and other out-of-school activities

Boxing	Judo / etc.	Dance	Riding	Orchestra	Swimming

Out of school awards, work experience and so on

Carer	Work experience	Duke of Ed	Scout/Guide	Etc.

Teachers may not have time to make such detailed records; they can be given a list of pupils in the class and be asked to put a star beside the name of any pupil who shows some higher learning potential (*) or creative potential (C) or both.

Lower attainers

These make up a significant portion of many classrooms for the reasons set out earlier, but there is one group who can too easily be overlooked. This is the group of slower learners who make up a third of mixed-ability classes. Some teachers and schools have maintained that all their pupils fall into this category, which is of course untrue. Some lower attainers are slower learners needing more time and support to construct meaning from what they experience. They are said to be of low ability and have IQ scores in the below average bands. This makes teachers expect much less of them, and they are given work that is less challenging and often much less interesting. It has however been shown that there is hidden potential for much higher achievement amongst these pupils if the current teaching methods, especially those in the 'transmission' mode, are changed (Montgomery, 1990; Watson, 1996; Rawlings, 1996). Examples are to be found in Chapter 5 under the title of CPS (cognitive process strategies).

Gender and disadvantage

In the past, girls were disadvantaged by lack of expectation from parents and teachers. They were able to leave school at 14 and then 15 before taking national examinations that would enable them to qualify for higher education and better jobs. Now they can compete on equal terms with boys when schools treat them equally. Often, it is the girls' attitude to STEM subjects that deprives them of the widest range of careers. In many schools, especially co-educational ones, these attitudes still persist, and boys' entry to the arts is not so well encouraged.

However, it is now boys who are found by national statistics to be underachieving by comparison. The main factors for this are regarded to be attitudinal and 'boy code'. However, schools and their curricula and pedagogy have been found capable of addressing these matters. In addition, it is suggested here that developmental differences and co-ordination difficulties play a more significant part in boys' lower achievements than has previously been recognised (see Chapter 5).

A factor not so often recorded in the present period is the lower amount of attention and information given by teachers to girls in co-educational classrooms. It was found that boys expected to receive two-thirds of the teacher's attention and time, or they complained they were being discriminated against unfairly (Spender, 1983). They were also given more information than girls (Good and Brophy, 1986). In girls-only schools, the take up of STEM subjects is much stronger not only because they do not have to put up with bullying from boys but they also have more opportunities to engage with the practical work and receive their fair shares of time and information.

Class, culture and disadvantage

Saxon England and the Celtic cultures of Scotland, Wales and Ireland are said to have enjoyed an egalitarian system of organisation. However, after the Norman invasion in 1066, the class system based on the Norman style began to spread. The 'upper classes', the wealthy Norman landowners and their acolytes, spoke Norman French; the rest of the English spoke Anglo-Saxon. Much of the French vocabulary, as well as their cultural habits over time, were absorbed into Old and then Middle English.

By the 19th century, the class system – upper, middle and lower – was well established, and it was considered appropriate that you were born and married into your class. The structure was deemed immutable and 'God given'. However, Darwin's publication (1859) of *On the Origin of Species* and later the understanding of genetics caused the class system to begin to be questioned. Despite this, it was not until universal education in 1897 that the 'lower classes' had access to education and opportunities to rise 'above their station'. This began to increase and improve throughout the 20th century.

Even in the late 20th century, despite secondary education for all and higher education open to anyone who could qualify for it regardless of wealth and position, a class notion still operated in the UK. It was maintained by the private school system with the major 'public schools', such as Eton and Harrow, open in the main only to children of the very wealthy and those with high positions and offices or titles and lands. The upper classes (social class 1) could thus maintain their positions and networks and learn to speak 'Oxford English'. The wealthy, originally local gentry and landowners and merchants (social class 2), or the upper middle classes, could aspire to join them, and even a few working-class children gained access by scholarships and joined the higher-status professional groups.

The rest made up the working class, which sociologists divided into social classes 3, 4 and 5. Social class 3 consisted of the lower professional groups, solicitors and teachers and so on; social class 4 was made up of the 'upper working class', who had trades and skills; and social class 5 was of an unskilled class of labourers. Below this was an underclass of itinerants (social class 6).

Access to the grammar school system of the 1950s to 1970s created a great wave of social mobility, and the class system was widely breached. Now, whilst the old system still exists, another based on meritocracy is also in operation. As the new meritocrats rise, they merge into the old system and become middle and even upper class, often with pretensions, or they rise and rise and maintain they are still 'working class'. Many people with a steady income, an office job, a car and a roof over their heads now like to consider themselves 'middle class'.

High-level professionals and many of the new wealthy still like to think they remain in the working class. Since most of us work or are seeking it, many of the old barriers have been removed, and the prejudices against others that were engendered are mainly a matter of attitude and ignorance.

Class in the 21st century in the UK is thus much more complex than it once was and more in the eye of the beholder and in the media than real. Perhaps only the vestiges of an upper class are left, and all the rest of us are best seen as workers of various kinds. Unfortunately, a new system leading to advantage has developed based on an old structure. Joanna Williams of the Sutton Research Trust (2019) reported that 7 per cent of UK children attend private fee-paying schools but occupy 70 per cent of all the higher-level posts in the professions and the arts. More pupils from the top eight private schools secured places at Oxbridge than those from 3,000 state schools. Advantage brings more advantage, and you can pay for it.

There is certainly no need to regulate society by a class system anymore, so pupils should not be brought up to think of it or define themselves by such limiting structures. It is an offence to their self-esteem and their potential. Nevertheless, governments and universities, for example, are finding it difficult to deconstruct the old system and attitudes.

It is the work of schools to counteract the disadvantage of classification by class by

- Raising the quality of the education they provide
- Developing children's critical faculties so they can challenge outmoded concepts of class, race, gender and disability purveyed by the media and the ignorant
- Having, modelling and teaching respect for all pupils and persons in general

Whilst the UK is busy trying to dismantle its class system through the permeation of good quality education, some immigrants from Asia have imported their own class system – the caste system. This means they define themselves and others by one of the four castes into which they are borne from Brahman to 'untouchables' or Dalits. The name and the village of origin back in the home country define social interaction. Children in the playgrounds learn to ask questions about these origins of peers. High-class individuals will exclude those of lower castes from jobs and will not accept coins from the hands of the 'untouchables'. Here is yet another complication for schools in areas with high densities of these families to deal with. Most important is to have positive parent liaison opportunities and structures in place so that there is an understanding on both sides of roles and responsibilities in the local community and the host society.

Culture, ethnicity and disadvantage

In the UK, there have been influxes of immigrants from the invading Romans and Vikings in the first millennium to the Normans in 1066 and others since then. A steady influx of refugees arrived throughout the 20th century. Others came to find work. Large numbers of economic migrants from various countries have arrived. The most recent are those from the European Union, particularly Eastern Europe, as their countries joined the EU. In 2018, there were 3.4 million people from the EU resident in the UK, and 1 million UK people resident across the 27 countries of the EU with most living in Spain (ONS, 2019). It is a compliment that so many people think it is good for them to join the UK, but it has caused a competition for school places and medical resources in certain parts of England, and funding has not necessarily been provided to take account of the changes and needs. It is a work in progress.

One of the main issues that arises for schools is whether to sustain a policy of immersion for new non-English speakers or whether support in the home language (L1) will speed up the inclusion process. English as an additional language (EAL) is a major system of support for these second- and third-language learners. What is known is that schools with good overall provision for EAL will enable these pupils to catch up in English after five years by the age of 11 in Year 6. SATs results will fall behind until this stage, affecting the school's position in the national league tables. Pupils arriving at a later stage will have more problems in catching up, as will any pupil having dyslexic difficulties or other learning needs in their first language.

Another issue is that the gender discrimination against girls is strong in some cultures, so that gendered education is sought and the sexes are kept separate. In mixed-sex schools, lack of segregation can become a source of conflict with the local community. Another current issue is the curriculum obligation of schools to create an inclusive attitude and information about individual and family differences because of LGBTQ (lesbian, gay, bisexual, transgender and queer) (DfE, 2019). This has caused conflict between school and government policies and some local groups, e.g. in Birmingham reported by the BBC news and other media over several months.

Intersectionality

Intersectionality is a recent term used to express the idea that an issue such as gender discrimination is more complex than just different or discriminatory treatment assigned to, for example, girls. Black girls and/or lesbian girls may be doubly or trebly disadvantaged and bullied, and their talents are missed. Some may have an additional need as well and are living in poverty or as a carer, and all this masks their talents and abilities if they are seen through one particular lens (Meyer et al., 2016).

Bilingualism

What is known is that training in skills and comprehension in L1 (first or home language) boosts the capacity to learn in L2 (English). The transfer possibilities speed up acquisition. Speakers of languages that lack the complexity of English and have a more transparent structure require specific language teaching at the earliest stage. Languages without a phonological base will prove more difficult for skills transfer, and specific synthetic phonics teaching in English is needed. Fluency in two or more languages enhances intellectual functioning and speeds up problem-solving ability.

Vocabulary

Another important consideration is that the new arrivals will quickly gain a good understanding of ordinary colloquial language and acquire a vocabulary of 2,000 to 3,000 words. However, what they and most culturally disadvantaged learners need is to be specifically taught the academic vocabulary of some 500 words that are commonly found in school texts and tests (Warwick, 2009). Warwick's REAL (Realising Equality and Achievement of Learners) project had some remarkable results with ethnic groups from disadvantaged environments when this vocabulary was taken into account and deliberately taught and when the teaching methods were designed to offer cognitive challenge and stretch.

Difference, poverty and bullying

One of the features of the English school system is that a significant amount of covert and even overt bullying takes place. It is the result of a coercive ethos that permeates some schools and some families, and thus policies and practices to overcome it must be made explicit to all staff and pupils. Pupils with SEND or additional needs are particularly at risk in such environments. Children of different ethnicity, culture and sexuality may also be picked on just for being different or poor. But it can apply to any white indigenous pupils who are regarded as different as well. This may even appear as an 'anti-boff' or anti academic attitude prevalent in some schools or sub-cultures and needs to be addressed as soon as identified. All children need to learn how to succeed and to experience the pleasure of success. This will help raise their esteem and reduce the antipathy to others' success.

Schools already help pupils from poor households with uniforms and payment for trips and the pupils should also be receiving free school meals. All of these helps need to be managed discreetly to avoid other pupils bullying the recipients.

The wider context is also significant. In education, there is a top-down persistent demand for one standard and then another, with a flow of hundreds of documents with rules for implementation and a round of Ofsted inspections, league tables and governors' meetings to check that the rules have been followed. This makes the whole system a coercive one in which teachers become anxious and can harass pupils by continually using SATs and school results to worry them into working harder. Stressed teachers and worried parents can cause stress amongst vulnerable pupils, and we have seen the rise in mental illness amongst them. To this effect is added the cyberbullying that can take place between pupils. A bullying system encourages bullying down through the structure despite schools having anti-bullying policies and practices. It is this 'hidden' curriculum that needs counteracting.

Self-image

Although individuals at all ages are vulnerable to attacks on their self-image, in the digital age, new problems have arisen and old problems have been magnified. Eight-year-olds are acting out what they see on *Love Island*. Body image and fatness have become obsessions in some groups, and the incidence of anorexia in both girls and boys has risen. One-third of girls and a quarter of boys report being cyberbullied (Pizalski, 2012; Sevcikova et al., 2012). All of these pressures on vulnerable children and young people can lead to anxiety and great distress that can end in self-harm and mental illness. In terms of Maslow's hierarchy, their socio-emotional needs are not being met, their minds will not be on the academic curriculum, and their former achievement will sink lower and lower.

Interrupted learners

Jordan (2001) used the Traveller paradigm to indicate the commonalities between groups of the disadvantaged and what can be done to help them. The key principle is that 'looked after' children, bed-and-breakfast families, excludees, refugees, Travellers, children with chronic illnesses, service children and young carers all have one feature in common, and that is 'interrupted learning'. They are seldom considered in the general literature, and they consist of a large number of children who often escape scrutiny.

They all have interrupted learning profiles in common (Jordan, 2001, 132). According to Jordan, they may also share a number of other characteristics: lack of respect and understanding, low expectations of them, harassment, racism and bullying from teachers and peers, lack of ready access to a school place, lack of personal support to stay in the school system, and unwillingness of local authorities and schools to build on successful projects elsewhere, especially distance learning projects

To these groups of underachievers, we might also add those with learning difficulties, behaviour problems, mental health issues and special needs and disabilities of any kind. They share similar problems, are bullied and are prone to underachieve. They are also more likely to have interrupted learning because of absences or from disapplication of the curriculum. They may have high learning potential, but with multiple disadvantages can never achieve this potential unless the cycle of disadvantage is broken.

Solutions identified for interrupted learners

As indicated above, a wide range of pupils experience interruption to their opportunities for learning, but there are strategies that can be used to help them such as the following:

- Developing genuine home-school partnerships
- Raising families' and teachers' expectations
- Replacing league tables with school self-evaluation
- Improving and broadening the content of Initial Teacher Training (ITT) and Continuing Professional Development (CPD)
- Open and distance learning provision for school-age learners with tutor support
- Acceptance of heterogeneity
- Accommodation to the needs and tensions in families
- Free lifelong learning opportunities for adult interrupted learners

(Jordan, 2001, 133)

These solutions would also seem applicable to underachievers and the disadvantaged in general, and many such solutions have been trialled in a range of projects, www.underachievement.uk. However, solutions are easier to define and recommend than construct. In addition, we must include low socio-economic status because pupils from these settings are seriously under-represented in higher education. Add to this the 60,000 children absent without leave from school on any day, and we have a huge underclass of underachievers (ONS, 2019).

There are however some schools, some departments within schools and some individual teachers who are recognised for their work in lifting underachievement.

The school effect

Smith and Tomlinson (1989) reported on 3,000 children in five years of secondary school in 21 schools. They found

1   In schools where children do well, black pupils did well. In this, the research ratified the concerns of the black parents in the London Boroughs that it is **good** schools that their children need.
2   The schools (or in certain cases the departments) in which all children do well are those that are managed well. Good management = good teaching = good learning.
3   Not only are the differences in attainment significantly determined by the *school effect*, but the differences themselves are astonishingly great.

The data imply that a child with a particular reading age (above average) might achieve a B grade at O level GCE in one school but only a CSE grade 3 at another.

> 'It is not necessarily pupils' colour then, nor even, within the range of 'normality', so much their ability, that determines the qualifications with which they come out of school. It depends far more on what school they went to in the first place'.
>
> (Klein, 1993,76)

In other words, what Smith et al. (1989) found was that measures that best promote the interests of black, Asian and minority ethnic (BAME) groups in secondary schools are the same as those that raise the standards of all pupils and education in general. Open enrolment to schools can permit discrimination against minority groups where racist attitudes prevail, and raw scores as school indicators of success will reinforce such values. Value added measures show what the schooling has contributed to the education of the pupils.

Recent concerns about the numbers of immigrants, especially economic migrants, coming to the UK have increased the amount of overt racism experienced by a wide range of UK residents, including those who are now third- and fourth-generation immigrants and are British subjects.

The difficulties faced by newly arrived immigrants are greater than those of already well-established families, but their gifted and talented children are rarely identified because the assessment procedures do not cater for this. Very rapid acquisition of the host language is one indicator but not for those with a learning disability. The shock of moving to an entirely different culture can also promote abreactions that damage ease of integration. Confusion and antipathy to the dominant culture may also be fostered by some external agencies.

The non-verbal Raven's Progressive Matrices tests can help give an indication of potential where vocabulary is limited or even absent. The tests could be much more widely used to help in assessment and provision for these disadvantaged groups.

Immigration status of refugee children

A refugee is a person with a well-founded fear of persecution in their country of origin for reasons of race, nationality, religion, political opinion, or membership of a particular social group.

–UN Convention Relating to Status of Refugees Article 1(A) 2

Note that this leaves out gender issues, where women for no other reason than that they are available or because they have been caused to be destitute or enslaved are raped and abused.

'At risk' factors or difficulties faced by immigrants and refugees

- Previous insufficiencies or lack of educational experience
- Securing a school place
- Racist bullying – the biggest obstacle
- Dismissive labelling by teachers
- Insufficient language support
- Difficulties associated with trauma, transition and loss
- Poor living conditions
- Expectations of the school
- Need for effective assessment
- Behavioural difficulties and depression

Disadvantaging schools – 'able misfits' or 'toxic schools'?

Teachers themselves often exert the strongest and most lasting influence on their pupils through their own personalities. This aspect is particularly important for those children who lack appropriate model figures in their own family. Underachievers have been shown to perform better with supportive, encouraging teachers than with those who simply demand high standards of work.

Sometimes teachers can fear the questions and challenges that some pupils can present. This can lead to open hostility and, especially in secondary schools, an environment in which the pupil is set to be seen as 'the problem' rather than the teacher.

This kind of rejection and hostility leading to neglect of the pupils' needs can give rise to or provoke negative or aggressive responses in some or withdrawal and disaffection from others. In either case, it is the pupil whose life chances are damaged.

The term 'able misfits' (Kellmer-Pringle, 1983) reflects earlier concepts of giftedness and was applied to those who would not conform. Today, across the ability range, there are pupils who refuse to conform. But should they conform? We might consider the school as the misfit or ill-fitting environment, and this frequently results in challenging behaviour (Sisk, 2003) from a wide range of pupils. Changes to teaching methods and contents that create better relationships between teachers and the taught can be found in Chapter 7.

Among the remedies, improving the self-concept and morale of the underachiever and enlisting parental interest and support occupy pride of place. Community, neighbourhood and peer group attitudes towards intellectual achievement may also need modifying, but this is inevitably a long-term goal. In school, the opportunity to work independently, to explore individual interests in depth and to develop or perhaps rediscover a sense of commitment and excitement about learning have been found to be prerequisites for rehabilitating any 'misfit'.

Characteristics most commonly found in children named 'able misfits' by Kellmer-Pringle in the *Needs of Children* (1983) were the following:

- A sense of inadequacy and limited ambitions
- Dislike of school and book learning
- Poor work habits
- Unsatisfactory relationships with peers
- High incidence of emotional difficulties (cause or effect?)

These attributes can apply to any learner. They apply in the sense that the pupils involved are much more capable than their everyday performance might reveal.

School factors that can put children at risk

A range of school factors have been put forward in researches that have caused children to be put at risk. These can be summarised as follows:

- A repressive and coercive régime
- Hostility in relationships between staff and pupils
- Exclusions, fixed-term or permanent and 'off-rolling'
- Rebellion fomented
- Didactic curriculum and pedagogy
- Underestimation of pupils' abilities
- 'Strong', unbending discipline

- Rigid authoritarianism
- Bullying by staff and/or pupils
- Divided staff
- Blame and scapegoating
- Heavy pressure on so-called 'academic standards' and pursuits
- Disruptive behavioural responses
- Negative attitude to many pupils
- Many pupils being regarded as socially deprived
- Disaffection and truanting

All these factors represent a **coercive** schooling ethos, which when faced with difficult or awkward pupils, immediately rules them as out of order, blameworthy, problem pupils and to be excluded from that school. It is characteristic of large secondary schools, where, with so many staff and so many pupils, no one really has time to get to know each other or the pupils or perhaps do not choose to.

When there is an over-emphasis upon academic goals and a neglect of personal needs, more children seem disposed to fail and become 'problem children' in the school's eyes (Rutter et al., 1979; Hargreaves, 1984). These differences cannot be attributed to the catchment areas that the schools serve. The implication is that the number of pupils regarded as having special educational needs on the basis of their difficult behaviour depends more on the school they happen to be attending than on the pupils themselves or their families (Galloway and Goodwin, 1987).

The main difficulties are that these are socially disapproved behaviours, the prognosis is poor and the onset appears in early childhood. The Gluecks (1968) maintained that they could identify pre-delinquent behaviours in two-year-olds. Over time, this appears to have been borne out, and the Sure Start programme and parenting classes were designed to help remedy this. Teachers were mostly concerned with pre-delinquent or non-delinquent problems that are 3:1 more common in boys (Rutter et al., 1970), for example, fighting, disruption, bullying, aggression, defiance, destructiveness, attention seeking and lying. Those pupils whom their teachers regarded as more successful tended to be given far greater attention than the others. The teachers interacted with them more frequently and paid closer attention to their activities, subtly structuring and directing their efforts in ways that were noticeably different from their relationships with pupils less favourably categorised. (Sharp and Green, 1975, 115). The same was found by Good and Brophy (1986) and Spender (1983) in relation to attention in classrooms given to boys rather than girls.

Mongon and Hart (1989) emphasised the 'role of fear' in schools. Although we are often most concerned by pupils asserting themselves and challenging the teachers' discipline, they draw attention to the fact that despite the kindliest intentions on the part of teachers, fear is the central debilitating characteristic of many pupils' school experience. They stated that the effect of the hidden curriculum may be a legitimate criticism of the schooling process that exerts a destruction of dignity that is so massive and pervasive that few subsequently recover from it.

If we put together these lines of discussion, we find that pupils with behavioural difficulties suffer from a massive lack of self-esteem, and this is recorded in much research. The worse the behaviour the lower their self-esteem. At the same time, the schooling process is at work steadily undermining them and many others, destroying their tenuous hold on self-esteem. It is no wonder that few adults have wholly positive things to say about their schooling experience. Even students at university confess to having been nuisances and frequently bored whilst there.

Self-esteem is a barometer of school life, well-being and success as well as a vulnerable entity to be protected and built by positive experiences if the person is to be successful, well-adjusted, fulfilled and self-actualised.

All of these conflicts in interaction generate emotional distress, which makes the behaviour more difficult to deal with. Thus, it is that the term SEBD (social, emotional and behavioural difficulties) is generally used. DfE reversed this to BESD because it thought the behavioural difficulties were key, when in fact the social interaction is the significant attribute, according to the experts, such as Professor Paul Cooper (1999) and the SEBD Association.

Behavioural difficulties that arise from emotional stress and emotional illness are less responsive to behavioural management strategies until the deep-seated emotional problems are addressed, usually in therapy (e.g., school phobia, depression, abuse, anorexia and bulimia, obsessive-compulsive disorders). In the last ten years, the increase in anorexic conditions and self-harm has been growing – most among girls but also increasingly among boys. This is proposed to be a result of current media promotions of and obsessions with perfect body images and the effect of trolls who disparage others' differences under a veil of anonymity. In extremis, the harm that this can do is to lead to desperate attempts to commit suicide that may often be successful.

To this list, we can also add the effects of Internet grooming of children and young people that can lead to lifelong harm. In some areas of the country, networks of abusers have targeted vulnerable young people, groomed them for sex and exploited them. Young girls in care have been particularly vulnerable responding to the initial apparent warmth and care they are shown. It has been indicated that these problems are not confined to particular areas but are widespread across the country.

Social disadvantage

Croll and Moses (1985) found that the home background was the most significant factor in predisposing pupils to problem behaviours. Three social factors were associated with poor attainments and problem behaviours: atypical families, low income and substandard housing.

Problem behaviour or SEBD is especially related to underachievement. Some schools cope poorly with it, and pupils curtail their own opportunities for learning because of it, thus anything that causes problem behaviour to increase will put pupils at risk from UAch whatever their levels of ability.

The NCB survey by Wedge and Prosser (1979) showed that social disadvantage had an enduring effect even in children of high ability and its effects worsened at secondary school. These factors can be regarded as putting pupils at greater risk from an unhelpful curriculum and teaching ethos. There is a range of such factors.

'At risk' social factors

- Socialisation – reward and punishment regime is inconsistent, too lax or too severe.
- Models and social learning are deviant.
- Socio-economic factors and values are poor.
- Enculturation and subcultures are deviant.
- Temperamental inheritance is difficult or unpredictable.
- Emotional relationships and tone are of poor quality.
- Physical relationships are of poor quality.
- Family relationships are dysfunctional.
- Illness and medical conditions are frequent or chronic.
- Nervous health is precarious and illness likely.
- Mental health and illness are possible long-term consequences.
- Dysfunctions are cerebral and relational.

Dysfunctional families or personalities?

The following have been found to be common denominators in disruption and delinquency by many researchers from 1922 onwards (Robins (1966), West (1967, 1982), Rutter (1985), Farrington (1994), Cooper (1999), and Cefai et al. (2015).

Disruptive behaviours often emerge under stress or at crisis points in a child's life, such as the following:

- During family discord and quarrelling
- During family break-up and divorce
- During severe parental illness and hospitalisation
- When a new baby is born
- In families where there is a lack of affection and support
- In families where there is abuse and neglect
- At puberty with mood swings
- Under peer group rejection

- As a result of a learning difficulty
- As a result of early psychiatric disorder
- As a result of cyberbullying

The themes that emerged from a survey on pupils with social, emotional and behavioural difficulties in schools and units for SEBD by Cole et al. (1998) about family background were very similar to those of the earlier studies and tended to result in emotional as well as behavioural difficulties. They include the following:

- Broken marriages
- Lone parents struggling to cope financially
- Problems encountered with pupil's siblings (e.g. delinquency, learning difficulties or health problems)
- Relationship problems with mother's new partner or step-siblings
- Unsuitable models for child (e.g. parents involved in drugs, alcohol or recidivism)
- Psychiatric difficulties (e.g. mother depressive and has attempted suicide)
- Physical abuse in some households

They also commented,

> In contrast to the articulate nature and successful education of some, many parents were reported to have had educational difficulties of their own which have left them with bitter memories from their school days. This in turn colours their perception of their children's schooling and teachers and suspicion and hatred may stand in the way of building positive relationships. This may explain the aggression and hostility which was reported in our survey as often exhibited towards staff.
>
> (p. 37)

It is of note that few researchers in the SEBD literature discuss the utter boredom of some classrooms and the lack of cognitive challenge in the ordinary curriculum. This only tends to be found in the gifted education literature, but it is the school experience of so many, as shadowing pupils will show.

'Toxic families' and abuse

Every now and again, a case comes to public knowledge where an infant or school-age child has been so seriously abused over a short or long period of time that he or she dies. The abuse may be physical battering, emotional and sexual abuse or extreme neglect leading to starvation. It could be a mixture of all of these. Two children a week are thought to die at their parents' hands. This terrible rearing environment is the tip of an iceberg below which many more children are brutalised by one or more members of their family.

Such were the cases of Mary Bell, who killed two young boys in 1968 (Sereny, 1999), and Robert Thompson and Jon Venables, the two young boys who killed Jamie Bulger in 1993 (Smith, 2017).

Families in which children are physically battered by a drunken father or stepfather and allowed to watch pornographic videos may also be unsupported by a drug-abusing mother. They can model what they experience and act out their family life or what they see on videos and games. For years, they may have been uncontrollable in school and in the local area, and the family are known as a problem family to Social Services.

Only early removal from such a toxic environment and being put into a safe foster home would help them. Instead, they become housed in a secure unit for young offenders, and their only hope is to experience a supportive mentor and befriender with therapeutic support of the kind that helped Mary Bell leave prison and attain a normal life.

Very bright children can also be born into such environments, and the consequences for society can be very serious indeed. They are likely to underachieve in schools and be disaffected or become pupils who are excluded because of their problem behaviours. They may easily take to street life, organising local gangs, graduating over time from minor to major larceny and serious crime. Because they are clever, they may avoid detection for a lifetime. They will have learnt to be cruel and lack empathy and concern for others. They can become gang leaders, and those who can kill without compunction. The early signs of these disturbing patterns can be seen in children who are unaccountably and exceptionally cruel to animals and to younger children, especially when unobserved. They are said to be 'sociopaths' or 'psychopaths' in the making.

Language and disadvantage

One of the defining characteristics of the class system and its modern manifestations is the limitations that are placed upon linguistic development in impoverished cultural settings. Poverty of itself is not necessarily an indication of cultural or linguistic disadvantage. Some very poor people live a rich cultural life through the free library system in the UK, books, music, museums, free entertainments, and social and cultural informal groups and free education.

Teachers have been becoming concerned over the last decade and more about the level of language competence of children entering school. They articulate poorly, do not speak in sentences and have a very limited vocabulary knowledge for common everyday objects and events. Some parents are not aware of how essential it is to speak to their babies and have waited until the child begins to speak of his or her own accord. They do not realise that babies need to hear language in order to 'pick it up'. Busy parents often dress their children when they should be helping them learn how to dress themselves. Others now keep their infants in modern absorbent nappies so that they arrive at school still not 'potty trained'.

The response to these needs must be to decrease the numbers of children in the early years classrooms so that more speaking and listening activities can be employed. In severe circumstances, nurture groups may need to be considered (Bannathan and Boxall, 1998) for at least the first two terms.

Children with speech difficulties and disorders are widely bullied in our schools and need extra consideration and language support, including speech therapy especially on starting school.

In the late 1960s, Bernstein (reprinted 1970) wrote a paper titled 'Education Cannot Compensate for Society'. He proposed that poor cultural environments disadvantage children, and schools cannot help them recover from it and achieve their true potential. Labov (1970) wrote a reply to this entitled 'The Logic of Non-Standard English' showing that the language used in black cultures had deep structures and meanings that did enable the user to think and express abstract ideas but not in the formal 'middle class' language of the schools.

The controversy raged for many years, and each side's position is still implicit in many attitudes today. However, what we now know is that an education that promotes critical thinking can compensate for society's limitations. The implication is that if schools do not use these approaches, learners are disadvantaged and they are reinforcing linguistic disadvantage. Successive HMI reports plead for more opportunities for legitimised talk in classrooms at all levels. Without it, we are creating underachievers.

The language of 'grunt' and 'whatever' was complained of by the Secretary of State for education at the turn of the millennium. In the interim, concern has been expressed about language development in the home, and projects such as Sure Start were implemented to help parents understand the importance of language and how to promote it with their children.

Now research has shown that more children are arriving at primary school still unable to communicate adequately, and children from low-income families were usually a year behind when starting school (Sutton Trust, 2010). An initiative to address this was 'Stoke Speaks Out', and in a Radio 4 programme, 'Why Can't Our Children Talk?', it was discussed with Jean Gross (5/2/2019), researcher and psychologist, and the use of tablets and video games to amuse and occupy very young children was blamed for the problem. Teachers have reported seeing the infants pressing shop windows, glass screens and pictures to 'make them work'.

Since then, it has been recommended that children under 2 years should not spend more than one hour a day watching screens, although the evidence of any actual damage is awaited.

Behaviour, disaffection, disadvantage and UAch

As already discussed, underachievement can lead to stress in the learner, and disaffection can spread quickly from a single subject to the schoolwork in general, especially when no help or recognition is given to the problems. Learners frequently respond to these stresses by becoming a nuisance in class as they try to avoid or evade exposing their difficulties or as they become excessively bored waiting for something interesting or relevant to be imparted. They can begin to misbehave or withdraw into an internal world.

There is frequently a continuum of behavioural difficulties to be seen in any classroom, and an individual pupil may move forward and back on such a continuum in different lessons and with different teachers. Behavioural difficulties in this context are those that teachers generally regard to be a nuisance and prevent the normal progress of work in the classroom or the normal work of an individual. These behaviours range from chatting and attention seeking at the mildest level to disruption, aggression and violence at the other extreme.

Minor attention-seeking behaviour can be seen to be exacerbated by other 'at risk' factors and can result in the pupil responding to the extra stresses by becoming more disruptive and finally being excluded from school.

Disruptive behaviour is

> That which interferes with the learning and opportunities of other pupils and imposes undue stress upon the teacher.
>
> DES (1979), Elton (1989)

The problem behaviours disaffected pupils exhibit are of two main kinds:

* 'ACTING OUT' Attention seeking, chatting, calling out
* 'ACTING IN' Withdrawal and passivity

Withdrawal and passivity are more likely to be linked to the development of emotional difficulties. 'Acting out' behaviours are wide-ranging and overt and more

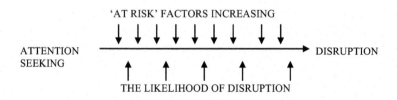

Figure 2.1 The 'Richter scale' of disruption

often associated with extrovert temperament and males. There are other behaviours equally challenging but which have a more serious medical or emotional basis, such as vandalism, violence, fire setting (arson), precocious sexual behaviour and psychotic behaviours.

Children with emotional and behavioural difficulties characteristically also may develop learning problems because of their lack of time on task over years of misbehaviour. Some develop behaviour difficulties secondary to a learning difficulty that has not been diagnosed and account taken. Older dyslexics, for example, frequently learn to read well, but as soon as they are required to write fear failure and evade, avoid or become agitated and are singled out as a behaviour problem rather than having a learning need.

Rutter et al. (1970) in their 'Isle of Wight Survey' found that

- A third of boys referred for behaviour problems had specific reading difficulties.
- Many showed serious educational backwardness.
- Their IQ was usually in the normal range, but if it was lower than average, this was associated with an increased likelihood of aggression, antisocial or delinquent behaviour.
- The ethos of certain schools and styles of teaching and discipline may predispose to or protect certain children from conduct disorders.

They said that **'the influences are, however, poorly understood'**. This is perhaps the most significant factor, and I think we can claim to understand this a bit more today, 50 years on.

Behavioural problems and problems of definition

The main difficulties are that these are **socially disapproved** behaviours, the prognosis is poor and the onset appears in early childhood. Teachers are mostly concerned with pre-delinquent or non-delinquent problems that were 3:1 more common in boys (Rutter et al., 1970), for example, fighting, wandering away, disruption, bullying, aggression, defiance, destructiveness, attention-seeking and lying. Today with the developing 'ladette' culture of girls, the ratio may be smaller.

Classroom disruption by various forms of attention-seeking behaviour and distractibility is the problem behaviour of most concern to the teachers who were involved in a range of studies. The attention-seeking and disruption took many different forms, depending on the pupil's personality. The main problem for the teachers was the continuous low-level chatter (Elton Report, 1989; DCFS, 2009b), and it continues to be the case. Underlying many of these problem behaviours, there seems to be a general inability to relate to peers, the teacher or the task set; hence, they are entitled social, emotional and behavioural difficulties (SEBD).

Personal 'at risk' factors from giftedness

Being gifted or talented can bring about its own problems and a range of these is listed here and appear widely in the literature (Reis and McCoach, 2000; Sisk, 2000; Niehart, 2011; Blaas, 2014). But many aspects also occur more widely amongst learners who are not 'gifted':

- Perfectionism
- Goals too high
- Persistence
- Overactivity
- Clowning
- Disruption
- Emotional tenseness
- Boredom
- Lack of cognitive challenge
- Independence
- Questioning
- Daydreaming
- Knows too much (!)
- Independence
- Creativity
- Stubbornness

Although some of these factors are also positives, it does depend to a large extent on how they are expressed, for example, the tone and frequency of questioning, the appropriateness of the clowning, the manner of dealing with personal frustration and the aggression of others, independence, how disturbing the behaviour can be to the routine of the teacher. Largely, there is a social dimension to all of these so that socially skilled pupils will get away with far more than those who are not. Thus social skills training will be part of the intervention systems considered in the next section.

A checklist for identifying the onset of behaviour problems with an emotional base

- Sudden deterioration in standard of schoolwork.
- Restlessness and inability to concentrate in class – poor work
- Irritability and sulkiness
- Aggressiveness often with little provocation
- Acts of delinquency, particularly stealing articles of little value to give away, despite punishment
- Attention seeking behaviour (e.g. repeated clowning as a means of attracting attention)
- The emergence of a speech defect
- Excessive day-dreaming
- A tendency to rapidly changing moods
- Failure to keep or make friends (e.g. over-shy or inhibited)
- Over-sensitivity when criticised or corrected

Current Internet 'at risk' factors – IGD (APA DSM-V, 2006)

The effects of grooming and trolling facilitated by the Internet have been widely discussed, but there is another current and common concern. This is the amount of time that some children devote to their devices, such as their phone. 'How long is too long?' That is a common question, as is 'When is it too early to give such access?'

This has been of such concern that the American Psychiatric Association issued mental health guidelines on the subject of Internet gaming disorder (IGD) in its update of DSM-V 2013.797. It states that IGD arises from video-gaming and Internet-based virtual communication. Like 'one-armed bandits', they set up intermittent reinforcement and habituation that is hard to disconnect from.

The guidance is that in a 12-month period, five out of nine of the following are present for diagnosis:

- Forms the dominant activity in daily life
- Abstinence causes withdrawal symptoms
- Tolerance builds up
- Lack of success in controlling participation
- Loss of interest in previous hobbies
- Continuous and excessive despite knowledge of the problems

- Deceitful about participation in gaming
- Deceitful information on amount of regular use
- Jeopardises marriage and career or school attainments

As can be seen, these criteria can apply to current concerns about betting that can be another gaming disorder. Most recently, the concerns centre on 11- to 16-year-olds, 45 per cent of whom admit to viewing pornographic images regularly.

Hillman (2014) described cases of people who had been referred to her for counselling. Characteristically they were adolescents who were spending more time on gaming each day than schoolwork to the extent of six or seven hours and two hours or more on texting. They were getting six or seven hours of sleep, which was not enough. They had become irascible and overactive and could not concentrate on schoolwork. Some who had joined virtual communities had been given roles, sometimes dangerous ones, such as those that inspired two girls, not in her caseload, to set out to murder a third.

Knife crimes

The origin of knife crime and its ethos is likely to be found in many of the factors discussed earlier, and research on its participants will no doubt help show its central causes and remedies. Youth gangs have always been with us, and many of us have joined them and fought other gang members usually over (irrelevant) territorial disputes but not usually with knives. Today, additional considerations may be necessary, such as purveyance of media violence, criminal models, drugs and density problems, as well as failure to achieve and connect with current educational practice and work ethics.

On 15 July 2019, a study for the mayor's office in London showed that the poorer an area of the city was, the higher the rates of youth violence are likely to be. Richmond upon Thames had the lowest level of youth violence in the capital – and it is also the least deprived borough in the city, based on official figures (Radio 4 News, Today Programme).

Conclusion

Disadvantage is an extremely complex set of factors that can lead to underachievement in schools, and poverty is only one of its many contributors. Nevertheless, some low-income families defy this trend, and their success needs to be investigated and used as a model for others.

What seems to emerge from a consideration of the range of disadvantaging factors is the importance of the interactions between parents and carers and children and between teachers and pupils in their care. One of the ways in which the parent-child interactions may be improved would be by an education for parenthood in schools. This is not a new suggestion but was seriously being promoted in the period 1985–1990 by the Fawcett Society Education Committee, and some schools were trying to support this. It was an initiative swept away by the introduction of the National Curriculum, but it has been shown once again to be an important consideration for current and future education policies now that families live in more isolated conditions and there are increasing numbers of 'blended families'. 'Life skills' courses are to be reintroduced to pupils in secondary schools to prepare them for independence at university and in employment.

The interactions between pupils and teachers show how crucial these are in the promotion of ability and talent in those whose backgrounds have been less than supportive. It is a last chance for many of them before the 'slough of despond'. In government's eyes, it appears that recruiting the cleverest to become teachers by selecting those having the best degree results from universities and putting them through a one-year training period has been the answer. 'Teach First' initiatives have not provided the answers either, and even the many three- and four-year B.Ed. programmes have not provided solutions. This is not to deny that many teachers and some schools do succeed, but more of them are needed.

From the study of disadvantage in education, it is noted that the structure of establishments themselves can conflict with the educative goals. Of prime concern are the transition years – reception and year 7. The biggest fears of children are that they might be bullied by the 'big' children. The problem for teachers is that it is difficult to get to know and work individually with classes of 25 to 30, and in reception, the language work and motor and social skills needs cannot be addressed from the outset. Year 8s lose momentum as a result of year 7's experiences.

It is suggested that transition year classes are half size with not more than 15 to 16 pupils in them, as is the case in many private schools. This investment will have long-term benefits in integrating and settling all the pupils.

A method successfully tried by one large West London comprehensive was to run an integrated curriculum in year 7 in which the pupils stayed for over half the time with one teacher. It was disbanded following the NC and after complaints by year 8 staff that the pupils came to them from the integrated system too confident and wanted to question what they were taught too much.

The selection and training of teachers for the needs of future generations is of more importance and sophistication now than it has ever been. But the current pattern and process has not been fit for purpose. Research has shown that teachers can make a difference, they are 'the key', but it is essential that their education and training is changed to prevent so many children becoming distressed and underachieving.

Examples in later chapters will address these needs, and each chapter will provide a CPD resource and suggestions file.

3 How schools can raise achievement

Introduction

Underachievement is widely defined as the failure of individuals to live up to or meet their potential. However, success in English schools is currently defined in the narrow terms of success in SATs, GCSEs and university places, not potential for developing as a fully rounded and fulfilled human being as once used to be the case. Concentration now is focused upon producing an educated workforce equipped to meet the needs of industries of the future. But the extent to which this can be achieved by a bookish university programme needs to be questioned. What should happen to the 50 per cent who do not go to a university? What should be their career plans and programmes?

The UK 'gold standard' for success in school was five A* to Cs in GCSE examinations at 16 years old, now converted to grades 9 to 1 with grade 1 the lowest. Annually, around 58 per cent of pupils have achieved the gold standard. On closer examination, DfES (2006) found that 38 per cent of white girls did not achieve this standard, 47.6 per cent of white boys did not; nor did 48.6 per cent of black girls and 59.7 per cent of black boys. Chinese children performed best of all, and Caribbean, Bangladeshi, Pakistani and white working-class boys worst of all. Thus, although potential may be equal, opportunity was not, and this pattern has persisted over time.

It is expected that the scores on IQ tests will be normally distributed, but attainments tests, such as SATs and GCSEs, are not. These depend much more upon good teaching and learning practices, individual strength of motivation and effort and home-school support rather than just intellectual ability.

The 'home' effect, according to Ofsted (2006), was around 10 per cent and stronger than school effects. Marking systems that use criterion referencing also tend to result in non-normal distributions of scores, as can the use of project work. The normal distribution is a distribution of errors in question setting, marking and so on.

Some state schools achieve 100 per cent at the 'gold standard', others 13 per cent and up to 600 schools have been categorised as 'failing' – that is, not achieving 30 per cent at the standard. Some schools in disadvantaged areas are high achieving, whereas others in exactly the same situation are not.

Regularly, it has been found that our children are the unhappiest in Europe and that they are forever worrying about SATs, for they are some of the most assessed in the world. Testing regimes can have unintentional consequences in rewarding a few at the expense of the many and assessing inappropriate targets. An assessment-driven system such as ours reduces intrinsic motivation (Ryan and Deci, 2000), the desire to work and achieve for its own sake. It causes standards to decline (Feller, 1994) as teachers learn to teach to the tests. Because of the UK's testing regime, the curriculum has indeed been narrowed by many teachers as they have learned to teach to the tests to boost their school's position in the league tables.

An assessment-driven system added to an objectives-based approach to school inspections can also encourage a coercive, authoritarian system that induces widespread bullying and gives rise to unrest and underachievement (Mongon and Hart, 1989; Galloway and Goodwin, 1987; Montgomery, 1989). It therefore does little to promote respect and self-esteem. This analysis and prediction have indeed been borne out, and bullying and underachievement are widespread in English schools so that many government initiatives are constantly being funded to overcome them. The underlying causes are never properly addressed, and schools are bombarded with over 100 initiatives, guidelines and regulations each year. The spectacle of members of Parliament bullying and shouting across the House is also an unacceptable model for the behaviour of the young.

The results of highly didactic and assessment-driven systems were researched by Gregory and Clarke (2003) in England and East Asian schools. They were shown to generate an elite of winners and an underclass of losers. In the Asian schools, they found that one in three primary school children said they found life not worth living; four in five spent three hours or more per day on homework; and seven out of ten had extra classes after school. They concluded that the biggest problem in Asian schools was fear created by the cumulative and detrimental effect of high stakes assessment and an unhealthy focus on school grades.

Singapore, frequently top in the academic league tables, was found to produce teenagers who

> exhibit a narrow mindedness, tend to be smug and egocentric, and see the paper chase as the means to a good life . . . they make good employees, but few can think out of the box, much less lead.
>
> (Cited in Heng and Tam, 2006, 172)

How could even gifted individuals worldwide from these settings solve the problems we are even now beginning to face? What of the development of wisdom and what some call spiritual needs? Interestingly, this has recently been recognised in some of these 'Tiger' economies, and they are trying to modify their education systems and methods to promote more creative and challenging learning environments.

Statistics have also revealed that boys in the UK by comparison with girls are performing 10 per cent less well up to GCSEs, especially in subjects requiring a lot of writing (HMCI, 2007; Montgomery, 2008a), and few from lower socio-economic groups, especially boys, gain a place at university or if they do, maintain that place. At A levels, the performances become more equal, and then in employment, young men outperform young women. This has been revealed by requiring companies to publish the gender differences in pay and in the roles and ranks occupied by men and women. Most recently, investigations of gender stereotyping reveal that this appears to have strengthened in infancy rather than been relaxed, and the Fawcett Society (2019) is investigating this. Later, girls only make up 10 per cent of the pupils taking STEM subjects at advanced level, and this will exclude them from many important careers, such as 'coding' and engineering in the information age. STEM take-up in all-girls' schools is much higher than in co-ed schools.

Underachievement in schools would also appear to be an international problem, especially for the disadvantaged and those of low socio-economic status, whether or not they are gifted (Passow, 1990; Wallace and Eriksson, 2006).

Early years gaps – Sutton Trust Research 2010

Children growing up in the UK today from the poorest fifth of families are already nearly a year behind those children from middle income families in vocabulary tests by age 5, when most children start school. The gap between the poor and middle income children is more marked than between middle and higher income children. Children from the richest fifth of families are 5.2 months ahead of those children from middle income families in vocabulary tests by age 5 – despite the fact that the income gap between the middle- and the top-earning families is 2.3 times larger than the income gap between the middle- and bottom-earning families.

Parenting style (for example, sensitivity of parent-child interactions and rules about bedtimes) and the home environment (factors like parental reading and trips to museums and galleries) contributed up to half of the explained cognitive gap between the lowest and middle income families. Just under half (45 per cent) of children from the poorest fifth of families were read to daily at age 3, compared with 8 in 10 (78 per cent) of children from the richest fifth of families. Nearly half (47 per cent) of children from the poorest fifth of families were born to mothers aged under 25; just under two-thirds (65 per cent) did not live with both biological parents by age 5. Over a third (37 per cent) of children from the poorest fifth of families were born to parents without a single A-C grade GCSE between them; only 1 in 12 of the poorest families contained a degree-educated parent compared with 4 in 5 of the richest families.

Twenty-eight per cent of the poorest mothers were employed when their child was aged 5, compared with 73 per cent of the richest mothers. Comparing children with the same family income, parental characteristics and home environments, those who were read to every day at age 3 had a vocabulary at age 5 nearly two months more advanced than those who were not read to every day. Regular bedtimes at 3 and 5 were associated with gains of two and a half months at age 5.

Comparing children with the same parenting behaviours, characteristics and home environments, those from the poorest fifth of families were on average three months behind those from middle income families at age 5. Similarly, a child at age 5 with a degree-educated parent was three and a half months ahead of a similar child with no parent with a grade A–C GCSE or above. Children at age 5 whose mothers were aged 25–29 at the time of the birth had a vocabulary three and a half months more advanced than similar children of teenage mothers.

Proposals for practice and policy from this survey were that children's centres should offer effective parenting programmes. Sure Start early learning practitioners should work in partnership with health professionals to support families, including home visits and outreach projects for the hardest to reach children and to contact vulnerable families. Nursery education should be extended to 25 hours a week for all to 2–4-year-olds from the 15 per cent most disadvantaged families.

As reported in Chapter 2, increasing numbers of primary school children are arriving at school in 2019 not toilet trained and hardly able to speak in sentences. This is especially true of children in the most disadvantaged areas of the country.

Raising the achievement of able underachievers

Reis and McCoach (2000) concluded that the research showed that the most important factor in raising achievement was to identify the underachievers as able and to tell them and then support them against and through the many pressures and stresses that they encountered. As will be seen, holding high expectations of all children, identifying their strengths and supporting them will raise their achievements (DCFS, 2009a). They need someone to listen to them and believe in them. The effect of telling teachers that particular children were more able was originally investigated by Rosenthal and Jacobsen (1968) and was termed 'Pygmalion in the classroom'. Every book on managing behaviour problems since demonstrates the positive effects of raising our expectations of children and the power of CBG (catching them being good) and CBC (catching them being clever) (Montgomery, 1989, 1996, 2015; Wheldall and Merritt, 1987; Long, 2005; Rogers, 2007).

Boys' Achievement

Boys in the UK were found to be on average 10 per cent behind girls in their achievements at GCSE in England, and this caused a flurry of research and a concerned outcry in the media. However, boys have been underachieving for over three hundred years. We have not noticed this until national statistics were collected and until girls have been obliged to stay at school to the same age as boys and have been offered the same curriculum and ostensibly the same opportunities. At A levels, these differences largely disappear until entry to work, when discrimination against females appears to set in again in their failure to gain equal representation in employment and equal pay for equal work.

What has followed from this concern is that an analysis has been made of situations in which boys become better engaged with schoolwork and gain results comparable to girls. In these situations, teacher-led, fast-paced, challenging classes, strictly enforced uniform, punctuality and attendance policies, equal treatment and equal opportunities are recommended by head teacher Arnold (2004). Arnot and Gubb (2001) found that girls were more flexible learners and more able to work with different styles of teaching and assessment than boys, and this contributed to their greater success.

Assessments such as course work appeared to favour girls' more persistent and consistent attitudes to work. Thus, course work was discontinued from some significant exams, and so boys were favoured again.

Some general reasons put forward for UAch in the UK are

- Media values and models
- Rise of feminism
- Teaching methods
- Attitudes of parents, teachers, peers
- Cultural, subcultural and local values
- Lack of relevance of school
- School, books, tasks, girl-orientated
- Influence of 19th-century public school system in 21st-century schooling

Many reasons have been put forward for underachievement in boys and girls, and these do need to be understood if we are to do something about it. The following lists indicate some of these more specific reasons:

Reasons for UAch in boys	Reasons for UAch in girls
Boy code – uncool to be seen to try	Girl 'cool'
Construction of English masculinity	'Little lady' syndrome
Lag in language skills	'Soaps' syndrome
Attitudes to language work	Year 7/8 pubertal changes – the feminine
Stereotypes of 'boy' and 'lads'	'Ladettes'
Types of assessment	Structural discrimination

Reasons for UAch in boys	Reasons for UAch in girls
Style of work set	Secondary schools – subject stereotypes
Bullying of 'boffs'	'Boys are teachers' pets', they bully and
Rise of feminism	harass girls, get more time, attention and respect

However, we have to bear in mind that boys have been said to be underachieving for over 300 years, and some concern was expressed about it by the Board of Education (1923, 20) as follows:

'It is well-known that most boys, especially at the period of adolescence have a habit of healthy idleness'.

With this attitude, a complacent tolerance of boys' idleness is encouraged, but girls would be treated differently and rejected for it. The influences that can give rise to underachievement arising from the lists can be seen to be multidimensional. Their effects work more strongly on some children than others, whilst some children are vulnerable in particular ways. The results of underachievement are not only apparent in the pupil's failure to learn at an appropriate level, but there are often behavioural consequences that can be quite concerning. In fact, the behavioural patterns are sometimes the only indication that all is not well. These patterns or typologies may fit any underachiever. Many frustrated and bored young children can become very disruptive indeed. They yearn to go to school, they enjoy it for a week or a fortnight, and then it all becomes too slow and repetitive. Unable to escape, they become frustrated, angry and disruptive. Eventually, the disruption may lead to depression, or they present a profile of high activity/motility and become incorrectly labelled as hyperactive.

In a survey of six primary and six secondary schools identified for their good provision in the NACE (National Association for Able Children in Education) Challenge Awards system, some types or patterns suggested for investigation were

* Coasters or cruisers
* Daydreamers
* Impatient inattentives
* Overactives
* Rhinos (Really Here in Name Only)
* Risk avoiders
* Disruptives
* Twice exceptionals

The study found that these types were not in evidence or considered by the teachers except for children who might be coasting (Wallace et al., 2009). Thus, even in good provision, UAch could be missed among the overactives, the disruptives, the doubly exceptionals and the non-participators.

The case of Alison

Daydreamers withdraw from lessons in whole or in part because the daydreams are more interesting and engaging, or they are troubled and have difficult events or emotions to deal with. Alison was a case in point, as in year 8 and 9, she began to slip down from a place in the top ten of the class to near the bottom in achievement. She was told that if she did not improve her performance, she would lose her place in the fast-tracking class and be moved 'down'.

She would miss her friends and lose self-esteem. She decided to stop daydreaming so much and to try to concentrate for full lessons to see what would happen. In the next set of reports, she came fifth. Having established the reason and maintained her place, she decided she could relax again and just 'pull out the stops' as and when necessary. This pattern continued, and in mock A levels, she played noughts and crosses and drew pictures but gained A's in the finals. This harmed the predictions that the school could make for any application to higher education or a job. Once in a job in the real world, she made quite startling progress. Alison revealed this background when she referred her son to the LDRP writing project in 2016 and took part herself. Her son was underachieving in year 7.

In a government-funded initiative to lift underachievement, Hackman (2005) identified those who had 'stalled' in year 7 and 8 as follows:

* Don't see the point; lack personal goals and motivation
* Experience education as something done to them not something that is personally significant or having transferable value
* In secondary, miss having one teacher
* Hesitate at conceptual staging points
* Are skilled in avoidance and concealment strategies
* Crave attention, direction, purposeful teaching

The case of Lee

Lee was 13/14 in 1980. He lived on a council estate until he was 5, and then the family moved to a private housing estate a few miles down the road. He went to the local secondary school. His mother did not work, and his father joined an American manufacturing company as a machine operator and worked his way up to become managing director over 15 to 20 years. Both his parents came from poor backgrounds and were less concerned with abstract ideas about life and the future and more concerned with practical activities for the job market – trades, specifically, they felt were the thing to aim for.

Lee wrote,

> My early years at school are somewhat hazy now but I was always pretty good at most of the subjects and found it quite enjoyable. On the move to the secondary school things changed slightly due to being part of a bigger school but I still performed well academically, even if most of my reports still contained plenty of references to 'being able to do better'.
>
> Nothing seemed terribly difficult I had the subjects I was really into, such as Physics and English. Anything to do with rote learning didn't grip me, such as history and mathematics; in physics I could see an application to the calculations whereas in maths it was just doing sums for no discernible reason other than to show 'working out'.
>
> Things changed around 13/14 but I can't put my finger on what happened, there was no conscious turning away from school, but I just felt I had less and less in common with my contemporaries, parents and wider family. I felt a growing sense of isolation, whereas previously I had a wide social circle this narrowed significantly and I stopped taking part in sports that I'd previously enjoyed.
>
> I just didn't feel a part of things anymore, I think that was the beginning of the slide downwards, but to this day I don't really know why it happened, it wasn't an overnight change, perhaps over the course of a few months. To this day, and knowing what I know now I am still confused and saddened by what happened and feel utterly powerless to effect any long lasting comfort from the knowledge.
>
> I left school with a handful of CSE's and so the only work I could obtain was mainly unskilled repetitive factory work, but although I was earning all it really did was drive me insane. The sheer boredom of life was devastating and the desperation of looking down a lens of where I'd be in 20/30/40 years' time was something I just couldn't comprehend.
>
> To take the pain away I self-medicated through drink and drugs which ultimately cost me another two or three years of waste but it was a relief from my day-to-day life. Through desperation I sold up and worked abroad for a year; returned to Surrey and after more manual work joined the Armed Forces.
>
> At 28 I saw an advert to join MENSA and after passing the test I became a member. This was a seminal moment as for the first time I began to understand more about myself and who I was.
>
> I left the Armed Forces in 2000 and since then I have obtained BSc and MBA degrees and am currently undertaking a professional doctorate. The Mensa test

was life changing. I have a debt of gratitude to Mensa I can probably never repay, without that I don't know what I'd be doing today.

If you have a failed education that is not something you recover from in a couple of years, in fact I don't think you ever recover and so I live the damaging output of that on a daily basis.

What were Lee's responses to the Hackman questionnaire today?

Don't see the point; lack personal goals and motivation?
'Yes, for me once I'd learnt the subject as taught I was more interested in learning more about the subject in depth. I could see examinations as being valid for those people aiming for university but it never occurred to me I'd even be able to attend 6th form let alone university. And given my careers advice was really centred on obtaining a trade and/or job I didn't necessarily see the point of qualifications'.

Experience education as something done to them, not something that is personally significant or having transferable value?
'I always felt that teachers were talking at me, not engaging with me/us. When they did engage it was more to perform rote learning confirmation. If any attempt was made to discuss wider implications or thoughts then this was usually dismissed as being something for later education phases / years and not relevant to the current question.'

In secondary they miss having one teacher?
'Absolutely; I was lucky in that my 4th and 5th year form tutor remained the same so this provided some continuity for me. I struggled when new teachers joined the school and also when stand-in teachers took some classes (for regular teacher illness cover etc.); even if they were better teachers I found the disruption distracting and especially if they taught a lesson out of schedule. The down side was that my form tutor knew a lecturer in Physics at Loughborough University, she suggested that I would benefit from speaking to him as I had an obvious 'gift' for Physics; this was a revelation to me that anyone would feel that I had the ability to attend university or be seen as having some potential to. I was deeply excited by this and was restless for weeks, unfortunately she informed me a few weeks later that the lecturer thought that it would be better to wait until I had obtained my O Level results before having any conversations.

Looking back I think this was a seminal point in my downfall, it's hard to articulate the sense of loss and hopelessness I felt, it was as if the lecturer had confirmed my own thoughts that university was not something I should be thinking about. I distinctly remember giving up on higher education at this point; it seemed futile to continue if such an expert felt there was no point in even having a conversation with me. Although I can now see my form tutor did this with the best of intentions I wish she had either not informed me of her idea until she had spoken to the lecturer or simply not bothered, as my outcome may have been different'.

They hesitate at conceptual staging points?
'Probably the opposite, I used to look forward to moving forward, I always hoped it would be the stage that deeper knowledge would be exposed'.

They are skilled in avoidance and concealment strategies?
'Yes, I tended to not put myself in front and always downplayed my academic ability; usually by saying how boring and pointless it all was. But I always felt deeply uncomfortable about this and instinctively knew that I was doing myself a disservice'.

Crave attention, direction, purposeful teaching?
'I wanted secretive attention; to explain, I didn't want the public visibility of attainment but I wanted the teacher to recognise that I could answer any questions raised but didn't put my hand up for fear of exposing myself and/or getting the answer wrong'.

Lee, did any of these statements apply to you?
'Absolutely, please see above.'

Inside Lee's story, we can see the power that teachers have to improve pupils' aspirations and performance by those small positive encounters. There is also the tell-tale sign: 'Could do better'. Someone needed to take him in hand and explain exactly how he could do better and why. They presumably had reports from primary and some ability test results even though he was in the secondary modern school in the comprehensive school period.

Equally parents need to learn how encouragement and improving their children's self-esteem can support them through school and build resilience.

The lack of intellectual challenge of Lee's curriculum is depressing and clearly harmed him, as it does so many children, including average and slower learners who will not become members of MENSA. The potential of six hours a day of boredom can create alienation, disaffection, disruption and truancy. It is often why some pupils will say they only go to school to be with their friends.

The answer to boys' lower achievement is not necessarily to develop more 'boy friendly' schooling and thereby disadvantage girls again but to develop more collaborative and co-operative learning that both can enjoy and is better for personal development and team-building. In addition, both boys and girls need to experience a challenging and interesting curriculum with opportunities to follow things in depth as well as in breadth. They also need to learn to develop the skills of resilience, self-regulation and autonomous learning so that they find a pleasure in learning for its own sake.

The want to learn will enable boys also to develop as more flexible learners and girls to find independence in learning. In addition, opportunities for creative responses and independent research projects of the students' own choice can lift the achievement of gifted underachievers (Baum et al., 1995). But what was suitable for them was found suitable for all learners in raising achievement (Montgomery, 1990, 1996, 2009).

What ordinary schools need to do

When we get down to basics, it is the school and its teachers that hold the key to the success or failure of their pupils. Whatever individuals bring to a situation, it is the role of the school to work with them and enable them to achieve. This is the first and foremost aim in education that all teachers seem to espouse. Yet confronted with an anti-authority, work-shy, 'bored' or disruptive individual, they tend to take it personally and seek to place the onus on the pupil to improve rather than review the range of factors that may be operating to cause this behaviour. They adhere to the 'within child' model.

Children who smile at us and answer our questions and do the work we set are seen to be reinforcing us in positive ways and gain our support and respect. The others are viewed as rejecting us and do not gain our support, extended information and feedback (Good and Brophy, 1986). Manipulative pupils are clever at benefiting from these situations.

Five steps towards lifting underachievement in schools

Step 1: audit the students' basic skills

When we do such an audit, we find that there are many areas of concern that do not emerge from the SATs results. SATs test pupils' knowledge of English in reading and writing, mathematics (and science). Pupils in Key Stage 1 are expected on average to achieve level 2 and at Key Stage 2 level 4 and so on.

There are however other considerations that can affect the quality and levels of performance that are not always assessed but are relevant in raising achievement. These are in the basic skills of reading, writing and number. For example, although reading skills are recognised as problem areas for some pupils, writing speed seldom is. But writing speed affects the amount children can write in test periods, and boys initially are slower and poorer than girls in this motor skill (Montgomery, 2008a, 2017a). It means they cannot write what they want to write and over time become disheartened and cease to try. Unfortunately, the research focuses almost wholly on motivating them to want to write (Wray, 2005; Wilson, 2019) when some basic skills intervention would raise their interest and boost their achievement. In all phases of school education and at university, slow writing speed contributes to lower grades (Berninger, 2008; Connelly et al., 2005).

Spelling problems are also widely involved. Poor spelling slows down the writing speed by an average of two words per minute and more in severe spelling problems (Montgomery, 2008a). Poor reading skills affect the ability to comprehend text questions and can handicap results in both maths and science as well as English.

DfE (DCFS, 2009a) and Sutton Trust (Jerrim, 2013) researches have shown that disadvantaged learners carry forward a deficit in oral and literacy skills of nearly a year and do not catch up. Many will fall further behind as they move through the phases and as adults turn away from education and lifelong learning (McCoach et al., 2017). A more detailed analysis of the pattern of skills of disadvantaged learners is necessary to find what needs to be done on a personalised basis to improve their life chances. Examples of the methods and effects of audits and interventions can be found in the next chapter on case studies and in Chapter 5 on teaching and learning.

Step 2: audit the provision

Schools that claim to make provision for their more able pupils usually only rely on one strategy (Montgomery, 2002). However, schools that have been shown to be effective in lifting underachievement of their gifted and talented pupils raise the achievements of all their pupils (HMI, 1992) and also use opportunities to include all the levels of provision. This was evident in the case studies of effective schools in the NACE/London G and T research project (Wallace et al., 2008).

Ordinary schools should audit their provision and make sure that all seven levels of provision illustrated here are available for all who might need them.

Now many teachers are using web materials to support their classroom work, particularly to illustrate the points they want to make. It can also be used to offer individualised and extended distance learning for those pupils who are well beyond the knowledge and skills of their peers. These programmes can often be found or developed as distance learning and extension programmes of universities and Wolsey Hall College. Schools should aim to make links with their nearest university or college so that access and new links can be forged.

In the past, acceleration as a strategy for 'gifted' learners was widely used. It operated in the grammar school system, where the 'A' classes pursued work faster and sometimes in greater depth than the other 'streams'. Now we see it in 'fast-tracking classes', 'accelerated' classes, 'setting' for some subjects and 'compacting'

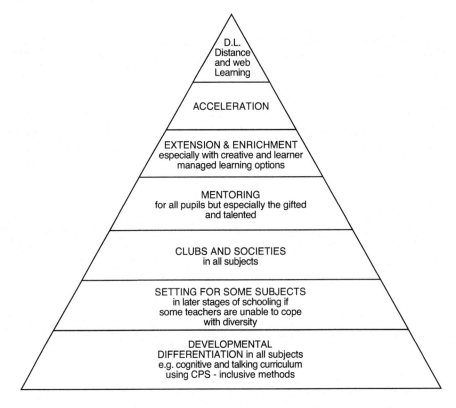

Figure 3.1 To show the seven levels of provision needed in every school

of the curriculum. In addition, individual pupils may be fast-tracked by moving them up a year or two. This is not always an easy option, as the more able child may be socially less mature than the new peers and may need extra support or a 'buddy' system to help.

Extension and enrichment have been the focus for much of the specialist work in the UK. In the past and even now in some schools, it is provided as a 'bolt on' provision to the ordinary curriculum for selected groups. It is often only given as more advanced curricular provision that would be met in subsequent years of schooling or at university and is what can be called 'accelerated content'. As a strategy, it creates problems in subsequent years when these accelerated content curriculum pupils will have already covered the topic and in more depth than the rest.

What some educators were seeking to do in enrichment was to develop more intellectually challenging curriculum activities that drew upon thinking skills and investigative learning opportunities that were 'intrinsic' to ordinary lessons. This focus needs to become government policy as the curriculum need for all children if we are to develop individuals who can cope with the needs of developed societies in the new millennium. However, it is not so easy to develop this approach, and teachers do need training support in general and in specific subject areas.

It is now policy for UK schools to offer a differentiated curriculum within the classroom (DCFS, 2009c). Unfortunately, the model has been borrowed from one that had already failed in the 1970s even though it has been widely used since then to try to cope with special educational needs in classrooms. The model is one in which the main ideas and concepts are taught to all the class, and then the most able move quickly through the basic work to do more advanced problem-solving activities, and the slower learners and learning disabled do more concrete work reinforcing the main ideas. The average do the standard work. This is known as differentiation by inputs and merely replicates the setting or streaming process of acceleration of content within a class.

Associated with this or as a separate strategy in its own right is differentiation by outputs. In this, the most able are required to read and write extended material, whilst the average learners work through the standard tasks and are expected to write less, and the slower learners and those with literacy difficulties complete charts, fill in blanks or draw their responses. Different marking criteria are also applied and not always shared with the pupils.

My research in classrooms using these input and output strategies showed that they were not fit for purpose. Instead, problem-based learning and teaching could be undertaken with all the class and proved more interesting and effective with all the learners. With talking support, the slower learners could join in the more problem-based work and learned more, and the most able working in mixed-ability groups had just as many opportunities for extended and enriched learning opportunities. It created a more equitable learning environment without damaging or holding back the more able (Montgomery, 1990, 1996, 2009). It was termed **'developmental differentiation'** and now is central to **inclusive teaching methods**. Hallam's (2002) research on mixed-ability teaching found similar results.

Hallam (2002) found that successful mixed-ability teaching can:

- Provide a means of offering equal opportunities
- Address the negative social consequences of structured ability grouping by encouraging co-operative behaviour and social integration
- Provide role models for less able pupils
- Promote good relations between pupils
- Enhance pupil/teacher interactions
- Reduce some of the competition engendered by structured grouping
- Allow pupils to work at their own pace

- Provide a sense of continuity for primary pupils when they transfer to secondary school
- Force teachers to acknowledge that the pupils in their class are not a homogeneous group
- Encourage teachers to identify pupil needs and match learning tasks to them.

(p. 89)

Hallam also warned that to engage in successful mixed-ability teaching, the teachers needed to be highly skilled and appropriately trained and have at their disposal a wide range of differentiated resources to match to their pupils' needs.

It is a mistake however to expect these resources to be readily available and wait for money to obtain them. Most publishers have not yet grasped the essential needs of developmental differentiation or problem-based learning in school subject areas, and the problems and resources are best when devised by the teachers to meet the needs in their lessons. Sharing these with colleagues makes the best use of them and enhances CPD within and between schools as a collegiate enterprise.

What sort of differentiation in the classroom?

Successful mixed-ability teaching is highly sophisticated; it is not enough to teach to the middle, give the slower ones worksheets to fill in and provide a few extra problems and ideas to keep the top group busy – input differentiation. All this does is reproduce a selective system of education within the classroom and perpetuate the inequality. Instead, developmental differentiation is recommended. The simplistic level of advice widely offered is that differentiation can take place in content, process, pace, product, grouping, support, outcomes, assessment and the learning environment. But it is a piecemeal approach lacking a coherent or integrative theory and practice.

The essence of **developmental differentiation / inclusive teaching** is that the learners should all be given the same problem-based or investigative task to do but that their input and knowledge should be included as part of the contribution to activities, and it is this that enables all of them to achieve higher learning outcomes. What this means is that individuals in pairs or in groups talk about the task and what they need to know and do as part of a learning spiral. By talking about what they know, they can gradually construct their own knowledge. Developmental differentiation is

> The setting of common tasks to which all students can contribute their own knowledge and experience in collaborative activities and so raise the level of output of all the learners.

(Montgomery, 1996, 84)

In this process, it is necessary to change the teaching methods rather than change the content of the curriculum – hence cognitive process methods.

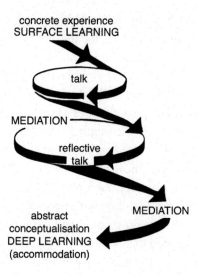

Figure 3.2 Cognitive learning spiral

The teacher input can also provide schema and scaffolds, such as the TASC problem-solving wheel (Wallace, 2000), or visual organisers (Swartz and Parks, 1994) and accelerated learning strategies (Shayer and Adey, 2002), enabling them to work on the new material and use it to acquire new information and concepts. Sessions are supported by reflections by the groups on what they have learned and also how they have done so.

In the process, the pupils follow a cognitive spiral of learning (Montgomery, 1994), as in Figure 3.4. In the first cycle, the pupils talk about the concrete aspects of the task and incorporate that into their learning, and then in the second cycle, they are enabled to reflect upon that learning process (Montgomery, 2009). It encourages metacognition, and this promotes learning and intelligence (Flavell, 1979) and is part of the cognitive process approach.

In Chapter 5, the cognitive and talking curricula are detailed so that an audit of the provision can include these aspects in each subject area's provision along with the effectiveness of the methods being used.

Step 3: audit motivation and communication

There are many ways of analysing motivation and communication in schools, and they usually involve questionnaires, surveys and Delphic oracle methods. However, in my opinion there are more useful and teacher-friendly approaches that can reveal a wealth of useful information that can be acted upon.

One example is classroom observation. When pupils are engaged in problem-based activities or collaborative activities, the teacher can stand back at intervals and observe and listen to the interactions. In addition, through the techniques of **shadowing** and **mentoring**, wider aspects of the functioning and ethos of the school can be seen. The first example is of shadowing Christopher. The school referred him for help and advice because of his language difficulties as part of our in-service development programme. The task was to follow Christopher to his lessons in the summer term of year 7, sit unobtrusively and observe what happened to him for eight lessons throughout one day. Christopher did not know anyone was watching him, and his teachers were told that he was being observed for his learning and behaviour during class, not them. The school had requested this shadowing day because Christopher had a speech impairment, and it had been recommended by the speech therapy services that he needed to be encouraged to talk more in all lessons so that he could practice. He seemed to have made no progress over six months, and they were concerned.

Throughout eight lessons, Christopher did not speak to any other pupil beside or near him. He did not put up his hand to answer questions and was not asked any. At three o' clock, one teacher spoke to him sharply and said, "Put that desk lid down!" It was evident that Christopher was going to make little language development progress in this setting. The teachers had all been told about his difficulties and his needs, but their methods did not involve much pupil talk except one-word responses to closed questions. He obviously was too fearful to become involved and did hide behind his desk lid when it appeared likely he might be asked something.

In addition to observing Christopher, there was an extensive opportunity to see eight different teachers at work and analyse their methods. They had been given in-service training courses on study skills and more open teaching methods, but although they had reported the sessions had been useful, it was quite clear that training days, even with follow-ups, had quite failed to change their teaching approaches. This is an important issue for CPD and reinforced conclusions that only long in-service courses involving practical work in their own classrooms could change teachers' methods.

Shadowing by teacher peers is a valuable continuing professional development strategy. It is comparatively inexpensive and can enable a wide range of audits to be undertaken as well as enable the shadower to see how others teach and children learn for them. Special needs provision can be analysed, as well as equal opportunities, teaching strategies, learning methods, assessment for learning, classroom control strategies and so on. Several shadowers, observing classrooms without the onus of undertaking appraisals, can share experiences and plan what needs to be done to improve teaching and learning in the school. It also sensitises them to their own teaching and learning methods.

A second example was shadowing Michael. On this occasion, the observer was just told that he was a more able pupil, and they wanted to find out if he was given any opportunities to match his ability. He sat at the front of each class. No one spoke to him during lessons, but he did put up his hand to answer questions and was allowed to on several occasions. He appeared just an average sort of learner, small, earnest and quiet. Only at the end of the day after the English lesson did he do anything unusual. He waited behind the rest and approached the teacher with a question, and they walked out of the room together talking.

In the staffroom, I asked the teacher what Michael had said, and he groaned. "He has set me my homework for tonight!" He explained that Michael, aged 12, had written two published books on great sea battles and had just come up with a question about an aspect of naval history to do with his new project, the Battle of Trafalgar. The English teacher also taught some history and had read history and English at university, and Michael often sought him out like this for a few minutes' talk and to look things up for him (this was before Google and *Wikipedia*).

Here we see Michael has found himself a mentor and was making good use of him. It was his only adult-level conversation of the day, and he would have benefited from more. Every pupil needs a mentor or a supporter to help him or her, especially through secondary school. Even with *Wikipedia*, it is inclusive and developmental for someone on the staff to take an interest in particular pupils' interests, discuss these topics with them in more adult terms and become their occasional mentor. Senior pupils can also be trained to take these supportive roles.

There are also a number of **schoolwide issues** that can be addressed by having mentors and peer support amongst the staff, for staff also need support. If the performance management system is positive, supportive and based in classroom observation and staff development, it can contribute significantly. These methods have a strong research base (Montgomery, 2002) and some details follow in the 'five-star plan'. Team teaching and peer review can also make a significant contribution to improving teaching and learning.

Observational methods can enable teachers to judge the motivational powers of different strategies and techniques, and they can also observe the nature of the communications in classrooms. The directions in which communications flow and the networks they engage can prove very revealing in an observation session. It enables the style of communication to be analysed for its positive and negative qualities so that the ethos of classrooms and schools can be understood and if necessary changed. When, for example, desists or negatives outweigh positive statements and support in classrooms, pupils begin to become disaffected and misbehave, creating class control problems (Montgomery, 1989, 2002; Scott MacDonald, 1972). Staff likewise respond well in supportive environments and improve their behaviour and positive responses to pupils.

Crowd management, school and class sizes, are also factors that play an important part in the life in schools and can too easily be overlooked for the stresses they create for individuals, pupils as well as teachers. Architectural features and space constraints may make some areas almost impossible to control without intense efforts from key staff. Classrooms that are too small for large classes or big individuals and one size furniture that does not fit all pose problems for attention, communication and motivation that are not always well understood by school architects.

Observation from key points in classrooms and schools can show where difficulties arise and what improvements need to be made. For example, simple things like the replacement of blackout paper on a corridor or shared windows with tracing paper can let in daylight. Curriculum integration projects can cut down pupil movement around tricky spaces and narrow corridors. Simple rules such as 'No running in corridors or classrooms' and 'No shouting' contribute order and calm but need to be monitored and reinforced by all staff.

Step 4: audit the behaviour management policy

In the UK, every school is required to have a behaviour management policy, and its operation is monitored in inspections (Steer Report, 2009; DCFS 2009b). However, once again, regular classroom and general school observation can be the starting point for gathering relevant data before and after behaviour management training sessions to monitor and if necessary change methods.

The DES (1979), the Elton Report (1989) and the Steer Report (2009b) all emphasised that most pupils behave well in most schools. Those who misbehave do not do so all the time. It was rare to find challenging behaviour, and those who engaged in it were usually from difficult and disadvantaged environments. Their needs, according to Steer, were becoming increasingly complex. The report confirmed that the major problem was still the low-level irritating noise identified by Elton. School leaders did not make sufficient use of the powers they had to intervene and withdraw early. All schools needed a withdrawal space or room. For the first time, Steer insisted that all schools should have a teaching and learning policy. It seems extraordinary that the schools did not have one in all the piles of required paper from the last 40 years.

The 'five-star plan' was developed and designed to improve teaching and learning and deal with the problem of low-level noise. It was also found to reduce disruptive behaviours in all but the most disturbed.

We can use classroom observation to:

- Count the positive CBGs (catch them being goods) versus desists to start the process of change
- Quantify the time-out, keeping behind, serious talk, on report, behaviour contracts, detentions and so on given by particular staff and received by individuals
- Collect information on ABCs (antecedents, behaviours, consequences) sensitively to help each individual pupil or teacher and identify problem areas

- Undertake teacher peer review using CBG and a positive constructivist coaching framework (Montgomery, 2002) to bring about changes in the ethos of classrooms and schools

The five-star teaching improvement plan (Montgomery, 2017c)

Positive behaviour management and classroom control was extensively researched in the observation and feedback to teachers in over 1,250 lessons (Montgomery, 2002). During this research, five interrelated strategies used by successful teachers for improving teaching and reducing behaviour problems were evolved. They were then used to improve student teaching in initial teacher education B.Ed. and PGCE programmes and shared with teachers in over 100 schools on CPD training days. As a result, funding for a research assistant was obtained for three years to test the plan and coaching system and to 'retrieve some failing teachers'. It proved as successful with the trained and experienced teachers as it had with ITE students.

The five 'stars' were

1. CBG (catch them being good)

The CBG strategy requires that the teacher positively reinforces any pupil's correct social and on-task responses with nods, smiles, and by paraphrasing correct responses and statements and supporting the student's on-task academic responses with such phrases as 'Yes, good', 'Well done'. Incorrect responses should not be negated, but the pupil should be encouraged to have another try or watch a model, and the teacher prompts with, 'Yes, nearly' and 'Yes, and what else – ', 'Good so far, can anyone help him or her out?' and so on.

At its simplest, CBG is one form of behaviour modification technique in which the teacher positively reinforces desirable behaviours emitted by the pupil, gradually **shaping** them towards desirable ends determined by the teacher without the children being aware of the goal towards which they are directed – there need be no cognitive input.

2. 3 Ms (management, monitoring and maintenance)

The 3Ms represent a series of tactics that effective teachers use to gain and maintain pupils' attention whatever teaching method or style they use. When teachers with classroom management disciplining problems were taught to use these strategies in coaching sessions, they became effective teachers.

MANAGEMENT PHASE

The teacher makes an *attention gaining noise* such as 'Right!', 'O.K. class 3', 'Good morning, everybody' or 'Uhummm!' or bangs the door or desk and claps hands.

Some teachers simply wait quietly until the noise subsides as the pupils notice she or he is present. Next, the teacher gives a *short verbal instruction*, such as 'Everybody sit down', 'Get out your English folders', 'Come and sit on the mat', 'Sit down and listen carefully' and so on. At this point, twenty of the pupils will do as requested and ten will not. The effective teacher pauses, looks round, spots those who are not doing as requested and quietly *names* these pupils and individually instructs them to stop what they are doing and to listen.

This is usually quite sufficient if a *check back* look is given to bring the whole class to attention. The mistake that the ineffective teachers make is to begin to shout 'Be quiet' and 'Sit down', as a general instruction to all pupils. Many give up the struggle and 'teach' over the noise so that the level of attention and achievement of all pupils is lowered.

Pupils often deliberately test out teachers' knowledge of these 'rules' and seek to undermine them if they do not know them. The effective teacher, having gained the pupils' attention and silence will immediately launch into the introduction to the session or begin reading the story. During the teacher talk or story, it is necessary for a range of attention-gaining and maintaining tactics to be employed, for example,

- Pausing in an exposition to look at a pupil talking until she or he stops
- Walking to a pupil and gently removing tapping pencil or note
- Pointing to mobile to cause it to be put away
- Asking the talking or inattentive pupil a question
- Repeating the phrase just given
- Adding 'and Goldilocks said to the three bears' in the middle of a sentence whilst looking pointedly at a pupil who is not paying attention (When attention is regained, resume explanation without comment.)

MONITORING PHASE

As soon as there is an activity change from pupils listening to getting out books and writing or going back to places to work, this is when disruption can and does arise. The monitoring strategy needs to be brief, perhaps lasting no more than 30 seconds.

As soon as the pupils are at their places, the teacher should move round the room to each group or table very quickly and quietly, settling them down to work. It is essential not to linger to give detailed explanations at this point but to say that you will come back shortly to help, going to the noisiest group first but making sure that all are visited. If there is not a lot of space to move round, then a vantage point should be selected and the monitoring directed from there by calming gestures and quiet naming.

In addition to activity change, monitoring should be used when pupils are engaged with tasks and the noise level and attention seems to be slipping. This can be noted at any time by the well-attuned ear and usually only requires that the teacher looks up and round the room to the talker.

Again, a pointed look or very quiet naming may well be all that is required. The important thing is not to nag and be noisy. Having told a pupil to be quiet, the teacher must look up and check back on the pupil within three to five seconds – the three-second rule.

MAINTENANCE PHASE

Once the pupils have been settled to the task by the monitoring techniques, it is then advisable for the teacher to move round the class to each individual to find out how the work is progressing. In the maintenance period, all the requests and queries of individuals can be dealt with.

During a lesson period or period of study within a curriculum area, each pupil should expect to receive some form of individual constructive and developmental comment on the work – PCI.

3. PCI, positive cognitive intervention

Positive cognitive intervention (PCI) summarises all the cognitive aspects of teaching and learning to encourage the teacher to use 'engage brain' strategies. The initials act as an aide-memoire for many substructures in this area.

Developmental PCI – The advice is that during the steady move round the room, the teacher should look at the work with the pupil and offer developmental advice which makes a positive statement about progress thus far and then offers ideas and suggestions for extension or through constructive questioning helps the pupils see how to make the work better or achieve the goals they have set themselves, cognitive approaches. When the work has been completed again, there should be written or spoken comments as appropriate and further ideas.

In addition to this form of developmental PCI, there is also the need to design lessons that do offer some cognitive challenge. Although open questioning is a favoured method, this is necessary but not sufficient. In addition, there needs to be a system of differentiation and the use of the cognitive curriculum and cognitive process teaching methods (Montgomery, 1996, 2015) if all pupils are to be more motivated and challenged.

The PCI strategy was derived from observational studies and interventions with slower learners and disaffected and gifted pupils in classrooms.

4. Tactical lesson planning (TLP)

Lesson plans need to be structured into timed phases for pupil learning, not teacher talk – for example, title/lesson objective or focus; introduction (teacher talk, Q/A) phase 1 (pupils reading); phase 2 (pupils doing practical work); phase 3 (pupils speaking – sharing experiences); phase 4 (pupils writing recording work and ideas); and concluding activity (Q/A reporting back to the class). Getting the TLP right improves the pace of the lesson and increases pupil time on task.

5. Assessment for learning (AfL)

When the talking approach to the cognitive curriculum was used with underachieving pupils, in their feedback, enjoyment and legitimised social interaction were not often connected in their minds with school learning. This meant that at each stage, they had to be shown in explicit ways that this was real schoolwork, how much they had learned and how their work was improving. Giving detailed comments on their work did this.

At intervals, the pupils were helped to reflect upon the products and the processes of their learning. Once they began to make these connections for themselves, they became avid learners, and other teachers began to notice a transformation and commented upon positive changes in their behaviour and attitude. It is in these ways that effective teaching methods and formative positive assessment can also be seen to be making a major contribution to achievement, classroom management and behaviour control. This is in addition to the general benefits created by a positive and supportive classroom climate and school ethos using CBG and CBC (catch them being clever).

The research shared the preceding details with the teacher, and then an observation of a lesson was arranged. The researcher made a factual running record of any of the preceding that were seen, and positive asides, questions and suggestions were made to support the teacher. At the end of the session, the record was simply read to the teacher with opportunities throughout for discussion and the sharing of ideas, the coaching input. Two to three targets were agreed, and another visit was arranged for three to four weeks later. The same procedure was followed. After each session, the researcher, assistant and teacher completed the college competency-based criterion referenced scale (maximum score 24 points). Pre- and post-scores showed each teacher had made significant progress, and, more important, the failing teachers no longer faced expulsion from the schools and were able to control their classes.

Step 5: reframing teaching and learning provision

Having identified the problems in the audit procedures described earlier, it is usually necessary to undertake some interventions. The locus of this that has proved most effective is in the improvement of general teaching and learning, the central aspects of the teacher's role. The difficulty is that the ways in which we teach and also learn are intimately linked to our personality and our own learning history. Such inbuilt propensities for action are difficult to change or modify once established.

It is therefore necessary that when we set out to reframe teaching and learning provision in schools, we must understand and also adopt the principles of learning in our work with teachers in order to do so. In this respect, lectures and training days are unlikely to produce change, for they do not meet the essential criteria. For learning (De Corte, 1995, 2013) to take place, it must be constructive, self-organised, situated and goal-orientated.

Learning strategies such as whether a deep approach or a surface approach (Marton and Säljo, 1984) is adopted can mean very different learning outcomes. These strategies are often defined and limited by our learning experiences in school; for example, didactic teaching methods (transmission) encourage and maintain surface approaches to learning. It follows from this that learning which is collaborative can be more effective because the interactions may induce and mobilise reflection and thus foster the development of metacognitive knowledge and skills, and these assist constructive learning.

Most experience of school learning has however been from a didactic perspective induced by an overfilled curriculum, and the learning strategies will be of the surface kind, geared to rote memorisation rather than anything of a deeper nature. There will have been few opportunities to construct meaning for an individual, and as academic work becomes more challenging, pupils will not have the capabilities to cope even though they have potential high ability and could benefit from higher education.

Constructivist approaches to teaching, learning and behaviour '**front-load**' learning and study sessions. This is because the learners are engaged in 'making meaning' or constructing their own knowledge (Desforges, 1998), for such pupils, a lighter touch is then needed on the revision accelerator. For teachers, a comprehensive CPD programme that involves them in designing, making and evaluating interventions in their own classrooms is necessary. This theory, research and practice in their own classrooms enables them to construct their personal theories (Whitehead and Huxtable, 2009) and practices in teaching and engage with the wider field of theory and research. It is only through changing the way teachers think that practice can be changed.

Social constructivism and personalised learning

The zone of proximal development, or ZPD, was a construct developed by Vygotsky (1978) and independently by Rey in 1934 with whom Feuerstein (1980, 1995) had worked and developed mediated learning and the learning potential assessment device (LPAD).

In ZPD, the learners actively build their understanding helped or 'scaffolded' by more knowledgeable persons, such as their teachers and mentors, until they become more aware and are able to regulate their own learning through metacognition.

In this context, personalised learning does not require a different curriculum plan and pathway or IEP (individual education plan, now an EHCP – education and health care plan) for every pupil – the mad bureaucratic end of PL – but is what the good teacher is doing daily. Implicit in this is also a teacher who has time for individual work with pupils. In a class of 30 with pupils you see two or three times a week as in secondary schools, this may seem problematic. It certainly is a problem if the teacher is the lead actor in everything that goes on – the 'Woodhead' classroom – teacher-led, teacher-directed, lively questioning, whole-class teaching (Woodhead 1998). (Woodhead was formerly head of Ofsted and chief inspector for schools.)

If however the methods involve the cognitive approach to the curriculum, then the teacher can often stand back, listen and watch or move round and help groups or individuals. There is time for reflection and time to work out how to adapt the strategies for the next lesson and the one after that.

Primary teachers most often spend most of the day with their own class. They have the opportunity to observe individuals perform in many different contexts and so build up a more rounded picture of individual needs quite quickly. Nevertheless, they still need time to stand back and observe and time to work with individuals. The cognitive curriculum and cognitive process strategies will help them too.

What has to be grasped is that the role of the teacher needs to change to become more flexible. It is difficult for many teachers to feel they have given a good lesson if they have not been talking and leading most of the time. New roles as facilitator, follower, supporter, manager, administrator, learner and socialiser need to be adopted easily and played out as appropriate. It is only in this way that pupils can be helped towards fulfilling their personalised learning needs and become autonomous learners.

As has already been explained, the theory and research behind the practices and principles of the cognitive curriculum, the talking curriculum and inclusive teaching lies in the constructivist area of theory of learning. It is therefore a good point on which to end by outlining social constructivism. Pupils construct their own learning, and they can be helped in this by sharing their learning and ideas with other pupils and together achieve higher learning outcomes.

According to Brookes and Brookes (1993, 2), there were 12 guiding principles in their constructivist teachers' approaches. They:

- Encourage and accept student autonomy and initiative
- Use raw data and primary sources, along with manipulative, interactive and physical materials
- Use cognitive terminology when framing tasks
- Allow pupil responses to drive lessons, shift instructional strategies and alter content

- Inquire about pupils' understanding of concepts before sharing understanding of them
- Encourage pupils to engage in dialogue both with the teacher and each other
- Encourage pupil inquiry by asking thoughtful, open-ended questions and encourage pupils to ask questions of each other
- Seek elaboration of pupils' initial responses
- Engage pupils in experiences that might engender contradictions to their initial hypotheses and then encourage discussion
- Allow wait time after posing questions (3–7 seconds)
- Provide time for pupils to construct relationships and create metaphors
- Nurture pupils' natural curiosity

Many of these same attributes are also needed if teachers are to encourage creativity in their pupils (Soriano de Alencar, 1995).

Mindsets about intelligence and performance (Dweck, 2011)

Mindsets are gaining significance in research about self-regulated learning, and it has become necessary to consider both student and staff mindsets in relation to it. Dweck (1999) identified implicit beliefs held by learners about learning. She termed them as 'entity' and 'incremental' theories. Those who held entity theory believed that intelligence was fixed and that you only had so much of it and nothing much could be done to improve it. They also assumed that education could have little effect on it.

Teachers/tutors who held entity views encouraged performance goals, believed that the products of learning were important and in feedback encouraged students to compare their work with the standards of others. This theory seems to be held throughout many education systems and by those administrators and politicians responsible for it.

However, Dweck did find people holding incremental theory beliefs behaving differently. They believed that intelligence or ability was something that could be developed through learning and that it can change and people can become more intelligent. Thus the more students learn the more they become capable of it and education can make a significant impact on intelligence. Teachers and tutors holding incremental theory beliefs encouraged learning goals. They focused on the process of learning and used assessment and feedback to encourage improvement based on individual progress.

Changing pupil's entity beliefs can be considered to be an important part of their learning experience, but it is not easy and needs systematic and constructive developmental work in each domain. The ability to learn from failures is a key component.

According to the research of Stoeger (2006, 36), the mindset beliefs of pupils in German gymnasia were better predictors of their achievement than quantitative cognitive abilities. Given the research of Cullen et al. (2018) discussed in the introduction, changing the mindsets of disadvantaged learners will be crucial to closing the excellence gaps.

Conclusion

The examination of recent research on underachievement in schools shows how it is assessed and the limitations in use, especially of objectives-based and didactic systems of teaching and learning. Gaps in provision and pupils needs are identified, and two case studies are detailed to show how talent may easily be missed. Examples drawn from studies of more able underachievers are found applicable to underachievers in general.

To address problem areas, the chapter presents five audit steps that schools can easily undertake to retrieve any failures and lift the achievements of all their pupils but underachievers in particular. The first step involves auditing the pupils' basic skills to check if they can cope with the curriculum and then auditing the provision, motivation and communication; the ethos and climate; and the behaviour management policy. This enables the school team to work on reframing the provision so that it is made appropriate for purpose in the 21st century. Details are presented to show how a five-star plan can improve behaviour.

The chapter ends with an analysis of constructivist teaching and teacher behaviours involving deep learning and the zone of proximal development.

The English inclusive model set out in the preceding sections is very different from that adopted in many other countries, and unfortunately, there has been and still is a conflict between it and the model intrinsic in the national curriculum documents. Over the decades, there has been a slow and expensive retreat from the original design and one that is still ongoing but not soon enough for the stressed pupils and teachers and all those underachievers it is creating.

Case studies in diagnosis and intervention of UAch

Introduction

Over the last three decades since SATs were introduced, there have been few advantages derived from them by pupils. One advantage is that children's underachievement has been more easily identified and attempts have been made to address it. The underachievement has however not always been connected to the correct cause nor the underlying problems addressed.

Most noticeable has been the concern about boys' underachievement in writing, and this, among other factors, will be addressed in this chapter. A trio of boys will be placed under scrutiny. They are real cases with name changes. They had high learning potential and were chosen because this makes their difficulties easier to demonstrate and because they are typical examples. However, there are vast numbers of pupils with low or average ability whose underfunctioning is less easy to identify but for whom the same interventions would raise their achievement just as much.

The case studies of girls show just as many problems, but because less is still expected of them in gender stereotyping, they pass under the radar unless a relative becomes an advocate and questions their treatment. Even so, boys are referred more frequently to the LDRP (www.ldrp.org.uk) in the ratio of about five to one for diagnosis because of parental concerns. Despite girls having more success at school than boys, the ratio is indicative of widespread gender stereotyping and a view that girls matter less and are not as able as boys.

Today, they must matter equally. Attention in class should be equally directed to them, their interests and their needs. Glimpses into their barriers to learning show that the ratio of dyslexic boys to girls is still thought to be four to one respectively. But this is the typical ratio in referral clinics for subjects needed for research. Community studies show that the ratios are in the order of three to two boys to girls (Rutter et al.,

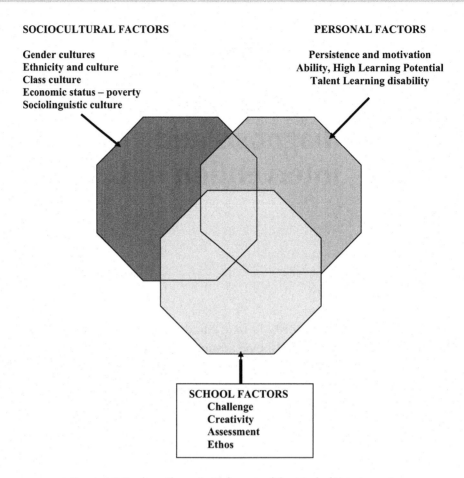

SOCIOCULTURAL FACTORS

Gender cultures
Ethnicity and culture
Class culture
Economic status – poverty
Sociolinguistic culture

PERSONAL FACTORS

Persistence and motivation
Ability, High Learning Potential
Talent Learning disability

SCHOOL FACTORS
Challenge
Creativity
Assessment
Ethos

Figure 4.1 To show the potential areas of the triad of impairments

2004; Montgomery, 2008a). We need to think of the real situation as roughly equal numbers of boys and girls except that their profiles of difficulties may be different. This is because girls tend to keep quiet, blame themselves and work hard to overcome their problems, especially in reading.

If girls' spelling is examined, their dyslexic problems can be found and in roughly equal numbers to boys. The treatment they get is to blame them for carelessness and stupidity. Dyslexic students on B.Ed. and masters SEN/SpLD programmes recorded such personal experiences. Teachers' comments in reports and on pupils' essays display the same attitudes today.

Summary of the range of UAch factors in the Triad that can be addressed by schools

- Anomie, alienation and identity – issues that beset many in large schools
- Potential for failure

- Writing issues
- Teaching methods
- Learning opportunities
- Motivation and effort
- School culture and ethos
- Learning disabilities
- Equality issues
- Sociolinguistic factors
- Mentoring and buddy systems

In other words, schools have a large number of factors that give rise to underachievement and that they can address within their control.

A trio of able underachievers – case examples

To examine the nature of underachievement and the influences of a range of factors, three case examples have been identified. All are boys, as they are frequently the focus of concern in the UK. All three boys have IQs of 120 points on full-scale WISC-IV without significant differences between VQ and PQ scores.

1 Gary 11 years; SATs – Eng. 4, maths 4, science 4
2 Wesley 11 years; SATs – Eng. 3b, maths 5, science 5
3 Robert 11 years; SATs – Eng. 3a, maths 4, science 4

Here, we see their SATs results in national examinations taken at the age of 10/11 years at the end of year 6. This is the end of Key Stage 2 and prior to entry into secondary school. Level 4 is the government's target level that 85 per cent of pupils are expected to achieve at the end of KS2. As our three boys are in the potential gifted range, they should all be placed on the school's register for the gifted and talented, and we should expect them to achieve at least at level 5 in their SATs. What we do not know is to what we can attribute the trio's successes and failures; for example, is it

- Teacher effectiveness?
- Booster group effect?
- SATs validity issues?
- Marker variability?
- Personal effort or lack of it?
- Personal ability or lack of it?

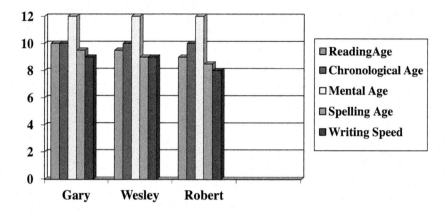

Figure 4.2 To show the pattern of abilities and disabilities of the trio

If we look at where they have come from, we find that in junior school, they

* Were the top dogs, the 'big' boys
* Were known by everyone
* Had a home base classroom and desk
* Had one class teacher most of the time
* Had a supportive classroom ethos
* Had responsibilities and an identity
* Were allowed some autonomy and choice
* Were used to group work and discussion

When they arrive at secondary school, they find themselves in a very different world. They become tiny fish in a huge pond, continually moving from room to room. They have a score of different teachers and learning experiences. They become nonentities, vulnerable, and they are unknown.

Our trio, in the English assessment-driven system, already regard themselves as losers. They lack self-esteem, and their motivation to work and succeed is failing. On entry to a large secondary school in Year 7, where initially no one knows them, they will be vulnerable, sure candidates for alienation and disaffection. It will take very little for them to fall further behind peers and seek other sources than school learning to gain esteem, such as in the peer group and the gang.

Their school should place them on the 'G and T register', but they are only on a shadow reserve list and have not been told about it, nor have their parents. This simple form of recognition was found to give a 15 per cent uplift in one school's SATs results (Head of Year, 2007).

Researchers in this field have contributed to a list of characteristics by which we can identify underachievers and our trio. Their findings are very similar (Kellmer-Pringle,

1983; Whitmore, 1982; Rimm, 1986; Butler-Por, 1987; Silverman, 1989; Wallace, 2000; Montgomery, 2000). The resultant composite checklist is

- Large gap between oral and written work (Gary, Wesley, Robert – these are their pseudonyms)
- Fails to complete school work (WR)
- Poor execution of work (WR)
- Persistent dissatisfaction with Ach (GWR)
- Does not function well in groups or with peers (GWR)
- Complains everything is boring (W)
- Lacks concentration and effort (WR)
- Poor attitudes to school (WR)
- Dislikes drill, memorisation, and writing (GWR)
- Misbehaves or plays class clown (WR)
- Low self-image (GWR)

We can also add in the case of many more able underachievers:

- Satisfactory work in all areas (G)

As can be seen, our trio score in most of these categories, and even Gary, whose work is satisfactory in all areas, should be performing at a much higher level, given his IQ and general cognitive ability. It is important that teachers **raise their expectations** for these three, for each of them should be performing in all areas closer to their mental age level rather than at their chronological age.

Social, personal and cultural information on our trio

Gary: only child of elderly shop-worker parents; social class 5; Caucasian; live in terraced house in town centre; G. is timid, works hard, bullied by certain peers

Wesley: has an older unemployed sister, mother a community nurse; father absent; family live in urban second-floor flat; Afro-Caribbean; social class 4–5; W. born and brought up in the UK; is big, brash, noisy and avoids work whenever possible

Robert: youngest child of six (three of hers all married and left home, two of his still at home, and R, who is theirs); parents Caucasian, self-employed 'company directors' of plumbing and central heating firm; live in detached house in own grounds; social class 4 (father also dyslexic, ex SC 6); high income; R is dyslexic, spoilt, prone to temper tantrums and playing 'class clown'

Gary's profile – his reading is at his chronological age level, but his spelling and writing are six months and 12 months behind this, as we would expect because they are more difficult skills to acquire and mature. His teachers are not concerned by his results, as his SATs are at level 4 and his literacy skills are at the grade level of peers. However, they should be concerned because his intellectual ability is 20 per cent higher, and we should expect his reading age to be at least at or around his intellectual age level. Given his limited cultural and social background, we can identify the problems in linguistic disadvantage and recommend that he needs an extended opportunity to discuss his work and practice oral communication and presentation.

If Gary had been sent to a public school (private education), he would be given such opportunities in the smaller class sizes (16 pupils on average) and by mixing with pupils using extended vocabularies. If he were at boarding school, his linguistic experiences would be considerably enhanced.

What ordinary schools can do instead is to ensure that there are class sizes of only 15 to 16 pupils in the transition years, such as reception and year 7. Schools that have done this have improved the life chances of their disadvantaged pupils and reduced alienation and disaffection (Basildon Headteacher, 2009). Small class sizes can increase the expert attention each pupil receives and permit more extended communication by pupils in response to teachers' questions and between pupils. This is critical in the reception year when pupils are learning to read and write and in year 7 when most pupils move in to the big secondary school. Another strategy is to change to teaching methods that promote speaking and listening (Chapter 6).

Wesley's profile is also of concern. He too should be reading around his mental age level (12 years old) but is six months below grade level and a year below level in spelling and handwriting. He does not work as hard as Gary and has little opportunity outside school to develop his reading skills. He needs strong motivation to read for reading practice. Getting the right storybooks and other texts that will really make him want to read best does this. He probably needs to see men reading to identify with these models. A male mentor, perhaps an older pupil, needs to be found to support him or, as in many secondary schools, he will gradually slip further and further behind and emerge at 16 years with literacy skills no better than when he entered. He will have few prospects for employment, a poor attitude to work, and disaffection from school. His behaviour may develop to challenging levels, and exclusion may be an early result. Otherwise, truancy will be a possible outlet for him if he is in a coercive school environment (Galloway and Goodwin, 1987) and may also lead him into trouble with the police.

Robert's profile is a classical one too. He is dyslexic but bright enough to cover his serious difficulties so that he reads at the nine-year-old level, a year below grade and age level. This will mean he does not meet the criterion most schools set for remedial help – that the pupil is two years behind peers. However, Robert's reading is three years behind what it should be in relation to his ability, and his spelling and handwriting are four years behind. He is in desperate need of specialist help. When checked, it will be found that he does know most of the sounds of the letter symbols and spells phonetically when it is not a very familiar word. He uses a very restricted writing vocabulary and also has a limited linguistic background that was hampered by some delay in his early language acquisition and development. As the 'baby' of the family, he was spoilt, and like his father is prone to temper tantrums.

Although he has had some extra reading help in primary school, this has not been effective, for it did not address the underlying difficulty in dyslexia, the spelling and word-building problem (Montgomery, 2007). He needs a specialist word-building pro-gramme based on HMLC (the Hickey Multisensory Language Programme) (Augur and Briggs, 1991) or TRTS (Teaching Reading Through Spelling) (Cowdery et al., 1994) and then to be moved on to the cognitive process strategies for spelling (CPSS) (Montgomery, 2007, 2017a). His father, also a bright dyslexic, will no doubt absorb him into the company, but with the right intervention, he has great potential, for his scores on the IQ test will have been depressed by at least ten points by his disability (Silverman, 2002).

In addition to his literacy difficulties and linguistic disadvantage, he has a mild handwriting co-ordination difficulty that a small, systematic amount of training could overcome (Christensen and Jones, 2000). His gross motor co-ordination and ball skills are not affected.

Most schools do not check the handwriting speed of their pupils, and this is an important omission, for the association of speed of writing and good composition has long been established (Roaf, 1998; Berninger, 2004; Connelly et al., 2005). It is only when writing skills become automatic that the brain is set free to think about content and be creative.

Key Stage 2 English SATs results from national statistics after seven years of the National Literacy Strategy (NLS) underlined the need for serious intervention in the area of writing skills, for example,

Reading – 87 per cent of girls peaked at level 4 in 2005
              82 per cent of boys peaked at level 4 in 2005
Writing – 72 per cent of girls peaked at level 4 in 2005
              55 per cent of boys peaked at level 4 in 2005

Although Tymm's (2004) analysis of the literacy research showed that standards had not really risen since 1956 and only 60 per cent actually reached level 4, there was still the disparity between the results of boys and girls. Fifteen years on, boys' reading level has increased slightly, and both groups have improved in writing, but there is still a significant gap between them in the region of 10 per cent. Whether these improvements are real has not been tested.

The focus of the NLS had emphasised reading more than spelling and writing, and teachers especially put much energy into reading teaching with spelling very much in second place and handwriting a poor third. It is therefore not surprising that our trio had disproportionately poor writing skills for their ability level.

Boys' writing SATs were 15 per cent lower than girls, and both were still well below the 85 per cent target in 2006–2017. Although 85 per cent is clearly the incorrect target for writing because of its greater complexity and because of its link to spelling and composition, we have to question why boys are poorer at it than girls. Could their problem with writing lie in more poorly developed handwriting skills, especially at year 7 when growth spurts begin?

In research, poor spelling skills lowered the speed of writing significantly, presumably as pupils puzzled over spellings or selected different words they knew they could spell (Montgomery, 2008a).

These results were obtained in a 20-minute speed writing test (Montgomery, 2008a). There would appear to be a significant problem in these schools with writing speed, for Roaf's research (1998) found that **25 per cent of secondary school pupils** were unable to write faster than 15 words per minute in her ten-minute test. These were the pupils who were struggling in all lessons using

Table 4.1 To show mean writing speeds in secondary school

Allcock (2001) 20-minute writing test (N=2701)					
Year	7	8	9	10	11	12
	13.9	14.6	15.7	16.3	16.9	words per minute
Dutton (1992) 30-min test (N=100)					
	12.5	14	16	17	18.5	words per minute

Table 4.2 To find if there is a problem with writing in year 7s after 2, 4, and 7 years of the National Literacy Strategy (NLS)

School	Numb.	wpm	Mean Sp Err	Dyslexic
A (2000)	106	13.97	12.73	10.0%
B (2002)	160	13.64	12.18	18.5%
C (2005)	251	12.44	10.79	15.6%
Total N	517	13.10	10.90	16.7%

writing. She also found that poor writing was linked to low self-concept and underachievement.

The writing speeds of our trio also show some serious problems

Gary 12.0 wpm   Wesley 11.4 wpm   Robert 8.0 wpm

Each of them is writing at a speed well below the mean for their age group. In addition, the speeds are much below the 15 wpm that Roaf found necessary to meet the needs of the secondary school curriculum. Poor writing attracts a great deal of criticism and lack of understanding from many teachers. They regard untidy writing and writing that is difficult to read as a 'crime', demonstrating lack of care and attention, even a personal insult to a hard-pressed teacher with a large marking schedule.

In the year 7 sample of 517 scripts, many slow writers had difficulties with motor co-ordination and letter formation, and some had poor spelling. A similar number of poor writers could write rapidly but not legibly. At least 30 per cent had significant difficulties with handwriting. The ratio of boys to girls with these problems was roughly three to one.

School C: results in year 7 (after 7 years NLS [N=251])

- Cohort C is writing slower than the mean 12.4 (13.9)
- Boys write 19 per cent slower than girls (11.4 to 13.69)
- One girl writes at 26 words per minute
- 1 per cent write fast enough 20–25 wpm (20 wpm in the 20-minute test)
- 37 per cent write at 13–20 wpm (32 b. 62 g.)
- 63 per cent write too slowly – 25 per cent slower
- 19 per cent write very slowly – 40 per cent slower (13g: 35b)
- Three boys write severely slowly – 2–6 wpm
- 32 per cent fail the HMI spelling criterion (no more than five misspellings in each 100 words)
- 16 per cent are dyslexic (2:1 boys to girls – ten plus misspellings per 100 words)

What this data suggest is that boys' handwriting difficulties could well account in a significant way for the difference in English SATs results of boys and girls in the national tests, despite the range of other reasons put forward to account for it. A huge amount of research and funding has been addressed to the motivational problems of underachieving boys, and it could well be missing its biggest target. The failure is in the recognition of the contribution of spelling and handwriting to higher-order compositional skills.

Writing at two levels

Writing involves spelling and handwriting (lower-order skills) and composition (higher-order skills). The two best predictors of good composition in primary and secondary schools have been found by Berninger and her colleagues over two decades (Berninger, 2004, 2008, 2015; Berninger and Graham, 1998):

• Speed of writing the alphabet (in 15 out of 60 seconds)
• Accuracy of coding the alphabet (spelling)

To write good composition, a brain needs to be free of lower-order skills problems. We need to have achieved automaticity in order to set the brain free to think and compose. It is thus important that we help pupils achieve this much earlier, such as by the end of year 3, not year 6. For example, by the end of year 3, they need automatic spelling of a common core vocabulary and to write at 15 words per minute so that by **year 7, they can easily achieve a speed of 20 wpm** in extended writing.

The data show that in English schools, there is a lot more to do about handwriting and spelling that the NLS did not achieve. Notably, the speed of pupils' writing in private schools is significantly faster than that of those in the state sector (Lyth, 2004). In Table 4.3, the year 9s' data are from a selective school for the arts, and writing speed is faster than in the non-selective school data of Allcock (2001), see Table 4.1.

The provision audit for the trio shows that they have been exposed to the current overfilled curriculum in which the pace has not been too fast intellectually, but their written work has been of poor quality because of their slow handwriting skills. Gary's response is the best of the three, as he works hard and generally manages to keep up and hand in completed work. It does not match his potential ability, but the teacher is not aware of this. Wesley's progress has been unsatisfactory, according to his teacher, as he seldom completes work and does too much talking and playing about. His writing is difficult to read, and his work is poorly presented.

Robert's spelling and handwriting are poor, so not too much is expected of him, and he is allowed to avoid much of the written work and fill in easy worksheets. This

Table 4.3 To show some comparative data (N=1085)

YR (N=)	wpm	Co	F/Co	Sp Err	Dysl.	HMI fail
5 (137)	9.2	21.7	74.6	9.6	(33.9)	54.3
7 (576)	13.1	15.6	60.9	10.9	18.7	33.4
9 (372)	18.0	18.7	67.8	8.4	8.3	17.1

KEY: Co = co-ordination difficulties apparent (more than five scores on a co-ordination deficit checklist – see appendix)
F/Co = still using print script, overlarge writing, scoring on some co-ordination difficulty items

consigns him to the lower work sets, and not surprisingly, he quickly becomes bored and plays 'class clown'.

The cognitive curriculum provision is not much in evidence in their classrooms. There is an overall didactic teacher-talk approach with occasional differentiation by input (different levels), and the talking and reflective opportunities are minimal because of the concern to 'cover the syllabus' in time. Wesley is in the top 'set' for maths. This means he worked at the top table in primary school and was sometimes given harder work to do. It usually means the set are expected to complete more of the work and with less help. Robert sometimes gets in-class help with his reading, but now in secondary school, he does not qualify.

Gary, for example, needed a 'buddy' or a mediator to help him counteract the bullying. Wesley needed an older boy as a behaviour mentor and a member of staff who would be a supporter and maybe counsellor if things got difficult. Robert needed a spelling peer or partner and a remedial specialist who could help improve his literacy skills and support him through other lessons. He also needed a gifted education mentor to identify his high ability and communicate this to his teachers and parents and then support and encourage him to engage in more challenging work to help cater for his potential very high ability.

The results are that our trio, now in secondary school year 7, are losing their interest and engagement with schoolwork and will be vulnerable to anomie and disaffection, as the same methods continue. It is also evident that any vulnerable pupils, such as our trio, would probably sink without trace in such a school. They could easily become disaffected and alienated in such an environment, and they would feel just as Hackman (2005) described.

The trio of cases described here represent part of a population that is considerable, and it will be a huge loss to a country in economic terms if their life chances are not enhanced. Each boy comes from a linguistically and culturally limited background. Most primary schools in the UK do not give IQ screening tests, so school attainment, SATs and reading ability too frequently guide expectations, and for our trio, this has resulted in too low expectations being set. If teachers were better trained, they would be able to identify high learning potential based on curriculum provision (identification through provision – ITP), and an IQ test would not be needed.

There are alternatives to the standard IQ tests, such as the Wechsler Intelligence Scale for Children (WISC-IV), administered by psychologists and trained staff during statementing (since 2014 – Education and Health Care Plan – EHCP) procedures. Instead, there are group tests developed for teacher administrators, such as cognitive ability tests and the British Picture Vocabulary test (Dunn et al., 1998), that can be considered as indicators of higher ability and learning potential. They are less accurate than individual tests but useful tools. Raven's Progressive Matrices tests (Raven, 2010) are especially useful non-verbal tests to identify potential ability in dyslexic pupils or those with limited language skills and non-English speakers.

Another test useful as an indicator of ability and reading skill is the Neale Analysis of Reading Ability (NARA, 1998). This is because the test gives scores for reading accuracy and reading comprehension, and as a rule, children of high ability gain higher scores on comprehension than they do on accuracy. This difference can be converted to give a rough IQ estimate, for example,

$$\frac{Reading\ Comprehension\ Age}{Reading\ Accuracy\ Age} \times 100 \frac{12}{10} \times 100 = 120$$

Some of the most effective and interesting ways to identify HLP is to do so by providing curriculum-based problem-solving opportunities. This method is often called authentic assessment and is something every teacher can carry out as ITP.

Some case studies of girls' underachievement

The girls in this section were referred by parents to the LDRP for a second opinion after school and other reports did not seem to reflect their perceived potential. Even when some girls had been formally assessed, the diagnosis had not revealed what the real problems were or how they should be addressed. The Learning Difficulties Research Project is a not-for-profit organisation established in 1981 to promote teacher research in classrooms. The analysis and advice is given without a fee in order to promote understanding of learners' needs.

Many desperate parents find their way to the LDRP website, and typically few children are referred from the poorest and most disadvantaged communities. Referrals from teachers however have come from them. The following underachieving cases have been referred by parents and are thus the tip of a very large iceberg. They have applicability to disadvantaged learners as well. It was noticeable in the writing research surveys discussed earlier that pupils from schools in more advantaged areas wrote more speedily and had fewer writing difficulties. The coastal area schools showed more handwriting problems than schools in other areas, except some rural and inner-city disadvantaged areas.

The case of Niamh, 10.3 years, November 2014

The following cases include direct quotes from their various case notes and each case has been given a pseudonym.

In my opinion, Niamh is a very able child with a mature approach to her several difficulties and an overview of her situation and the people in it that shows a good intellectual grasp. I would expect her real potential to be in the order of 130 IQ plus. My reasons for this are

i) The reasons given in the school report – maturity and intellectual grasp of situations and ability to keep people 'in play'
ii) Literacy difficulties, such as shown on the reading and spelling tests, depress IQ subtests and item scores. Silverman (2004) advises adding ten points at least to the IQ score to take account of this
iii) Her much higher comprehension than accuracy score on NARA
iv) Her early 'glue ear' condition that can affect both language acquisition and literacy learning – more details of this would have been helpful, e.g. onset, length of time, interventions
v) Her low BPVS (British Picture Vocabulary Scale) score suggests that the 'glue ear' had a significant impact
vi) Her life in two language environments – this can slow language development minimally at first and often not at all, but the added problem of 'glue ear' would have made language acquisition and development less easy

The literacy difficulties – developmental dyslexia?

There is clear evidence of her reading difficulties and even poorer spelling. The extent of her difficulties puts her in the 'dyslexic range', but the problems could equally have been the result of delays due to the glue ear and bilingualism. The results look the same – delayed literacy development – and the interventions need to be the same.

A multisensory approach is not enough. A multisensory APSL programme, such as HMLC (Augur and Briggs (eds) 2nd edition – not the later editions, or TRTS (Cowdery et al., 1994) is necessary. Looking at her skills level, she should be started at a more advanced level in the programme based on an analysis of what she already knows.

If this is not possible because of lack of such expertise in the school, she could be introduced in an informal way to CPSS (cognitive process strategies for spelling). Every teacher can learn to use these and iron out most spelling problems. This will also transfer and improve reading as well.

The numeracy difficulties – developmental dyscalculia?

I do not see evidence of classical dyscalculic problems in understanding the concept of quantity and number. Instead, she shows typical problems with operations and general understanding of arithmetical vocabulary and concepts.

97

This is common amongst dyslexics and those with delayed literacy development. It is possible that during the early years, she was still struggling with the language labels and concepts and missed out on some of the specialist vocabulary and concepts necessary in maths. Many children experience this, and their knowledge is insecure, but the teaching moves on. This exposes them to failure, and they develop a fear of maths as in Niamh's case.

What needs to be done to help her

i)   I would not recommend the Tony Buzan rote memorising strategies suggested in the report to extend her working memory. We already know she has sufficient capacity for her schoolwork. As reading and spelling improve, so will her working memory (digit span) because it is dependent upon verbal processing in which her literacy scores show she is delayed.

ii) Instead, the person designated to help her needs to do a 'Miscues analysis' of her maths errors (a practice sheet of typical errors is enclosed for the tutor to try). More sums can be generated to diagnose other problems, and Niamh can bring her own errors to the tutorials.

iii) The tutor needs to engage in a 'sum story' practical approach to clear up the errors and establish the concepts one at a time. Different creative strategies need to be applied until she securely understands the operation and concept and has the 'Eureka' moment. See examples the chapter by Mary Kibel in Miles et al. (1992).

Developmental co-ordination difficulties – developmental dysgraphia

It is clear from the samples that Niamh has some handwriting difficulties. Also noted in the report was 'hypermobility'. This needed amplification (e.g. what form does this take, bendy finger joints?). Are there any gross locomotion difficulties? Visuo-motor difficulties? Overactivity? Inattention? We needed to check penhold (dynamic tripod grip?) and finger strength, paper position and so on.

i)   Because of the co-ordination difficulties, she should have been taught a joined hand (i.e. cursive) from the outset. If at all possible, she should be persuaded and taught to change to cursive now. Because of the dysgraphia, this will not be easy, and she needs to understand why it is important to her in the long term, an appeal to logic.

ii) She has done well to learn to write as much and as fluently as she does, but the speed for her age is too slow and dysfluent. I suggest that she learns to write the most frequent common single-syllabled words first as single writing units (e.g. *the, and, come, so, was, It* and then, *why, what, when, where, who* plus words of her choice). Taking her back to single letterforms would be too babyish and slow.

iii) If lead-in strokes are too much for her to bear, then they can be shadow lead-ins.

iv) The rest needs to be associated with the CPS strategy – she must write in cursive over the area of error to correct it and lay down a new motor memory as well as the new lexical entry/correction.

It will probably be hard for her to learn a new motor programme, having already established the print script one, but it will help improve and consolidate her spelling. Although it is not generally realised, DCD can delay the development of literacy skills, especially spelling, but also will impact reading and number. For this reason, I have said that Niamh has had several difficulties to contend with, and her underlying ability is not adequately captured by traditional tests. The most important thing is that her confidence on entering secondary school should not be destroyed. Her current difficulties can be overcome. However, I suspect that Niamh's personal qualities that come through what people have written will enable her to become a high achiever, despite all the difficulties – although her life will be made a lot easier if they are cleared up soon.

The case of Catherine, 8.4 years, right-handed tripod grip, Jan. 2016

Transcript

Once upon a time, there was a small Karmarlo(?) called Sunny who was quite famos and wanted to discover what humans were 'they are Big for one thing' hissed a snake and very tasty to a dirgo(?). But I'm not a dirgo' Sunny iameditly replied 'That my friend is erelivent so screw your head back on you wanted to know.

'But I dident ask you' he shouted, Well I Can Read Minds!' snake yelled as loud as a rock hiting a planet at high speed eavery thing in the whole world was silent you coud heare a rein drop hit the ground but soon after a stange//'

Writing skill

Catherine has written 108 words in ten minutes, a speed of 10.8 words per minute and 43.3 letters per minute. This is an average speed for this age. If she is a very able child, we could expect her to be writing at nearly twice the speed and accuracy.

The script is joined with lead-in strokes. The letters are variable in size within words, and some words float above the lines whilst others sit properly on it. There is also variation in pressure with light and dark letters. The general appearance of the writing is spiky and not quite under control, lacking in fluidity. It was noted that 'this writing was much neater than her usual work'. It may be that this was done earlier in the day or that she was really working hard at motor control in a specially required task. I think she would benefit from developing a little more speed and fluency (see following suggestions).

Suggested handwriting interventions

To improve legibility, there are two important strategies i) making all the bodies of the letters the same size, as in the LDRP style in Figure 4.3 and ii) making all the ascenders and descenders face/slope the same way.

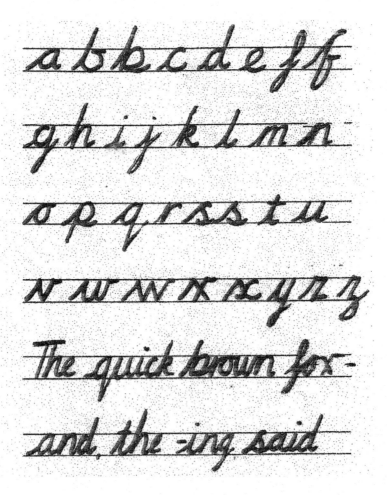

Figure 4.3 Example of ovoid sloping LDRP cursive

In Catherine's case, the first thing to help her with is getting the bodies of her letters the same size.

- Draw a half page of triple lines, see following, to suit the size of her writing.
- Explain what the task is and why it is a good idea to try it.
- Demonstrate the first word on each line.
- The task is for her to repeat it to the end of the line.
- Start with only three easy, common, short and useful words.
- Examine results together and discuss how easy it was or not.
- The next day, she should choose two or three more words to write within the lines.
- Repeat with new words every day for six days.
- Day 7, Catherine should try to do the task with only one line for guidance to sit the words on.
- Discuss. Decide together whether she needs to continue for just one more week.
- Stop after the 14 days in any case.

_____

_____

_____

Use three-letter words first, such as *the, and, why*, in cursive to start, and then use longer words, such as *come, said, when*. Add words from her misspelling list: *hear, famous, would, could, should* and so on.

When developing speed and fluency, some people find practising to rhythmic music can help.

(A 't' is a small letter and does not go up to touch the top line. Adjust the spacing of the lines to suit her handwriting size. Any 'i's' and 'j's' should be dotted at the end of writing the word not during.)

Spelling skill

famos, iameditly, erelivent, dident, hiting, eavery, coud, heare, stange

Her train of thought is consistently followed through with some interesting imagery in her MS. There is a rate of nine misspellings in 108 words. It is above the target level of HMI of no more than five per 100 words in SATs in year 6. It is more than expected of a more able or gifted child and suggests some difficulties that she needs help with. We should expect her reading and spelling to be at least at the 10/11-year-old level.

Suggested spelling interventions

1   Ask Catherine to reread her piece of work to see if she can identify and correct any of her misspellings. If so, she should put a ring round the area of error and concentrate on correcting that segment.

Only tackle two errors in a session, and ensure she has learnt them before moving on. Tell her she is going to learn to be a 'spelling detective'.

2   **dident** – She needs to say the word correctly for spelling in citation mode – 'did not', did-n't.

Some of her errors result from using an advanced vocabulary, and she will gradually acquire the correct versions from contact with print. Some need correcting now, but go carefully in case she is not yet ready.

3   The vowels have two different sounds, a short sound and a long one in which the vowel 'says its own name', as in A E I O U.

hiting – Can Catherine detect the short vowel sounds in one-syllabled words – *hit, cap, run, hop* – as opposed to the long vowel sounds in *bite, cape, rune, hope?*

HOP and HOPE

If so, the *rule* is that after the short vowel sound (in a closed syllable – CVC) when we add – ing, then we must *double* the consonant (e.g. hit-t-ing, hop-p-ing, run-n-ing and also hitt-er, hopp-er, runn-er).

The silent 'e' at the end of the word 'hope' is to tell us to make the long sound of 'o'. When we add – ing to this word, we must drop the silent 'e' and just *add –* ing (e.g. hop-ing, mak-ing).

(These are called suffixing rules, and there are four main ones – *add, double, drop, change.*)

She could try counting how many examples there are of the doubling and drop rules in a page of her reading book or a newspaper article to help remember the strategy.

4   **heare** – This is an overgeneralisation of the long vowel/silent 'e' rule. When 'two vowels go walking, the first one does the talking' (CVVC), and they make the long vowel sound anyway, so we do not need the silent 'e' to tell us this.

5   **eavery** – The 'ea' is the long vowel sound (two vowels going walking). Spell 'very', and just add the short vowel 'e' as in 'e-very'.

6   **stange** – This may be a slip of the pen or a slight articulation error. Check that she pronounces the three-letter blend 'str-' correctly and can feel the difference in the mouth between 'st-' and 'str-' and also hear it.

7   **famos** – This is a nearly correct spelling. The *baseword* is **fame**. There are three spellings of the 'us' sound at the end of words – us, -ous and – ious.

- After nouns, we use – us (e.g. crocus, locus, circus, bonus, virus – nouns are the names of things).
- The suffix – ous is an adjective ending, telling us how something is (e.g. famous, nervous, generous, dangerous).

Keep this one in reserve in case she needs it later:

- If the word has a 'sh' sound before the 'us', then we use – ious (e.g. vicious, malicious, fictitious, anxious).

8 **coud** – The spelling rationale for this one is lost in the mists of time. A writing strategy is recommended (e.g. for 'could' and 'would' and 'should'). See the writing practice suggested in the following section.

   The next two are best dealt with by getting them nearer to the correct version. Identify the baseword, and articulate it clearly.

9 **erelivent** – Start with correct articulation, 'relevant', and syllabify i-rele-vant. Later, point out the double 'rr' after the short vowel sound.

10 **iameditly** – im-mediate-ly (prefix + baseword + final stable syllable)

    She is using a visual strategy from reading to spell, and so the order of letters is muddled. She needs to pay more attention to the articulatory sequence in words and syllabify them for spelling – im-e-di-at-ly. This gives the basic skeletal structure on which the correct version can be built.

The case of Millie, 12.9 years, right-handed rigid tripod, Nov. 2018

N. B. The text is transcribed as it appears to the reader as though it is misspelt, although it can be inferred that she spells most of it correctly. The problem is not the spelling but the incomplete letter formation and incorrect construction and joining of letters.

Transcript

Max ran, ran ran. Behind him he could her, the pounding of 'One black Manal, gang. As he sprent Orough the streets he Oought about where he should take them. Do iase them. Mabye throogh broad street?

   He was snepped back to reclity as a lerge stone wall loomed before him. It was a decel end. A whipped around to see Morah mcliciously layhing at him. Sh was trapped.

Max clcsped ai siver B X studded win emerclds in one hand and reld for gold hand sparkling with rubies in his trouser pocket. Morch leerecl at him as deg slowly strutted oven. Neg knes neg heel won. Behinar sttod his gang of cronies, holding sling shots, knives and club like pieces of junk wood.

March was only a metre away now. Max knew he only had one oprion.

'Take xx one more step tnd I throw these beuties' indicating to m too pieces of priceless jewlrey, also the secred symbols of the bleck hand gang. 'Into the river!' Bothe Macx cni Morch knew nct//

Writing skills

Millie is writing at a speed of 17.5 words per minute and 76.1 letters per minute. This is a good speed and above average for the age group (i.e. 14 words per minute). She should be aiming towards 20 words per minute over the next year.

The writing is small, and the spacing between words is large. Rivers of space run down the page. She uses a mainly unjoined print script. Ascenders are frequently too short, but descenders' 'tails' are generally adequate. The 'tails' and 'sticks' tend to slope in different directions. There is a tendency to drag words below the line.

There are four types of handwriting:

i)   A fast running hand for personal notes
ii) A fluent, speedy style for teacher audiences, exams, SATs and so on.
iii) A slow, careful script in semi-print for form-filling
iv) Calligraphy or 'beautiful writing' for posters and exhibitions, possibly using Italic or Gothic style

The sample of Millie's writing shows a fast running hand useful for personal writing, but it is not good for exam use. In exams, she will be under pressure to write at speed, and this is when the poor construction will disadvantage her and be at its worst – when externals try to read what she has written.

The pencil grip (Figure 4.5) is not clear from the photo, but it seems to be with the index finger over too much and the pencil too thin in a weak grip. Paper angle is 45 degrees and may need to be smaller. The paper should be moved up the desk so that the arm rests by it and the arm is at the same angle as the paper.

The best grip to try to work with is the flexible tripod grip. She could start with the rigid tripod – this is index and middle finger on top. Plastic and clay moulds can help develop the correct grip, and some pens that have the tripod guide structure built into them can be bought.

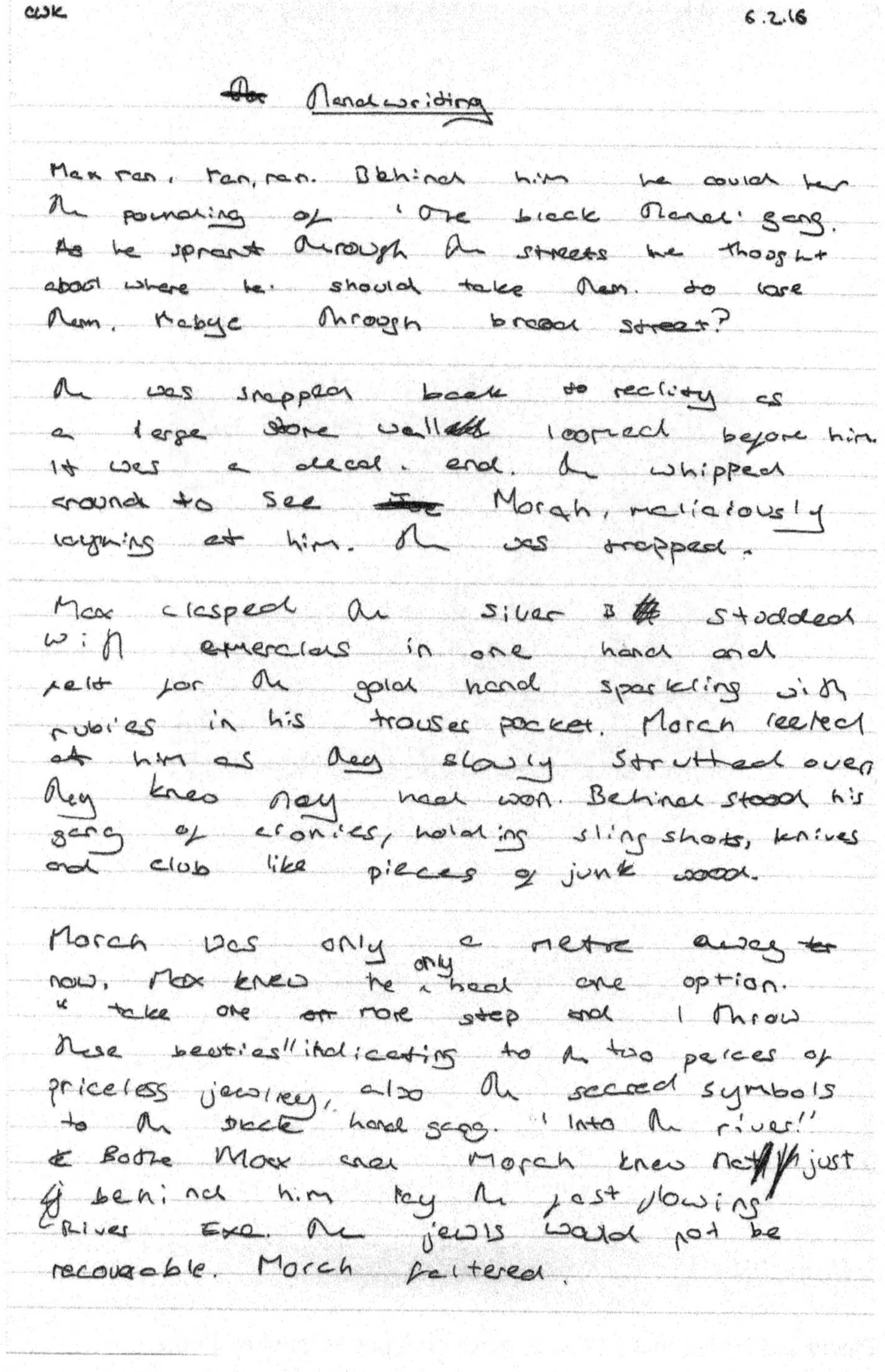

~~the~~ <u>Handwriting</u>

Max ran, ran, ran. Behind him he could her
the pounding of 'the black Snake' gang.
As he sprant through the streets he thought
about where he should take them. to lose
them. Maybe through broad street?

He was snapped back to reality as
a large ~~store~~ wall~~ed~~ loomed before him.
It was a dead. end. He whipped
around to see ~~the~~ Morah, maliciously
laughing at him. He was trapped.

Max clasped the silver ~~ ~~ studded
with emeralds in one hand and
felt for the gold band sparkling with
rubies in his trouser pocket. Morah leered
at him as they slowly strutted over
they knew they had won. Behind stood his
gang of cronies, holding sling shots, knives
and club like pieces of junk ~~wood~~.

Morah was only a metre away to
now, Max knew he only had one option.
" take one or more step and I throw
these beauties" indicating to the two pieces of
priceless jewlrey, also the sacred symbols
to the ~~state~~ hand gang. " Into the river!"
& both Max and Morah knew ~~neth~~ just
if behind him lay the fast flowing
river Exe. the jewls would not be
recoverable. Morah faltered.

Figure 4.4 Millie's writing, an extract

Figure 4.5 Millie's pencil hold

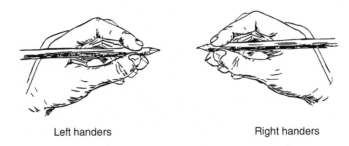

Left handers   Right handers

Figure 4.6 Flexible tripod grip

Spelling skills

Misspellings? Her for hear, beuties, pieces and peices, jewlrey, bothe.

There are possibly three spelling errors, although 'beauties' may not be misspelt but is a writing formation problem. Dictate all five words separately to find if Millie can spell them correctly; she probably can.

- Beuties – beauty, beautiful, from the French 'beau'
- Jewlrey – the baseword is 'jewel' – jewel-ry means jewels in general. Check that she says the word correctly, not as it is spelt.
- Bothe – She has over-generalised the use of silent 'e' to show the long vowel sound is made in 'both'. This is an exception to the rule (c.f. moth). We probably used to say it with the long vowel sound once or just dropped the 'e' over time in writing.

Millie's spelling is good, but it could be misunderstood, as I have illustrated in the transcript.

Suggested interventions

Determining a useful intervention for Millie is problematic. She has not been taught how to form her letters and words efficiently for speed and legibility in the early years and has developed her own style. It is hard won and embedded now, and she may be reluctant to change or find it too difficult.

Some fatter and light pens may help in strengthening the grip. Try several different sizes and shapes, and ask her to write the 'fox' sentence with them to see how the script looks and feels.

'The quick brown fox jumps over the lazy dog.'

In Figure 4.7 is the Test of Handwriting Form and Legibility (T-HFL) that shows a typical range of errors that pupils make.

There are two ways in which some improvement in legibility might be made without sacrificing her speed and personal style.

i) Targeting keywords and letter combinations, such as
    - 'the', which is mostly illegible in her MS, starts from right to left and often looks like a circle and squiggle
    - always joining 'ou' and 'oo' in words (vowel digraphs)
    - double letters (e.g. in all, stepped)
    - digraphs (e.g. th, ph, ch, wh, sh), consonant digraphs
    - always join suffixes such as '-ing'
    When she can consistently do these tasks, she can move on to other letter combinations or work on the length of ascenders and the consistent slope of them.
ii) Practising a slow, form-filling style that can be used for multiple choice tests requiring one-word answers using the LDRP model, which is very different from her own script (It will be interesting to see if she can learn a modified structure.)

Over the next few years, she ought to be able to assimilate these changes in a modest way that will make her script more legible but not compromise speed and fluency.

Test of Handwriting Form and Legibility (T-HFL)

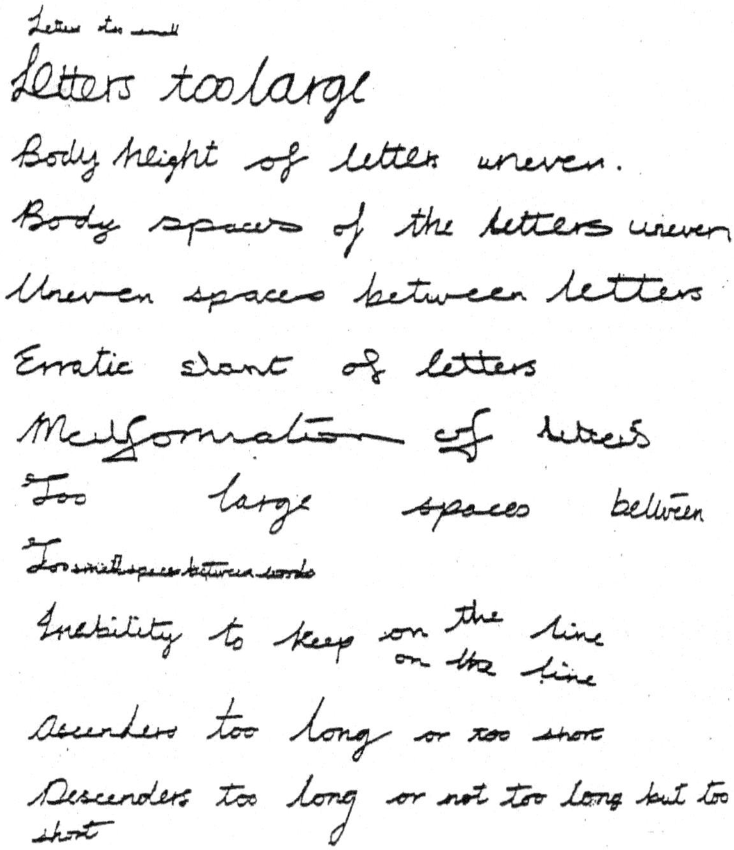

Letters too small

Letters too large

Body height of letters uneven.

Body spaces of the letters uneven

Uneven spaces between letters

Erratic slant of letters

Malformation of letters

Too large spaces between

Too small space between words

Inability to keep on the line on the line

Descenders too long or too short

Descenders too long or not too long but too short

Montgomery (1990)

Intervention Procedure

1. Whatever the errors identified give the pupil some double lined paper and ask him or her to write name and address between the lines. The target is to get the body size of letters all the same. Note any malformed letters.

Figure 4.7 Test of Handwriting Form and Legibility

The case of Tara, 8.1 years, left-handed tripod grip, Dec. 2017

Transcript

Once upon a time there lived a e girl called Goldilock. She lived with mum in the little cottage on the egde of a forest. On the side of the forest there lived three bears. A big one, a middle sized one a and a baby one. One early morning Goldi// locks

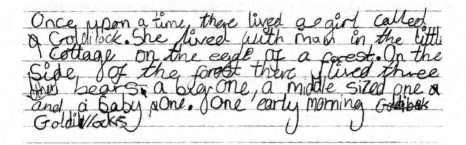

Figure 4.8 Tara's handwriting

Writing skills

Tara is writing at a speed of 5.4 words per minute and 20.9 letters per minute. This is a significantly slower speed than the average at her age and suggests there are some problems and one of the reasons she does not enjoy writing. The average speed at her age is nine to ten words per minute, and many of the ablest pupils write at a speed of 15 words per minute.

Her writing form is a large, mainly joined script without lead-in strokes. The descenders, 'tails', are very long on 'g' and 'y'. The letters slope forward and back. The bodies of the letters vary in size within words and sometimes are as large as capital letters. Letters such as 's' and 'z' that are more complex to make are often too large and look like capital letters. The overall appearance of the MS is that it is cramped. All of these features make the script less legible than it should be and suggest a mild coordination difficulty.

Spelling skills

* 'egde' – She is spelling all the standard vocabulary well for her age.

'Edge' is not a common word, and her attempt is a good phonetic equivalent. From visual memory, she recalls all the letters but not in quite the right order. She may even be able to correct it if she proofreads her MS. Ask her to do this to check. More careful articulation should enable her to feel the differences between ED-ge and EGde.

If she does not find and correct the error, point it out to her. Ask her to put a ring round the area of error – the misplaced 'g'. Then ask her to overarticulate the word as 'ed-ge'. She should then try to write it three times from memory, covering the previous word each time and *naming* the letters (e.g. E-D-G-E), simultaneous oral spelling (SOS).

Ask her to try to think of some other words with this structure (e.g. rid-ge, frid-ge, mid-ge, brid-ge, badge, nudge, judge). Don't tell her these if she cannot think of them, but ask her to look out for them in her storybooks and make a little collection – 'her fridge words' – the 'spelling detective' approach.

Suggested intervention on handwriting

The most problematic area is Tara's handwriting coordination in relation to fluency and speed.

- Find some fatter pens and pencils for her to try. She might find one that suits her best.
- Draw some three-lined paper to practice for fluency. Only draw half a page of lines. Practice for motor skills should be little and often – not more than about five minutes per day:

————————————————————————————————————

————————————————————————————————————

————————————————————————————————————

- She must try to make the bodies of her letters sit on the bottom line and touch the line above.
- All the 'sticks' and 'tails' should slope in the same direction, either forward or back or upright.
- The sticks should touch or nearly touch the top line.
- Note that 't' is a small letter, and its 'stick' does not touch the top line.

Ask her to write three common words, such as *and* and *the* and *why*, in the top line and discuss how well she can do this.

- Next, ask her to write a whole line of each of the words as fluidly and speedily as she can: *and and and and and and*
  the the the the the the the
- Repeat the exercise several times more over the next few days and then after that with different words, such as *come, home, long* and so on.

The LDRP model (see Figure 4.2) is a fully joined (cursive) with lead-in strokes. The lead-in lines enable all words to begin in the same place on the line, which is helpful for children with difficulties. As Tara does not use lead-in lines, she does not need to change but use 'ghost-in' lines instead. Do not bother her with single-letter practice.

Keep the daily practice up for a fortnight with a day of rest in between each week, and then review her writing with her. Does it look better and please her more? What does she find difficult? What are her thoughts on the process?

She should now begin to try to use the strategies in her schoolwork. At weekly intervals after this, encourage her to have a practice session for speed. Then at the beginning and end of each half term, she should write the 'fox' sentence as many times as possible in **one minute** to see if she is speeding up.

The quick brown fox jumps over the lazy dog.

All the letters of the alphabet are contained in it.

The point of the regular discussion is to enable her to gain cogntitive control over the skill and know what she needs to do even though she may relapse at times.

Other things to check are for her left-handedness:

• Left handers should hold the pen a little further from the point than right handers so they can see the tip of the pen and the words they are writing.
• They should sit on the left of peers in the classroom to have enough free left elbow room.
• The paper for writing should be slanted more to the left – 30–40 degrees – than right-handers need to the right (20–30 degrees).

Figure 4.9 Above, paper slope for left handers

Some left handers write with palm upwards (hookers), even with the tripod grip, and may need to have their paper placed horizontally. It is best not to try to adjust this grip, as it indicates that the child has had to change hands for neurological or a hand structure differences.

One final point is the adoption by Tara of the 'Oxford i's'. These are the little circles or rings she uses instead of dots. She should know that it is a habit that will slow down her writing speed, and she should try not to use it, especially when she needs to write later for SATs. She may find this hard to give up, so she might try thinking of using it only in classwork and not in homework so that both styles become fluent and she can switch from one mode to the other when required.

Lilly, 6.9 years, right-handed thumb-over grip, Dec. 2016

Transcript

(This is about star monsters.)

> They can bounce high and low, play games and more. I have 109, My faviroute star monsters are Belbo, Urri, Suggi, Olara, Foxiju and more. I got into them in August. The crdotiouns I have are Rokton, RinKo Linguer, Vibrolin, Flimec and Umaji. Series 3 is going to be out next summer. They can come as capsules packets Tins and more. Series 1 packets are red. Series 2 packets are blue and I think series 3 packets will be green. Who knows? (Here are the colars I thought of). Green Orange black Pink burgundy and purple.

Overall analysis

Lilly has written 98 words in ten minutes. This is a speed of 9.8 words per minute and is a little above average for the age group (circa eight words). After eight minutes of writing, Lilly said her hand was aching and that she tends to avoid writing anything.

This script is typically faint, as seen in many types of coordination difficulties.

There are three misspellings – **faviroute, colar, crdotiouns**. This is a good standard for the age group per 100 words. Given her high ability and good literacy scores, it would be expected that her handwriting would be far more fluent and extensive. The main reason that it is not can be seen in the penhold she has adopted to control the pencil, which is between a full fist and thumb-over grip. It is a very inflexible hold and requires a large amount of effort because it requires a whole hand movement and control from the wrist and arm rather then from the finger

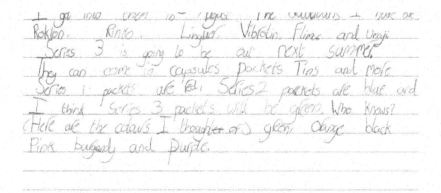

Figure 4.10 Extract from Lilly's MS

Figure 4.11 Thumb-over fist grip

ends to make the letters. The pencil is almost in the upright position in the second picture.

It will be essential for her to be helped to change the pen grip if she is to speed up her writing, not feel pain and begin to enjoy the activity.

In addition to this, she has not been taught to form her letters correctly with ligatures so that she can begin joining them in words. This print form she is using is also slowing her writing speed and fluency. But for these factors, she would have a mature writing style for her age that is pleasant and legible to read.

Both the index finger and the middle finger are on top of the pencil and guide its movement at the point. The middle finger joint is 'bendy' – bent backwards, indicating the joints are not yet fully developed. The left hand holding down the paper also shows slim and not well-developed top joints on the fingers. The hands have the appearance of a much younger child not in size but in the soft outlines and bendy appearance. This often requires young children to adopt the fist grip and then the thumb-over grip, as seen in the photos. It is often accompanied by a weak grip and lack of muscle strength in the hand. This can make the writing faint because of lack of pressure.

Paper position

The paper should be sloped at about 25 degrees to the right parallel with the writing arm.

The penhold needs to be changed towards the tripod grip

This is essential to reduce the amount of effort involved in writing and make it easier and more enjoyable. In order to do this, a much fatter and lighter-weight pen should be tried. Pencils are too thin for her at present. Collect a range of pens for her to try – look at the Stabilo and Osmiroid ranges for example. She will quickly chose one that suits her best and enables her to match the flexible tripod grip. At first, this may only be for short periods. It has to be thought of as daily practice as for running a race, getting faster and stronger each day.

Finger-strengthening exercises are also recommended, such as in the use of finger exercises (playing the piano or the same types of in-air exercises).

Using eating tools and cooking preparation activities, play tools, finger painting, drawing and painting and manipulating clay and dough will all help this. She needs to be taught how to join her letters in words beginning with the short common words such as *the, and, why, said, come* and so on.

For example, draw some double lines for her size of handwriting and ask her to copy a line of joined up 'the' using tripod grip.

All the 'bodies' of the letters should just fit between the lines. As an alternative, a flat end yellow marker can be used as a guide instead of lines.

Each day, she could write a line of a different word from the set above.

After the weekend, in the following five days, she could try to write two lines of words each day for the week and then three lines the third week and see how she gets on. In the fourth week, she could try to write all five different words on the five lines. See LDRP cursive example (Figure 4.6).

The exercises will help with the finger strengthening and tripod grip, but do not force the pace. She may need longer for the joints to develop and the fingers to grow stronger. Lilly may prefer to use 'ghost' lead-in lines on words from the line.

Lilly's writing above can be used for the reader to practice diagnostic assessment and think about intervention strategies.

Although the preceding cases were all referrals by parents and contained case information and background details, it is possible for teachers to learn to do sufficient useful analysis based on essay writing. For example, SENCos and English teachers could, with a little training, do the following when given no information about the cases but just a written narrative from a mock examination.

The next two referrals are from a school in East London. No other information was provided

The document (New GCSE Additional Science Assessment, 2012) stated that the answer is to be awarded six marks, and the assessment will have regard to the quality of written communication. There is no guidance on how the marks will be assigned for the facts (4) or the quality (2). These two pupils had just taken a mock exam in year 11, and the results caused concern to their teacher who asked for advice.

Case: Tehmina 3 May 2014

OCR paper: 'Describe intensive farming and discuss its advantages and disadvantages'

The pupil has written the following:

'The advantages of in tensive farming is that it produce a large amount of crops and increase the yeild. and for alot cheaper as as well. One of the methods of Intensivee farming is battery farming. One if the advantages of battery farming is that chicken in the battery do not move around so there energy spent en respiraision and mure energy spent fo Growth and Reproduction thus you fatter meat for cheaper. The disadvanteys are that Battery famers only chicken have space the same size as A4 sheet of paper. The boiler chicken weight is heavy for their legs so the collapse and they struggle to do basic thing like drink water.

'Another advantage of intensive farming is that there is less workers needed to attend the crops'

The sample has 128 words plus 12 words crossed out = 140 words in total in 10 minutes.

There are 15 misspellings, including five missing plurals and some confusions arising from incomplete letter formation (e.g. mere [more]) and squiggles. There is a range of syntactic errors related to plurals and connector word omissions.

Study skills

T needs to be taught the 'rule of three' and how to tackle an exam question. For example,

1   Circle and number the different parts of the question, often three as here: e.g. i) Describe intensive farming; ii) Advantages; iii) Disadvantages. This format can be used to check that all parts of the question have been answered.
2   Time needs to be reserved for proofreading

Cognitive skills

The answer has some rational structure defined by the question, but there is a lack of overall balance. For example, T launches straight into advantages without defining the term and then switches to battery farming in some detail but does not underline the ethical nature of what she writes.

There is no paragraphing except as an afterthought when another advantage is added at the end.

Together with a partner, it might help both if they have a model answer with assigned marks and then help each other mark their answers. They should use different colours to underline spelling errors and grammatical errors and then discuss their efforts with a tutor or another pair who have done the same task on their answers. A few such exercises will help them learn how to structure their answers better and bring more of what they know to the fore.

Language skills

The language structure is mostly syntactically correct apart from pluralisations (e.g. 'The advantages of intensive farming is that it produce'; 'One if the advantage of' 'chicken in the').

Proofreading her work should help iron out the difficulties in relation to the plurals but only if she makes them correctly in her speech. Thus her oral work needs to be monitored, and feedback should be given on it. It would help too if more formal oral opportunities were available to practice coherent and correct expression.

Capitals are introduced at unnecessary points within sentences (e.g. Crops, Growth, Reproduction, Battery).

Spelling

The misspellings were produce(s), increase(s), yeild, alot, intensivee, advantage(s), disadvanteys, chicken(s), there (their), Respiaision, fatter (fatten), reprodution, famers, the (they), workuuu, collapese.

These errors reveal a problem with the use of plurals and with a lack of clear articulation for spelling. She needs practice with oral work and citation mode as already indicated.

The real spelling errors here are as follows:

'yeild'– This is a common error in which there is an over-generalisation of the rule 'When two vowels go walking the first one does the talking' (except in yield, field and friend, for example).

'alot' – This is a failure to identify the baseword 'lot, and lots'.

'there' and 'their' – These are common confusions ('their' must be used when things belong to them – their energy).

'Respiaision' – may not be a correct representation of what was actually written as the handwriting form is not clear, or it may just be a confusion between -tion and -sion. In which case, the guideline is:

i)   -tion is the most common spelling of the (shun) ending, so when in doubt use -tion.

ii) Use -tion after basewords ending in the (t) or (k) sounds, whether they are spelled 't', 'te' or 'c' and 'ce' (e.g. reproduce – reproduction; dictate – dictation; produce, product, production; vacate – vacation; reduce – reduction; induce – induction).

iii) Use -tion after a short or a long vowel (e.g. ignition, volition, ambition; respiration, invitation, replication, duplication).

Misspellings 'respiaision', 'disadvateys' and 'collapese' may also illustrate
  i)   a lack of clarity in speech of some multi-syllabled words,
  ii) a lack of understanding of their construction from smaller basewords (e.g.
       respire, vantage)
  iii) a lack of use of syllabification to underpin spelling

She needs to be encouraged to use citation mode to assist spelling of these long words, and when the words are introduced, their construction from the baseword could be explained.

The rest of the errors are more to do with a lack of clarity of the writing form and are considered in the section on handwriting.

Overall, the number of misspellings is 5/6 in 140 words, which is just within the poorer but average range, and the nature is not dysorthographic.

Handwriting

T's handwriting is an area of some considerable concern. It is mainly in a joined style. This is good. At the beginning, the form is overlarge for this age of pupil. Halfway through the writing begins to grow smaller but also deteriorates, and a fatigue effect is noticeable. Letters begin to slope in different directions, and their size within words begins to vary.

Speed

In order to be successful in school and able to cope with the curriculum, a pupil of this age needs to be able to write at a speed of 20–25 words per minute in a ten-minute period. Other research finds the mean speed at this age is 20 words per minute, suggesting speed-up strategies would be widely relevant.

This pupil has written 140 words in the span of ten minutes allocated to the question. If this pupil is writing at a speed of 14 words per minute, it is severely slow, and she would need help to develop more speed.

Form

The form is a joined style. However, the letter formation and joining have not been well taught, and this leads to reader confusion. For example, 'farming' looks liken 'feming'; amount – amaint; cheaper – cheapr; farming – faming; struggle – smggle; to – te; and so on.

The particular problem is that some letters within words are incompletely formed or the join comes from the base but leads backwards and over not forwards. Many 'a's', 'd's' and 'g's' are left open. The 'a's' therefore look like 'u's'; some 'n's' are also written like 'u's' and 'r's' are often incompletely formed; 't's' are often joined from the bar and not from their base. All these errors and more contribute to decreasing the legibility of the script and making it look as though there are more spelling errors than there actually are. In public examinations, this can only lead to lower marks than the work deserves.

It would therefore be desirable that some input is offered to show the pupil how to diagnose these issues and then how to correct them without changing style and losing fluency. If the pupil is willing, this should not take her more than a few minutes' practice each day for about a fortnight.

Another concern about this script is that many letters in words vary in size so that they appear as capital letters. This is a phenomenon noticed when children have had mild handwriting co-ordination difficulties. Letters such as 's' and 'k' and 'w' are particularly difficult for them to form, so they are made larger. Other signs are when simpler letters, such as 'c' and 'u', appear small and large at random. These signs appear in this script. Other evidence shows in the fatigue effect that should not arise in such a small amount of writing at this age. It can be seen that after a pause for thought and a rest, the final sentence shows some recovery.

It would be advisable to check her penhold and writing posture and if she finds writing at length painful in any way. If the interventions do not bring about improvement, and writing is still difficult for her, it may be possible to obtain extra time in the examinations. In such cases, DASH would be a test to use.

Case: Zainab 3 May 2014

OCR: 'Describe intensive farming and discuss its advantages and disadvantages'

The pupil has written the following:

> 'The advantages of intensive farming is that it has fertisers that contain insecticides and hesepcides a insecticides kills pest prevents them from destroys the crops and causing diseases.
>
> 'Hesepides kills weed plant kuver which will decrease the amount of competition for light, water and space for the other plants. It also used biological farming this is when hens are traped in a tight space where they for eat and produce egg less movement occurs, less movement results in more reproduction of the eggs therefore there will be more energy for growth. The disadvantages are intensive farming the chemicals in fertisers are expensive to purches and there is no support for the tomatoe plant'.

113 words, plus 6 words crossed out = 119 in total. A writing speed of 11.9 wpm

There are eight different spelling errors, ten altogether and one missing plural, a total of 11 errors. There is a range of syntactic errors related to plurals, tenses and connector word omissions and one missing capital after a full stop.

The answer has no overall clear rational structure defined by the question but is an assembly of relevant facts, some poorly expressed. There are two logical sequences related to plant cover and the hens.

Study skills

Z. needs to be taught the 'rule of three' and how to tackle an exam question. For example,

1   Circle and number the different parts of the question, often three, as here, for example, i) Describe intensive farming; ii) Advantages; iii) Disadvantages. This format can be used to check that all parts of the question have been answered.
2   Time needs to be reserved for proofreading.

Language skills

Z. launches straight into the advantages and disadvantages without describing/defining the term *intensive farming*.

> Para 1: Contains some elements of correct information, but it is presented in a disjointed fashion that does not always make sense. The syntax is poor.
> Para 2: There is more correct connection between facts in this paragraph, but there are still syntactic errors, and the final segment is neither logical nor connected.

Proofreading her work will only help iron out some of the difficulties. In addition, it would be a good idea for her to read this piece of work aloud to a tutor and discuss the omissions and language structures to determine how capable she is of detecting the problems and correcting them by herself.

The script reads as though the pupil is a learner of English as an additional language, not one who has been in English education for ten years. This may be because the language of the home is different from that of the school, and although she may be competent in social, everyday language comprehension and expression, this does not extend to specialist terminology and the second-level or academic language of school examinations. These several demands place undue stress on the processing capacity so that previously memorised segments cannot be successfully integrated into the overall argument.

Alternatively, we may be looking at a different or related phenomenon. This may be the work of a diligent but quiet child who refrains from speaking in class in front of peers whenever possible. Over the years, she has succeeded by learning material by heart but not always seeking to understand it. Now the curriculum requires the application of higher-order academic skills of analysis, synthesis and evaluation, not just recall and repetition. Lack of practice in higher-order learning is now causing her problems.

Written communication is a complex and difficult set of skills and is predicated upon good basic oral communication. Lack of practice in 'citation mode', speaking clearly and out loud so that every syllable can be heard by an audience has probably not been part of her regular experience. This is not atypical, as many CHMI and Ofsted reports have pointed to the lack of enough opportunities for the development of formal speech in classrooms.

This pupil needs such help. Perhaps in her revision activities, time could be set aside for her to explain what she has learnt to an 'expert' listener. This should include answers to such questions as in the preceding not random, self-generated recall. The listener should be able to correct the language and clarify or at least question the constructs. It could be part of a revision 'buddy' or mentor system set up for the purpose.

Spelling

The misspellings were fertissers, fertisers, hesepcides, hesepides, kuver, biogical, traped, egg(s), wiu (with?), purches, tomatoe. Although the literacy skills have been checked and a diagnosis of dyslexia was not apparent, the spelling errors made by this 15-year-old are a cause for concern. The errors centre on specialist terminology and infrequent vocabulary. They are typical of the 'second-level dyslexic', one who has acquired the basic literacy skills in reading and writing but has systematic spelling problems with advanced vocabulary.

This work suggests a dysorthographic profile that is not generally picked up on standard dyslexia tests. It may be seen in recovered dyslexics or arise in the absence of any reading difficulties in gifted children who learn to read self-taught. They use their very good visual memories to learn to read but miss out on the phonological aspects of the skill, and this undermines their later spelling abilities.

The HMI criterion is that no more than five errors should be made per 100 words at year 7. Dyslexics at this age are making ten or more errors per 100 words. This pupil has made nine errors in 119 words at the age of 15 years, and so there is a serious issue to be dealt with.

In this case, the common lower-order errors are in incomplete syllabification. If the words are spoken in citation mode and then spelled syllable by syllable, this will help begin the correction process (e.g. fert-i-li-sers; herb-i-cide; and so on).

'Traped' is an example of a higher-order error involving knowledge of one of the four suffixing rules – *add, double, drop, change*. When a single syllable word has a suffix added to it, such as -ed, -ing or –er, if the word contains a single short vowel sound, we *double* the final consonant before adding the suffix:

e.g. trap – trapped, trapping, trapper; run, running; hop, hopping; pot, potting

If the word contains a long vowel sound (denoted by a silent 'e'), we simply drop the 'e' and add the suffix:

hope – hoping, hoped; cope, coping, coped

There are 15 such rules that can correct the spelling of some 20,000 words and 12 general strategies that all teachers could use to help correct misspellings. Look – cover – write – check does not correct a misspelling unless the error in the lexicon is also corrected by one of the cognitive strategies.

This pupil needs extra spelling support that begins with her self-generated errors, using CPSS (cognitive process strategies for spelling). The method/programme need only occupy a few minutes each day.

Handwriting

The handwriting is another area of concern. It is mainly in a print style with a few running joins. The form is overlarge for this age of pupil, and there are problems of legibility and speed.

Speed

In order to be successful in school and able to cope with the curriculum, a pupil of this age needs to be able to write at a speed of 20–25 words per minute in a ten-minute period. Other research finds the mean speed at this age is 20 words per minute, suggesting speed-up strategies would be widely relevant.

This pupil has written 119 words in the hypothesised span of ten minutes allocated to the question. This pupil is writing at a speed of 12 words per minute, severely slow. She needs help to develop fluency and more speed.

Form

The form is a print style typical of infant school models. It appears to have been self-taught and developed from copy writing rather than being directly taught as an efficient motor skill. The size and lack of systematic joining hampers the fluency and speed. The spelling problem will also slow down the writing speed.

The bodies of all the letters are roughly all the same size; this is good. The ascenders and descenders however are not always longer than the rest of the letters, and this hampers legibility. The reason may be that the form is so large it leaves little room for lengthening them. Some of the p's stand on the line, another hangover from poor infant school writing practice.

Some typical legibility issues are *will* (looks like uuu); *more* (mare); *kills* (rius); *of* (at); *support* (sipport). Many 'd's' look like 'a'; 'f's' look like 't's'; 'v's' and 'u's' merge into the next letters and become part of them – therefore looks like 'theretoe'.

When the work is marked quickly by external examiners, they will not have the time to work out what the real spelling is, and the work will attract lower marks than it deserves so it is essential that some attention is given to improving speed and legibility.

It could begin by giving lines to write between under timed conditions to show how much the size can be reduced and speed increased. Then ascenders and descenders will not tangle with letters in other lines.

Handwriting is a personal attribute, and Z needs to be convinced that some changes are necessary and will be useful to her; otherwise, she will resist.

Many pupils would benefit if the school had a handwriting policy in which print script was not encouraged and instead a fast-running or cursive form was used by all the pupils and promoted by the teachers. The difference this can make is in higher-degree classification and higher GCSE grades.

Print needs to be reserved for application forms, formal messages and calligraphic exercises, such as labelling and poster design. Feeder schools in particular need to be encouraged to work on speed and legibility in writing and early development of a joined script.

Conclusion

All the case studies in this chapter were referred for a secondary diagnosis because the pupils were perceived to be underachieving by their teachers or parents. In some cases, there had been no intervention. In others, interventions had been undertaken but no improvements had been seen. Because of previous research, an additional task was given to the pupils, and this was to write a story in ten minutes. A photograph was taken of the writing position and penhold. It was increasingly surprising that in nearly every case, the writing difficulties were the core difficulty, and there was a range of reasons that appeared to cause them.

Over the last 70 years, attention has been directed to the acquisition and development of reading skills and less attention has been given to spelling and handwriting in schools. By the 1970s, Peters (1967, 1985) observed that spelling was being 'caught rather than taught', and this has remained largely true until relatively recently after the Rose Report (2006). Whitehead (2004) an early years educator, affirmed that it was not necessary to teach spelling until year 2, for example. How wrong this is can be seen in the case studies.

To illustrate the needs of underachievers, the case studies of the three boys were selected specifically to illustrate different profiles, but all three were found to have had some writing issues. The girls were not specifically selected but were referred for advice for underachievement, and when the story writing task was given, all of them showed writing problems, as did the two underachieving year 11 students.

This suggests that more attention should be given to the teaching of handwriting in the early years and regard should be paid to the potential needs of those with difficulties. Instead, teaching handwriting, when it is undertaken, takes for granted that what is suitable is a method that assumes the subskills are all developmentally regular. Adults do not seem to realise how hard it is to learn to write, and one third of pupils may be expected to have some difficulties, especially in disadvantaged areas. Each school needs to have an agreed handwriting and spelling policy.

One test for teachers to make them understand has been to give them a short dictation in a training session. When pens are poised and ready, they are asked to change hands. They learn very quickly how hard it can be to write with the non-preferred hand, and only one or two in the 'class' can keep up with the pace. Some just scribble, and others become frustrated and angry and give up.

We need to start developing writing skills in pre-school and reception with games and skills that underpin writing and strengthen and correct penhold as necessary. Neurological research shows that this will support reading (James and Engelhart, 2013) and help build literacy skills in a developmentally appropriate manner. If we keep them separate, this does not allow them to reinforce each other and build together.

In the next chapter, the literacy teaching skills that all teachers need will be discussed and exemplified. But one final case to think about – the disadvantage of wealth: A 7/8 year-old boy is being waved off after half term by his family at Colchester station. He is rigid and stony-faced. As the train moved off his face reddened, he began to shake and tears streamed down his face, no sobs , no noise. Off to boarding school amongst peers, bullying and repressed emotions. What kind of judge or leader will he become?

5 | Changing early years teaching and closing the literacy gap

Introduction

In the chapters so far, underachievement and disadvantage have been shown to be the target of research and government policies in a number of investigations and initiatives. The conclusions were that teachers needed more support and targeted CPD. Some schools were effective in helping overcome disadvantage and underachievement, but most were not. It was concluded that the methods promoted by the National Curriculum documents, the assessment-driven system and league table competition enforced by Ofsted, rather than driving up standards were driving up levels of underachievement and endangering the mental health of pupils and teachers. The system was not fit for purpose and needed radical overhaul.

In this chapter, an examination and revision of basic skills teaching and learning is the focus for raising achievement. Teaching methods or pedagogy has an important history, but it is not well understood by those ministers and administrators who have the responsibilities for directing education in schools and colleges.

Mass education introduced in 1897 requires a complex set of classroom management and pedagogical skills if it is to be effective. If we teach pupils something, it carries with it the implicit assumption that they will learn it or at least most of it. Initially, the methods used were rote memorising, and it was thought that memorising large chunks of the scriptures, for example, would imbue children with moral virtue, memorising poetry would imbue culture, and so on. Reading and spelling were learned through rote training and in copywriting. As more colleges for teacher training were opened, a more developmental method became popular for nursery and primary school teaching. It tried to replicate the ways in which children learned naturally in the home (Comenius, Froebel, Montessori). The secondary school system had a different ethos, it followed the transmission model from the universities in a watered-down format (Barnard, 1961). It involved telling the pupils information and devising ways to check they had learned some of it. But telling and lecturing are not teaching, and new, more effective methods began to emerge by the 1970s. These were not always understood, and the progressive-traditional debate ensued.

Just as education techniques began to change and move in new directions towards problem-based learning (Montgomery, 1983), in the early 1980s, the government assumed control of the school curriculum and then teacher education and training. They brought the experience of adult university education to the education of children once again and did not appreciate the difference. Primary education was considered to be 'child minding', and a secondary-school style of curriculum based upon university curricular was handed down. It had ten subjects and specified levels at which age groups would be 'instructed', Key Stages 1 to 4. The teaching of reading was absorbed into the English teacher's curriculum, and so the difficulties began. In the colleges, methods teachers were dispensed with, as were primary experts and reading teaching specialists, and replaced by subject specialists. Reading was not considered to be a 'subject' (William Taylor, Chair of the CATE Committee, WEF Conference, 1986). The pedagogy was moved back again to favour the transmission model.

To support the move in the subject content direction, the triennial PISA test results are used as evidence that the methods of South East Asian schools are more effective than ours and we should continue to move in their direction. Their doctrinaire techniques and indoctrinating instructional methods with study time extended up to 18 hours a day by pressurising parents was ignored as well as the side effects of the system reported in Chapter 3 (Heng and Tam, 2006). What is evident today is that many of these countries are trying to improve teaching and learning from this 'concrete operational' style to a more open, problem-based and critical thinking model that the UK has tried to readopt. This history of pedagogy was likened to Piaget's (1952) model of intellectual development in children (Montgomery, 1981). It has moved from rote preoperational methods to concrete operation to 'abstract operational mode'. The reason is that it has been shown to be more effective in enabling learners to construct meaning and raise their achievement. These features will be examined in more detail in this chapter and Chapter 6.

Early Years basic skills teaching is the crucial foundation to combatting disadvantage, learning disabilities and underachievement set out in the previous chapters and exemplified by many of the cases in Chapter 4. The basic skills consist of reading, spelling, handwriting and number.

In 2010, Ofsted reported that there were approximately 450.000 pupils in English schools who had been identified as having SEN, when in fact, they had been misdiagnosed. They tended to be children with milder difficulties; they did not have learning difficulties but had emotional, social or behavioural difficulties that could be alleviated by better teaching and learning methods or improved health or social care.

With these factors in mind, the methods to be detailed should mean that most of the 40 per cent of pupils who do not achieve five GCSEs with grades of A* to C (nine to four) or an English baccalaureate will be enabled to do so. In addition, social, emotional and behavioural difficulties will be reduced and self-esteem will be raised.

General changes needed in early years teaching

In the UK, children enter the reception (foundation) year as rising fives, a year younger than in most other countries. Formal education is expected to begin then, although early years experts continually challenge this assumption made by government agencies. The current subject content or product-based education in the early years has replaced the learning as in the home that existed for most of the 20th century. The methods were based upon the best features of Froebel, Montessori, Pestalozzi, the MacMillan sisters and others. Modern theorists draw on this and promote the methods worldwide as in Bruner's (1968) spiral curriculum and in the Helix curriculum by Noguera and Rawlings (2019).

The essential proposal is that there is a need to return to more time for learning through play, experiential learning and more time for fantasy play in the early years of schooling. This means reinstituting features such as sand and water play and experiential learning. For example, when children are engaged in a cooking activity (experiential learning) following a sequence and set of instructions, not only are they developing motor skills and cooking techniques, but it is also an opportunity for language development in naming tools, ingredients and processes and in speaking and listening to other children and the teacher. It is also a social developmental experience. When they share and exchange and when asked questions such as 'What will happen if we . . . ?' they are engaged in thinking and problem solving. At the end, they talk about what they have done and what they have learned, and this involves reflection and metacognition. Four- and five-year-olds are perfectly capable of all of these in appropriate contexts. Nursery rhymes and singing games, music and movement, story-telling and role-play and so on. all have important parts to play in the education of young children. When they are engaged in fantasy play in the home corner, language and social development can be facilitated. Nature walks, outdoors play, colour, shape and number tables and found objects are all features of such classrooms.

The children's interests and experiences, such as the effects of last Sunday's gale or snow, can lead to the pursuit of science and art topics on air and water and so on. This curriculum is an integrated one with particular strands on the fore-, mid- or background of the helix. The methods need to take account of children's intellectual levels of development, such as their early pre-operational and concrete levels of thinking (Piaget, 1952) and how this may be developed through learning experiences and meaning making. These methods will help to close the vocabulary gap that is increasingly becoming of concern as more time in preschool is spent interacting with electronic devices (Gross, 2019).

This type of 'cognitive curriculum' was tested experimentally in Weikart's (1967) Perry Pre-school Project with disadvantaged groups (Blank and Solomon, 1969). Later, it was termed 'the Westinghouse Project' based on funding. With colleagues, Weikart compared the cognitive approach, the traditional 'on the mat' transmission model and the direct instructional system for teaching arithmetic and reading (DISTAR), a highly structured format. The early results at seven years showed that DISTAR was the most effective in improving the children's basic skills, but the long-term effects were more interesting. After 15 and more years, the groups that had received the 'cognitive curriculum' by contrast had mainly stayed out of prison and were in work. Many of them were back in education with the prospect of improving their careers. The conclusions were that the cognitive curriculum was in the long term the most effective, and it had created lifelong learners and kept many out of prison and poverty. There were also indications that the strict DISTAR format had induced emotional problems (Blackwell, 1991).

The reasons for the need for change from a formal curriculum style is that young children are in the phase of developing their concepts and skills. This needs a rich variety of direct interactions and experiences. It is the teacher's role to provide this enriching experience and to mediate the learning and develop interactions through talk. As concepts are developed, higher-order concept attainment, constructs and schema can be promoted, and this prepares children for more formal learning.

Implicit learning

The power of implicit learning tends to be ignored in our education systems. However, it is not only powerful in our lives, but it is highly sustainable. Children who are born into a word-filled environment, over their first six to 18 months, learn to speak the language of their home. Implicitly, they learn the names of important things – 'Mumma', Dadda', 'doggy' – in their environment and key command words, like 'want' and 'go'. They move on to grammatically correct two-word utterances and then develop sentences. Some bright children may even speak in sentences at six to eight months and learn to read self-taught at three and four years old.

Simultaneous bilinguals from birth, if spoken to in one language by one parent and in another language by the other parent, grow up speaking both languages fluently. Sequential bilinguals have a secure single home language (L1), but when they go to school are totally immersed in a second language (L2) and all the subjects are presented in L2. Some simultaneous bilinguals become multilingual by immersion in a third language at school. All this is acquired implicitly by ordinary learners, not necessarily those who have a particular talent for languages and may become polyglots.

Van de Craen (2016) found that implicit learning is not confined to languages and reading but that there is a wide range of skills and knowledge that can be acquired by this method. He went on to demonstrate through photographs of brain scans that the connectivity in the brains of bilinguals was greater than in monolinguals and discussed research that showed they were thus enabled to solve issues and problems faster, with greater ease and efficiency and less cognitive effort. Many poor and disadvantaged children live between two languages, the local street language and the language of the school. These implicit learning findings can also apply to them and accounts in some part for their ability to become very high and talented achievers if just given the opportunity.

In the context of literacy teaching, implicit learning has an important place. It means that the school as well as the home must provide a reading-rich environment. Thus teachers tell stories to the children, and they read to them as well as covering the walls with reading material and pictures. However, it is often overlooked that beginners may not have the vocabulary and concepts contained in the storybooks. Children may never have travelled on a train but have flown abroad. They may never have spent a day at the seaside. The most disadvantaged children were shown in the Sutton Trust research (2018) to come from these impoverished environments.

Good schools identify key experiences and fulfill the need. One primary school studied (Montgomery, 2009) took all 400 inner-city pupils for a day at the seaside. For all the children (and the accompanying parents), it was a hugely memorable outing, and the literacy work that emerged from it was extensive and excellent. The school was the family for all of them.

The implications of all this is that classroom learning can be too sedentary and confined to the resources inside four walls. Experiential learning outside the room with its capacity for wider, deeper and more sustainable implicit learning is a very important contribution to the literacy of all children, but it is life enhancing for disadvantaged pupils.

Closing the literacy gap: writing

Why writing is as important as reading

The reading and writing curricula need to be integrated with daily experiences and with the rhyming and singing games that are played and stories and news that are shared. There are also changes that need to be made to specific literacy teaching and learning methods. These are crucial to help disadvantaged children so that they do not underachieve throughout the rest of the school years as the Sutton Trust found. These methods should reduce the 11-month learning gaps that were found and preferably close them altogether. Steps in this direction are shown in the research that follows.

Custom and practice dictate that if children are not reading and writing by the age of 7 years, then additional support may be needed (Bullock Report, DES, 1975). It is also held that reading is the key skill to concentrate upon and spelling teaching follows on later (Whitehead, 2004). Despite these assumptions, the Sutton Trust (Jerrim, 2013) found that disadvantaged children were 11.1 months behind advantaged peers by the end of the reception year so something must be going wrong.

Dyslexia experts now suggest that dyslexia support needs to be introduced earlier if children are not beginning to read and write at six years (Snowling, 2019). This also needs to be challenged. Something needs to be done in reception to overcome these problems, and obviously the current methods do not do this and must be changed for the children's sakes. Disadvantaged learners and all learners need to have their literacy gaps closed by the end of the reception year.

In a writing research project, it was found that disadvantaged groups were five months behind advantaged groups after five months in school (Montgomery, 2017b). After reports on individual spelling and handwriting were sent to the teachers for the writing samples in October and then March, the school SATs for the disadvantaged schools rose for writing by 30 per cent over the previous three years and for the advantaged school by 10 per cent (their scores were already high). The reports showed how more attention should be given to the writing task and to clear speaking and the articulatory feel of key phonemes (sounds of letters) when writing the letters (graphemes). This was termed multisensory articulatory phonogram training (MAPT), whereas teachers normally use multisensory training to link the phoneme and grapheme (MPT) without connecting to the feel in the mouth of the letter sounds.

Developmental norms indicate that between three to five years, a teacher should be able to expect a child to

* Have established hand dominance
* Circle anti-clockwise and clockwise
* Make vertical strokes
* Form letters correctly
* Copy some letters
* Use one-handed tools

In disadvantaged groups, these skills may not be present on entry to school and so need to be diagnosed and developed by skills and strengthening exercises and games.

The best early predictors of dyslexia were found to be

a) Failure to develop sound-symbol correspondence by the methods used in ordinary classrooms
b) inability to name or say the sounds of the alphabet

> (Chomsky, 1971; Liberman, 1973; Bryant and Bradley, 1985; Snowling, 2004)

The best early predictors of later academic achievement in good composition were a) speed of writing the alphabet and b) sounding and/or naming the letters of the alphabet (Berninger 2004, 2008).

The tasks cited in this research suggested that handwriting and spelling skills on entry to reception and beyond should also be the targets for intervention. The advantage is that they are concrete and available for inspection and comparison in a quick and easily collectible manner. This is in contrast to what teachers actually do. Instead, they focus greatly upon reading, especially using visual memory methods despite recent DfE initiatives such as 'Phonics First' (Rose, 2006; DfE, 2014a). The Sutton Trust research showed that this too has failed and something more needs to be done.

Clay (1975) and Chomsky (1971) found that children's first impulse was to write not read, but schools do not seem to take advantage of this. What we know is that some gifted children learn to read and write by themselves in the early years before they go to school. They appear to do this if they are read to and are in an environment of words and books. This was termed 'self-teaching' by van Daal (2018). Disadvantaged children, who may not have experience of books, may quickly learn to read once they are in school and start to write news and messages without help. They did this even in the Look and Say system, which is fundamentally a method using paired associate memory training.

Skill diagnosis: miscues analyses applied to early writing

In Figure 5.1, the reception children were asked to write their news or a story after one month in the class without any help. From this, it was possible to learn exactly which reading and writing skills they knew and at what level.

> The errors children make when they write are neither random nor thoughtless – examined diagnostically they reveal systematic application of the child's level of understanding.
>
> (Rosencrans, 1998, 10)

Once they know some sounds and names, they can begin to use them to decode words for reading. It means that reading and writing can be taught simultaneously. Pupils need some synthetic phonics for spelling, showing how to build words from the outset and some Look and Say for reading or whatever method the teachers use that is structured and systematic. The sounds learnt can immediately be used as initial clues in decoding words in text.

In learning to spell, the features used are letter sounds and names and their graphic forms. However, the child needs to learn only about five or six sounds and their graphemes for them to be able to establish the spelling principle for word building (Solity, 2018). At the same time, as they are reading or being read to, a process called 'orthographic mapping' takes place (Ehri, 2018). These two attributes reflect the dual route to reading hypothesis (Coltheart, 1984), the visual and auditory routes. They need to be in balance for teaching success rather than education focusing on one or the other in the acquisition stage.

The research proposition was that if we can identify the onset of the use of 'phones' in early freeform writing, this would predict those children would not become dyslexic. Others who learn from a mentor within their zone of proximal development (Vygotsky, 1978) during the first term or semester will not become disadvantaged or dyslexic.

The term 'phone' was used to describe a situation in which one or two initial letters might be used to represent a word, for example, 'w' or 'wt' for 'went' 'bd' for 'bed'. It is typical that initial letters and then a consonantal skeleton appear. It was proposed that identifying poor writing skills and then using targeted MAPT interventions in reception could reduce the underachievement of those disadvantaged pupils throughout the school years by 'closing the gap'.

The reception/foundation year classes were given a month to settle in to the routines, and then the whole class was asked by their teacher to copy a sentence of their 'news'. Copy writing is a common daily activity in the reception year in many English schools. The scripts (N = 177) were collected and analysed. In the same week, the teacher asked the children to write a freeform story of news or any subject of interest. No help was given, and the materials were those typically used by the teacher. The 'message' the child was trying to write was written below it.

This research involved the development of a) a handwriting test (Appendix 5.1) and b) a spelling test (Appendix 5.2) so that by the end of the reception or the first years in school, teachers could collect a profile of achievement and underachievement. They would also have knowledge that would enable them to develop the skill levels.

In Figure 5.1, we can read,

a)   I do my homework after school. (scores 9)
b)   I had a little Kitty birthday cake. (scores 4)
c)   Red hen had some bread. (scores 5)
d)   I went to the cinema. (scores 1)

a) Sahana

Ido mY hom
wuck aft Sool

b) Abi I had a Hello Kitty birthday cake

t d albk

c) Harry Red hen had some bread

rhe hed
hdsmdh

d) Devon I went to the cinema

Figure 5.1 shows levels of spelling and motor skill combined (one-fifth size)

In the analysis of the spelling, a critical borderline at a rank of five was established. This point was where the child gave signs of using a form of skeletal phonics, showing the 'alphabetic code' had been broken. This was defined as the use of 'phones'. These were the single letters or collections of letters, usually consonants, representing words, for example, 'w' or 'wt' representing 'went'. Some scripts at rank 5 might also include some vowels by the orthographic mapping procedure – 'litl' (little) and druk (truck). In addition, commonly copied words might also be included, such as 'the' and "I' and 'and'. These were ignored in the scoring system.

Table 5.1 October 2012, mean ranks for entry skills

	Males	Females	
Motor skills	4.21	5.67	(top score = 10 − 5 + 5)
Spelling skills	3.51	4.41	(top score = 10)

Girls were shown to have higher scores on entry for both spelling and handwriting skills.

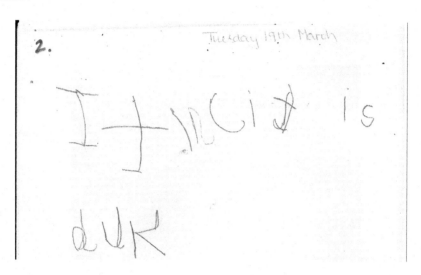

Figure 5.2a Freeform writing after 6 months in reception

I finc it is duk. ('I think it is dark 'in space'.) (scores 7)
(I go to nanny's) (scores 4)

Figure 5.2b Freeform writing on entry to reception

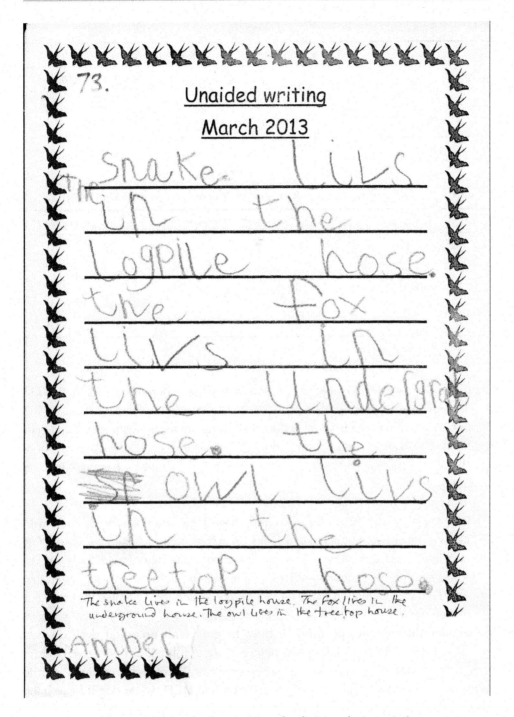

73.

Unaided writing

March 2013

the Snake Liks
in the
Logpile hose.
the fox
Liks in
the underground
hose. the
SF owl Liks
in the
treetop hose.

The snake lives in the logpile house. The fox lives in the underground house. The owl lives in the tree top house.

Amber

Figure 5.2c Above freeform writing after five months in reception

Table 5.2 Socioeconomic status (SES) and differences in skill status, October 2012

SES	N	Copy writing means	Free writing means	
A + B	58	3.52	2.65	Low SES
C	55	4.18	7.08	Middle SES
D	64	5.86	3.80	Private
	177	4.52	4.48	

Key: A+B are two schools in disadvantaged areas; C school is in an advantaged area; D is a private school

Table 5.3 Progress and numbers at risk for spelling after five months in Reception N-112

	Progress	N	Dyslexia/UAch	Dysgraphia/HW
A1	4.79	19	1 + 1	6
A2	1.86	19	11.0	7
B1	2.89	20	4 + 1	5
C1	0.65	29	0 + 5	9
C2	0.73	26	4 + 6	8
	2.18	113	33	35

The snake livs in the logpile hose. the fox livs in the undergd hose. The owl livs in the treetop hose. (scores 9)

The copy writing means show typical increasing advantage with increasing economic status. The free writing means show some special event taking place in school C. This was a special writing experience which was 'Taking our grandparents to school day'.

The private school D left the project.

Teachers of classes A2 and C2 seem to have larger numbers of children with poorer skills after five months than the other teachers, twice as many as B1 and C1. The teacher of A1 started from the same low base as the other low SES classes but achieved much more progress for the class. Inspection of the scripts suggested that she had paid more attention to the first set of reports and implemented the strategies more than the rest.

Gender differences The ratio of boys to girls with potential dyslexia was 3:2. The ratio of boys to girls with potential dysgraphia/DCD was 4.5:1. From UAch, 29.5 per cent were at risk, and some may have been dyslexic. While 31.3 per cent showed immaturity in HW and had DCD, some might have been dysgraphic.

Gifted writers at 4/5 – high learning potential (HLP) 12 children (9F and 3M) – 11 per cent scored 8–10 on entry to reception. These might be potentially gifted self-taught (HLP) or with home or preschool advantage. None of them appeared to have advanced their skills during the research period of five months.

After five months in reception, 37 out of 112 had spelling scores between 8–10, 33 per cent now showing potential HLP. The ratio of girls to boys in this category was 2:1 (24 F and 13 M). The inverse was that 67 per cent, or two-thirds of children, were already five months behind peers in writing skills. From the Sutton Trust reading research, we know that they will not catch up unless the teachers pay some attention to the second report and suggested interventions.

Follow-up studies 2014

On entry to year 2, the schools were asked to collect another sample of freeform writing from the project group in a ten-minute writing period test. This time, 94 pre- and post-matches were traceable. The results showed that every child had written a readable story. One boy showed dyslexic level spelling problems but wrote a long MS.

In 2015, the school SATs for Key Stage 1 became available, and the schools in the disadvantaged areas had improved the writing SATs by 30 per cent and the advantaged school by 10 per cent – there was less room for them to improve on their previous results. The data suggest that the targeted interventions were appropriate and could be used to help disadvantaged learners in particular as well as potential mild dyslexics, all of whom might have some HLP. The spelling assessment proved an important tool for identifying those at risk.

Children's marks on paper are not usually thought to be important or indicative of any kind of potential, and teachers are not taught how to use the knowledge the marks display to intervene and develop the skills observable.

This research indicated that disadvantaged children and those with learning disabilities can be taught to overcome their disadvantages by some focused teaching on the basic skills of spelling and handwriting using MAPT. Five high frequency letters, i t p n s, can make 25 words, and teachers can show children how words are built by using them in examples as in the 100 mini-lessons in *The Developmental Spelling Handbook* (Montgomery, 1997b). The handwriting interventions included use of lines, correcting paper position, posture and penhold with aids as necessary and finger-strengthening exercises Montgomery, 2017a).

Some comments on the EYFS (DfE, 2014a) programme

The EYFS is divided into five phases (p. 50).

'**Phase One:** Identify sounds in the order in which they occur in words'.

(We know from the research of Liberman et al. (1967) that this is not possible unless we can already spell them. A syllable cannot be split 'by ear' because the separate phonemes are shingled on top of each other in speech. Illiterate adults can clap syllable beats but not phonemes in a syllable. Dyslexics and controls were also unable to do this task correctly unless they could already spell the words (Montgomery, 1997a). The initial sound can be deciphered hence the effectiveness of the onset and rime strategy.)

Phase Two: 'Teach one set of letters per week in the order that make the most possible CV, VC and CVC words'. Some children can do this but not those from disadvantaging environments. If the set is not seen in the pupil's writing, then it has not been learnt although the teacher may have done her best to try to teach it.

(It took Omar 12 tutorials to learn to write small sized and read the letter 'i'.)

- Set 1: s, a, t, p
- Set 2: i, n, m, d
- Set 3: g, o, c, k
- Set 4: ck, e, u, r
- Set 5: h, j, f, ff, l, ss
- 'Say a letter sound (with the mnemonic and action if necessary) ask the children to write it saying the letter formation pattern as they do so.'

(This order of letters bears no relation to the difficulty children might have in constructing them such as 's', 'f' and 'a' or the confusions between similar shaped letters 'n' and 'm' occurring together and where in the mouth they can be felt for ease of identification, for example 'l'.

From the outset, the letters need to be used to make words. With i-t-p-n-s, beginners can make 25 words (see Appendix 5.1).

At least the vowels are more or less separated out. However, there are no initial or final blends taught, and they should be. Teachers complain that the four per week is too fast for most of the children, and they are right. They should not move on to the next set until the first one has been secured.)

Closing the literacy gap: reading acquisition

Reading is a recognition skill

This means that all the letters making up the words are already present on the page. The reading task is to decode the written symbols to find out what meaning the word or sentence makes. This means the reader already needs to know the names of objects and events, and by four and five years, most children are expected to have a well-developed grasp and use of the English language, its meanings (semantics) and its structures and tenses (syntax). Disadvantaged children seldom have a full range of these abilities. Language development in speaking and listening activities is thus of great importance in the early years and throughout education.

In reading, alphabet letters, like words, have individual patterns and features. We do not store images of the actual letters or words when we learn, but we apparently do store features in the brain and rules for recognition (Farnham-Diggory, 1978). Thus, the reading task is to identify the features that call up the word's meaning on a consistent basis. How the eye and brain do this features analysis is not fully under- stood, but most children in an environment of print can learn to read by 'paired associate' learning in a purely Look and Say regime. Thus, in this system, we do not actually teach children to read; we provide the right structured environment.

There are however two routes to reading (Morton, 1980), the visual and the audi- tory, but both are intangible and involve the use of abstract perceptual units (Ehri, 1980), the features rules and the sounds. It is sensible for teachers to make use of both systems' inputs rather than stress one, such as Look and Say or phonics. The previous section on writing shows how important this symbiosis is and that both need to begin from the outset.

Within the reading side of teaching, there are a number of additional strategies that can help children, especially underachievers, learn more easily.

Taped reading and audio stories

Following text in a book whilst listening to it on audio can be supportive. This is especially so when the pupils read into the recorder and then follow the text as they listen to their recordings. This is the ARROW (aural – read – respond – oral – write) technique found effective by Lane (1990).

Bedtime stories at home need to be promoted along with shared audio CDs where parents also may have difficulties – a school library of CDs that children can choose to take home or feeds they can download via their smartphones.

Onset and rime

Children reported they found it easier to blend single-syllabled words when the word was split in one way rather than another, for example, they found 'c – at' an easier way to blend than 'ca – t' or the traditional 'c-a-t'. Bryant and Bradley's (1985) research confirmed the effectiveness of the technique and named it.

Despite this, the DfES (2006) guidelines referred to a 'running blend through words' such as s – a – n – d and s – t – r – ee – t. This is not what dyslexics and other poor readers find easiest for reading. Decoding S – and/or STR – eet (S-TR – eet) are best for them.

Phonological Awareness Training (PAT) (Wilson, 1994)

This was used with dyslexics and improved their reading and writing skills. It involves teaching common rimes and getting children of seven plus years to generate some more examples so they begin to recognise the common pattern, for example, -and, -ing, -ent.

TRUGS – Teaching Reading Using Games (Jeffery, 2016)

Many programmes use games to reinforce learning, particularly of phonics knowledge, and this resource is a structured set of card games to enhance other phonics programmes designed by Joanne Jeffery, Principal of Dyslexia Access in Devon and Cornwall. It is constructed in 15 stages from basic words in Box 1 through to higher education levels, Box 3. There are four different types of card games to play, graded according to difficulty. Each is numbered and colour coded. It is focused upon improving reading skills and has become popular with SENCos.

Synthetic phonics and the Clackmannanshire study (2005)

The Clackmannanshire study (Watson and Johnson, 2005) compared spelling and reading progress at the end of Primary 2. Three hundred children were given 16 weeks training for 20 minutes each day in one of three programmes:

1 Synthetic phonics to blend letters for spelling words
2 Analytic phonics to decode words for reading
3 Analytic phonics and phonological awareness training

The results were that at the end of the programme, the synthetic phonics group were about seven months ahead of the other two groups and seven months ahead of their chronological age in reading. They were eight to nine months ahead of the others in spelling. Contrary to expectation, the synthetic phonics group was also able to read irregular words better than the other groups and was the only group that could read unfamiliar words by analogy. Thus, during the synthetic phonics teaching, they were learning and developing transferrable skills that the other methods were not providing for their groups.

Other useful supportive strategies in general use

- Pause – prompt – praise
- Paired reading and shared reading
- Language experience methods – the pupil writes/composes his or her own books with illustrations to read to friends, parents and the teacher
- Older pupils write illustrated storybooks to read to children in the early years
- Listening dogs – children read to real dogs trained to listen

Pattern recognition training for reading acquisition (Montgomery, 1977, 1979)

Four teachers in their reception classes in a disadvantaged area were observed teaching reading over a period of two years and raised the question about how children actually learn to read in a Look and Say environment.

Children were shown key words in the Rainbow Reading scheme, 'read' the picture books and moved on to the controlled vocabulary storybooks. They took home word tins with their words in them to practice at home. After they had acquired a sight vocabulary of 50 words by a process of paired associate learning using the 'flash cards', they were introduced to some phonics work by learning the sounds of the letters. Each day, they told the teachers their news and traced or copy wrote it until they were allowed to write it themselves.

Some of the children began to read very quickly, and others did not, but the question was how did anyone learn by this method of pairing written words and their sounds – association learning or 'paired associate learning'? Good readers would need to have good visual memories, but how did the brain perform this feat without any guidance? How might the poor and the non-readers be helped?

In brief, the answers were found in perception research and tank recognition studies. Perceptual studies showed that the eye and brain perform a features analysis on any input. The tank recognition studies showed that naïve subjects after doing jig-saws of a range of tanks were able to identify them very easily and much better than subjects shown pictures and told the main features of the separate tanks.

This posed a series of problems about reading. What were the relevant features in children's visual learning of words, and could they be taught by the jigsaw method to identify and learn them? What were the features that made up words and their letters?

Some of the early learners appeared to scan the words correctly from left to right, but others did so from right to left. If they fixated on the last letter when the teacher said the word, it would make it difficult to learn to read it. If they fixated as some did on a particular letter, such as the 'k' within a word, this would not help either, especially if they were expected to play the game 'I spy something beginning with . . .' What was the 'beginning' of a word for them? Did they know the meaning of 'beginning'?

The analysis showed that the lower-case print letters of the alphabet were made up of four main features: a circle, a stick (long or short) and a curved stick. In fact, the letters a, b, d, g, i, j, k, l, o, p, q, t, v, w, x, y, z could be made with circles or 'long and short sticks'. The children were given 'dot and stick' patterns to copy with counters and sticks. This ensured they could be taught to start on the left and work across to the right. They were also given jigsaws of words to make, and then they would say the word they had formed. This involved a close observation by the children of the features of the word they were to make. It helped them learn the words in their tins more easily.

In a controlled study, using 'dots and sticks' training patterns and non-word jig-saws, those in the experimental training groups had moved ahead several grades faster on the reading scheme than controls given paired associate training. Those who had hitherto not begun reading had also moved forward onto the scheme.

| WEEK 1 On red (pink) | | | | |
A1	A2	A3	A4	A5
G G G G ROROR YYGGYY RRRGGG OO GG OO	OO O OO YOYOY RRYYRR OOORRR YY RR YY	R RR R GYGYG OOYYOO RRRGGG GG RR GG	Y YY Y RORROR GGYYGG OOOYYY BB OO BB	GG B GG YOYYOY RROORR BBBYYY YY OO YY

| WEEK 2 On orange | | | | |
A1	A2	A3	A4	A5
B BB BB OR OR OR GGG RRR BGBGBG RRRRR	Y YY YY YY OO YY RRR OOO RYRYRY GGGGG	G GG GG GO GO GO GGG RRR GBGBGB RRRRR	R RR RR BR BR BR OOO BBB RORORO YYYYY	O OO OO GB GB GB YYY RRR GYGYGY RRRRR

Figure 5.3a Coloured dots sequences

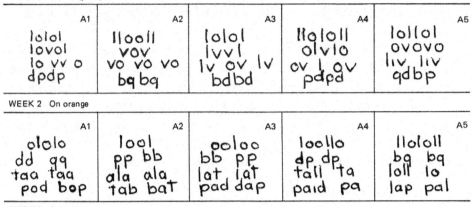

	A1	A2	A3	A4	A5
	lolol lovol lo vv o dpdp	llooll vov vo vo vo bq bq	lolol lvvl lv ov lv bdbd	llqloll olvlo ov l qv pdpd	lollol ovovo liv liv qdbp

WEEK 2   On orange

	A1	A2	A3	A4	A5
	ololo dd qq taa taa pod bop	lool pp bb ala ala tab bat	ooloo bb pp lat lat pad dap	loollo dp dp tall ta paid pa	llololl bq bq loll lo lap pal

WEEK 3   On yellow

Figure 5.3b Dots and sticks sequences

Week 3
CI

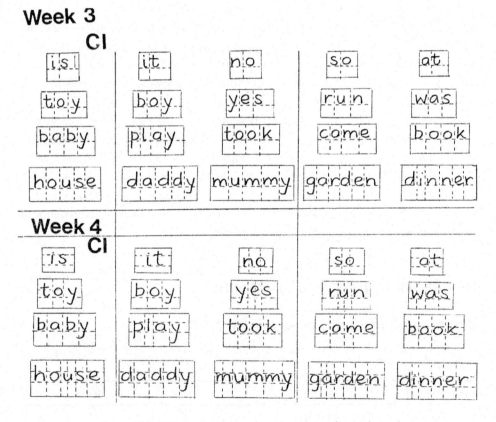

is	it	no	so	at
toy	boy	yes	run	was
baby	play	took	come	book
house	daddy	mummy	garden	dinner

Week 4
CI

is	it	no	so	at
toy	boy	yes	run	was
baby	play	took	come	book
house	daddy	mummy	garden	dinner

Figure 5.3c Jigsaw examples of some commonly used words

Figure 5.3 To show some of the 'dots and sticks' pattern recognition training materials

Source: (Montgomery, 1979, extracts from pages 22–24)

When pre-schoolers were also introduced to the 'dots and sticks' training and word jigsaws, they were able to enjoy them as informal approaches to literacy work. The manipulation of the 'dots and sticks' and jigsaw pieces enabled the teacher to see which features the child was focusing on and which ones needed to be modified. The handling of the pieces showed the readiness in fine motor skills and the speed of the process. All of these aspects are important in preschool and reception learning but also to potential dyslexics and other poor readers and writers. After the test development phase, pattern recognition classroom training materials were designed and tested. In case studies, 30 diagnostic points were identified showing problems that early readers might have and how they might be overcome.

A hearing reading inventory (HRI) – reading development

One of the common methods for helping young readers improve their skills is to hear them read on a daily basis. This becomes difficult when a lone teacher has a class of 30. Mrs D.'s method was to hear them in matched groups of three at her desk! She claimed that because she knew the texts so well she could hear when any individual made a mistake and would be able to go back and help overcome the error at a pause point. Her readers were the best of four other classes, but she was also the most organised and systematic teacher of reading.

The categories in the HRI presented here are, with their examples, mainly self-explanatory except for some of the more technical aspects, which are illustrated. The HRI can be used with any book that the pupil elects to read or which the teacher selects. There are three main categories in which the intervention can take place. These are word attack skills, comprehension skills and audience effect. The other categories can be used for intervention or to monitor the effects of intervention in the other areas.

An informal hearing reading inventory

Monthly progress record – using an HRI

Table 5.4

First name or code		At test	Post-test
Class:	Chronological Age:		
Date of Birth:	Reading Age:		
Reading Scheme:	Reading Test:		
Spelling Age:	Spelling Test:		

Dates	Examples (use ticks if possible)	Month
Text	Reading scheme book and page number. Criticism if any.	
Word Attack Skills	Guesses from initial sound	
	Tries blend	
	Self corrects, syllabifies Uses onset and rime	
	Uses analogy	
	Note two errors for later work	
Comprehension Skills	Can answer factual recall questions	
	Can predict using picture,	
	syntax or general meaning	
	Answers inferential question	
	Pauses at full stops	
Audience Effects	All one tone	
	Word-by-word reading	
	Drops voice at full stop	
	Reads in units of meaning	
	Speed	
	Takes account of speech marks	
	Fluent	
	Reads with good audience effect	
Behavioural Signs	Reading position close to page or distant.	
	Body posture	
	Finger or bookmark used above or below?	
	Hand not used	
	Smooth eye scan	
Emotional Signs	Tenseness cues: jiggling, breathlessness, nervous smiling, avoidance of task when possible, lack of fluency, monotone	
Other Comments	Select one thing to help the next week's reading, e.g., using initial sound to help guess word. Teach appropriate sounds.	

Example of the HRI in use

TEXT: The train is going under the bridge.
   CHILD READS:

   'The train is goin' under the . . .'

PAUSES LOOKS AT PICTURE ON LEFT HAND PAGE, FAILS TO DECIPHER IT, READS –

   'tunnel.'

BEGINS TO JIG, IS READING WORD BY WORD IN HIGH-PITCHED MONOTONE, FIXED NERVOUS SMILE, SHOWING BOTH UPPER AND LOWER TEETH.

During three pages of reading in this manner, she makes no use of initial sounds to help guess words in context. The substitution of tunnel for bridge is but one example of this. Even when it is suggested to the child that she tries the first sound she does not do so.

Reading development interventions

* Present **randomised letters** of the alphabet a few at a time to discover which sounds, if any, the child does know and then persuade her or him to use this information in the next reading session.
* Concentrate very much on confidence building and praising each small effort the child makes.
* Ask her or him to reread the text paragraph by paragraph, and find out if the fluency improves. Several re-readings may help here.
* Some readers may benefit by having their reading slowed down because they are reading too fast for their level of skill and so make errors and fail to comprehend what they read.
* Some will need you to select an easier text to match their reading ability if slowing down and rereading does not help.
* The finger-pointing is actually directing the word-by-word reading, and so after the word attack skills have been worked on, give a bookmark to place **above** the words and explain it is because she is making such good progress. The bookmark should be **above the words** so that the eyes can move on ahead and down to the next line so that meaning can be preserved and observed.
* Once s/he is comfortable with the bookmark and is using word attack skills as they are taught, attention can be turned to further aspects of the reading.

As confidence and skill build, the jigging and tense smiling will stop, and the focus can be on audience effects. Pausing and dropping the voice at the end of a sentence can begin the work on this.

Miscues analysis

Reading is a RECOGNITION skill and is best practiced in context by guessing new words from initial sounds and then attempting the rime or ending altogether. This strategy is supported by the sentence and prose context, for example,

She played in the school b-and
Let us go by tr-ain

- Multi-syllabled words can be tackled step by step, putting sayable clusters of letters or meaning units together as syllables.
  - **cat – er – pill – ar**
- Syllables are the BEATS in a word and can be identified when saying a whole word and act as a support for spelling, for example, cat-er-pillar!
- Splitting onset from rime is a way of cutting up a syllable c-at-er – p-ill ar.

From 1964, Kenneth Goodman began tape-recording poor readers in order to analyse the mismatch between what the text said and what they read aloud. The mismatches were termed 'miscues' (as opposed to 'errors'). 'Miscue analysis' then, far from being something mysterious, is simply an observation of the patterns and strategies used by the poor reader to process the text.

The view of reading implicit in using miscue analysis is that the process is not merely one of decoding but is in fact psycholinguistic. In other words, as *talking* is producing oral language, and *listening* is receiving spoken language, *writing* is the productive counterpart of talking and *reading* is the counterpart of listening. We speak and write in order to communicate; we listen and read in order to accept and understand others communicating with us. Reading, therefore, uses language to get at meaning. We always reconstruct the speaker's or writer's word in accord with our own experience. Much of what we see when we read is what we expect to see, or 'predict'. If our predictions prove to be wrong, we backtrack and revise. Reading becomes a kind of guessing game, based on our own understanding of context.

It is kwite possibel to raed thiss txet wtih a greta man y mistaeks becos we no hwat we expetc to rade; teh sense is ont afectid

Until we disturb the construction of the language –

moving by sentences words or about so not they correct are grammatically.

From this example, it becomes obvious that what counts is interpretation, or reading for meaning. It is thus an important element in reading and not to be ignored in teaching reading strategies.

Miscue analysis can show whether the poor reader is relying on decoding strategies of a phonic (sound) or graphic (visual) nature, ignoring contextual clues, in the struggle to get at meaning. It can also reveal the strategies used by the child who 'barks at the text' (i. e. appears to be fluent but makes no progress beyond the instructional level of reading towards clear interpretation and understanding).

It is quite easy to apply a simplified form of miscue analysis in the classroom, and, although it takes time, the patterns that emerge often reveal the overall emphasis of the methods used by a school to teach reading!

- Miscue analysis shows up strengths as well as weaknesses.
- Miscue analysis can be used with poor readers at any stage or age, using carefully chosen texts. Choose an interesting story that you think will prove a little difficult for the reader so that errors are generated.

147

- Make a copy of the text to record the errors and if possible tape-record the session so that you can check the errors.
- If you use the Neale Assessment of Reading Ability (NARA), then the texts are graded and the record sheets provide the space to record the errors, but some practice will be needed to do the recording quickly enough as the child reads, and so taping is a good idea.
- NARA also tests comprehension as well as accuracy and speed and gives norms for these.

The example of recording miscues in Table 5.5 is the same as will be found in NARA and derive from earlier research studies by Spache (1940). Time for an update?

- The more self-corrections made, the better the reader's level of skill.
- Whole-word substitutions and additions (e.g., mum for mother, come for came) indicate good prediction and the difference between the artificiality of the text and the speaker's language.
- Only intervene during the reading at instances of refusal or unacceptable substitutions.

The limitations of this scheme of analysing errors are obvious. The teacher needs to know **exactly what has been substituted, self-corrected** and so on in order to intervene correctly. The numbers of specific errors are not of major relevance. What is needed in order to intervene is the precise word attack skills that the pupil has or has not mastered. This enables them to be specifically used in the intervention plan to improve the range of skills.

Table 5.5 Typical analysis of miscues table

Type of error	Code	No. of Pos	No. of Negs
Substitutions	**Underline word substituted**		
Self-corrections	**Write in original error add C to denote correction**		
Refusals – no Response	**Put dotted line under word**		
Pauses	**Put stroke where reader pauses for 2–3 secs or longer**		
Omissions	**Circle word(s) left out**		
Additions – Insertions	**Write in the additional word**		
Repetitions	**Mark word(s) with curved or wavy line**		

Closing the number gap: miscues analysis in number

In a numeracy recovery pilot scheme, (Dowker, 2001) described her research project with 62 children identified by their teachers as having arithmetical difficulties. The children were tested on

1   Principles and procedures related to counting
2   Use of written arithmetical symbolism
3   Place value
4   Understanding and solution of word problems
5   Translation between concrete, verbal and numerical formats
6   Use of derived fact categories for calculation
7   Arithmetical estimation
8   Memory for number facts

After weekly individual tuition targeted to the specific area of weakness of each child, the pupils were found to have improved significantly as a group, and teachers reported the children were enjoying the help and the materials.

Dowker reported that these types of mathematical weakness were common in primary children, and it was important to correct them before the consequences became profound.

What we need to know from any subsequent studies is if some pupils were unable to respond and improve their numeracy skills (potential dyscalculics) or if the methods and materials were not sufficiently good enough to help all of them improve.

Systematic errors

Some errors in arithmetical calculations: miscues analysis of algorithms

When pupils make errors in calculations, it should be assumed that the error is normally neither careless nor random. It then becomes a useful diagnostic example to examine the underlying strategy the pupil is using leading to the error answer. The early work of Grossnickle (1935) distinguished between constant and chance errors, and Cox (1973–1974) extended this work to define three basic types of computational error:

1)   **Systematic errors** occur in at least three out of five problems and show a systematic error pattern.
2)   **Random errors** occur in at least three out of five problems but contain no discernible pattern, which makes them difficult to remediate.

3) **Careless errors** occur in one or two out of five problems. The pupil knows how to perform the operation but miscounts, is distracted or has an attention lapse and error occurs.

The error examples that follow are drawn from children's mathematics books. What is helpful is to try to unravel what was in the pupils' minds when they made these systematic errors.

Examples of some systematic errors

The errors are easier to see when the sums are in columns, for example,

(1)   (a)   (b)   (c)
         83   35   43
    +   49   +   67   +   72
       1212   912   115

Error explanation: _____

_____

(2)   (a)   (b)   (c)
         46   372   154
    –   39   –   295   –   86
         13   123   132

_____

_____

(3)   (a)   (b)   (c)
         22   43   29
    x   3   x   5   x   6
    –   66   255   424

_____

_____

(4)   (a)   (b)   (c)
         39   28   15
    +   7   +   18   +   3
         32   10   12

_____

_____

(5)

	(a)	(b)	(c)
	76	27	48
+	9	+ 7	+ 5
	715	214	413

(6)

	(a)	(b)	(c)
	84	74	48
−	9	− 3	− 5
	65	61	33

(7)

	(a)	(b)	(c)
	81	30	44
−	6	− 7	− 5
	85	37	41

(8)

	(a)	(b)	(c)
	35	72	64
−	19	− 45	− 17
	26	37	57

(9)

	(a)	(b)	(c)
	324	612	215
−	46	− 69	− 87
	328	603	278

(10)
(a) 506 x 3 = 1548
(b) 201 x 8 = 688
(c) 390 x 4 = 1564

_____

_____

Sum 'stories'

When a pupil appears to be making systematic errors or errors of any kind, ask him or her to 'tell you the story of the sum'. Pupils are often reluctant to explain their workings out because they feel vulnerable and exposed to ridicule for not knowing the 'correct' way or the teacher's way of working it out. Sum stories help them put the sum at a distance and tell its own story. Sometimes their idiosyncratic methods will prove successful, particularly on simpler levels of calculation with single or double figures. When working with three columns of figures, the load thus placed upon the memory can prove too much and the errors then occur. Telling the story of the sum can be a more relaxed method of getting over this problem.

When children use their fingers to support their counting and carrying, quite often, they can forget to add these in at the appropriate stage and may carry the tens on to the hundreds column by mistake.

e.g. 94 + 19 = 203

The crooked finger representing the carried 10 from 4 + 9 is not added into the 10s column 9 + 1 + 1 but is forgotten and added in with the other crooked figure representing 100 hence the 'answer' 203!

An example of teaching about how to overcome such difficulties as these is described by Mary Kibel in a chapter in *Dyslexia and Mathematics* (Miles and Miles, 1992).

Analysing past learning

Any serious commitment to helping children with their number difficulties must of necessity involve talking with them to establish when and where the breakdown in their performance occurred. There may have been a period of absence from school or some trauma that prevented the acquisition of the correct methods. Tracing these can often release the pupil from tension about this number work that could eventually permeate the whole of mathematical learning.

In the CPD masters SEN and SpLD programmes at Middlesex, teachers were asked to describe one teacher who had really helped them with their maths and one who certainly had not. The pen portraits were set to be 300 to 500 words long. It was not entirely surprising that some teachers (N = 100) were entirely unable to think of one who had helped them. The teachers were mainly women from the UK but some from around the world, and many of the stories were almost too upsetting to read (Montgomery, 2017a).

The main problem was that their maths sessions were the object of fear – fear of failure, fear of the teacher and the whole curriculum running too fast for them to catch up. It seemed that most of the difficulties arose in the early years basic skills teaching, when they were moved too quickly from work with concrete apparatus to abstract formal teaching of maths. Their failures were exacerbated at secondary school when it was assumed they had the necessary basic skills and arithmetical concepts and teachers would become irritated by their errors and push on regardless. Their best maths teachers, the 'stars', were not usually those who were gifted in mathematics. An in-service project with teachers who had no mathematical background found that they could become the best teachers of mathematics not least because they could understand the children's problems and thereby do something to help them (Askew et al., 1997).

The Mathematical Difficulties and Dyscalculia module (M6 Study Guide www. ldrp.org.uk) enabled them to gain perspective and some confidence in dealing with the basic skills aspects of maths and later learn to use some statistical analyses in their projects.

Conclusion

In the current era, many children's lives are much less free than they once were, and the opportunities for exploratory learning and implicit learning at home are much diminished. It is the teacher who can change and improve their lives by providing optimal learning environments. When subject content is introduced, it needs to be integrated so that sciences, arts, humanities and language are involved as project work, such as in the Helix curriculum outlined. This is a reworking of traditional early years teaching methods that were developed to meet the needs of children who were developing their concepts. It is argued that learning through play, experiential learning and implicit learning are not only essential for disadvantaged learners to provide a sound basis for later learning but also important for all young children. It is the nurturing environment that they need, one that allows them to explore and develop social and self-efficacy in a safe structure. It was shown how the literacy gap can be closed by an initial focus on learning to write. It also showed that disadvantaged learners were more likely to have less well developed handwriting coordination and need more subskills training and carefully guided practice. Teachers needed more training in this area to ensure that teaching assistants provide the correct form of support. Joining letters from the outset was found to be best for children with coordination difficulties and easy for the rest to learn. Widening the range of reading teaching strategies was advised, and miscues analysis was recommended and demonstrated for improving all three basic skills in reading, writing and number.

Appendix 5.1
25 words that can be built from i t p n s

I in it is pin sin tin tip tit nit pit nip sip pins sins tins tits pits snip pint -pint tint tints pints snips

Spelling ranks

10 Mainly correct spelling, legible, average size, word spaces
 9 Some correct spelling, skeletal phonics, meaning apparent
 8 Words, phonics, phonetics, meaning can be deciphered
 7 Skeletal phonics, words, letters, some meaning apparent
 6 Some phonic skeletons, word bits and letters, part meaning
 5 Word forms, letters, phone(s) evident
 4 Letters, possible phones
 3 Letter shapes, letters
 2 Marks, mandalas, occasional letters
 1 Scribble
 0 Faint random marks

Appendix 5.2
Handwriting ranks

Scoring 'first marks on paper' for copy writing and free writing

10 Letters all the same moderate size on a line
 9 With clear ascenders and descenders
 8 Spaces between words
 7 With appropriate capitals
 6 Bodies sit on the line, real or imaginary

5 **Letters formed in a single fluid movement**
4 **Distinct letter shapes**
3 **Drawn letters**
2 **Mandelas and letter-like shapes in a line**
1 **Some letter-type marks in a line across the paper**
0 **Random scribble and faint marks**

The first six items give the ranks in order. The upper four may be in any order, and the ranks would be 6 + 1, 6 + 2, and so on.

Appendix 5.3

Coordination difficulties may become confused with legibility issues because poor coordination can result in malformed letters and problems in positioning letters and words on the lines. There are however distinct indicators of coordination difficulties that observation of older children writing and the scripts produced can reveal. A list of indicators is as follows:

- Script drags in from the margin.
- Rivers of space run down the page.
- The script is very faint.
- The script is spiky.
- Words wave about above the lines and drag below them.
- There is a variation in pressure seen in darker and lighter letters and words.
- Pressure may be so strong ridges appear on the reverse of the paper.
- Script may be very large and faint.
- The writer may complain of pain after a few minutes.
- Particular lower-case letters may look like capitals (e.g. S, K, W, F) because they are more difficult to form precisely and small.
- Ts appear as capitals because the cross bar cannot be added precisely enough down the upright.
- Other letters, such as U and M and N, may randomly be formed extra large, as the coordination control is lost.
- There may be holes in and ink blots on the paper.

No wonder young writers might complain of pain.

Changing higher-order skills teaching, strategic approaches

6

Introduction

Higher-order skills are defined in literacy as compositional and research skills. They are the techniques we use when we are 'reading to learn'. Then we use the knowledge to organise and inform our writing.

The DCSF (2007a) report *Getting There – Able Pupils Who Lose Momentum in Years 4 to 6* showed these pupils had limited ability to orchestrate all elements of writing simultaneously. They had restricted opportunities for oral rehearsal, developed a preference for personal/private writing that was not shared with an audience, lacked confidence in the wider use of punctuation and were insecure in the planning of writing.

If pupils are delayed in developing their basic skills in reading and writing, as described in Chapter 5, then it is harder for them to engage in informational and compositional writing, especially writing of any quality and length. This is because the brain is too occupied with the lower-order construction of writing because it is lacking in automaticity and attention is directed away from the plan and the potential creative elements. They will suffer from cognitive overload as they try to summon up spellings and control their motor configurations. This means there is less cognitive space to address and engage in planning and developing creative and complex ideas. This causes the gap to form between the oral and written work and makes the pupils reluctant to write and to expose what they know are their inadequacies. Not only are more able pupils vulnerable to these problems, but so are the learning disabled and the disadvantaged. This will include most of the 40 per cent who leave school at 16 without five GCSEs and many in special schools for EBD and moderate learning difficulties (MLD). This was seen in the case studies in Chapter 4.

Limited language capacity because of disadvantage and lack of experience in speaking and listening can add to the compositional problems, and the pupil will tend to write to a formula that has proved acceptable before. The freedom from spelling and motor skills issues with the use of digital technology can reveal some considerable talent. Then the language experience and language capacity need to be dealt with. Experience can be provided to some extent by school-focused events and activities, by shared viewing of film excerpts and reflective discussion and debate on curriculum topics. But a major secondary source of experience is through text, the narratives and the stories that we read. Underachieving and disadvantaged pupils and especially boys will be less likely to read for pleasure than peers, so their experience of the world is further limited, and they become less capable of reading for meaning and engaging in deep learning.

The DfE (2016) SATs data revealed

- For pupils on free school meals (FSM) and not on FSM, there was a gap between white boys of 23 per cent on the Key Stage 1 writing assessment.
- Between boys and girls on FSM, the gap was 16 per cent.
- At KS2, in the higher expectations tests in 2016, the gender gap doubled from 4 per cent to 8 per cent.
- In reading at KS1, 78 per cent of girls and 70 per cent of boys achieved the expected 85 per cent standard.
- White boys on FSM achieved the lowest standard of any socio-economic group, and only 51 per cent reached the expected standard instead of 70 per cent.

The motor skills research in Chapter 5 showed that boys from poorer environments also had poorer motor skills in handwriting, and overall, boys' skills were poorer than those of girls from all the environments. It was also shown that with improved training, these skills difficulties could be overcome, except in the severest cases of dysgraphia, when assistive technology was essential from the foundation year.

Where the preponderance of research and concern has been focused is not upon the basic skills but upon composition and boys' unwillingness in large measure to write. It is encouraging that there are so many practical strategies that have been implemented to close the gender attainment gap, and these have been widely shared by DfE, Ofsted, trainers and teachers and on the web over the last 20 years. Some examples follow. Nevertheless, the gap has not closed although it has narrowed. This suggests the early years motor skills issues must be part of any intervention to close the gap, but it is also important to examine the higher-order reading skills that can extend and support the compositional work. These are variously called 'cognitive study skills' and 'research skills'.

From teacher education research with students in ITT and CPD, seven general principles for developing good quality writing emerged. These essentials were

- Experiential learning
- Motivation and interest

- Creativity and curiosity
- Looking and learning
- Listening and learning
- Language experience
- Oracy foundations

Experiential, situated learning

It can be surprising that some children's lives are very limited. They can travel by car to and from home without interacting with anything in between but their iPhone. Infants may read stories about buses and trains but never travel on either. Castles are discussed but have never been visited and a day at the seaside never experienced, except for a pool at a hotel in Spain. Children can write so much better if they experience some aspect of the project they are to write about. Students looking back on their school years remember the school outings in detail, whereas they rarely remember a significant aspect about any lesson. Television 'soaps' or football may be the dominant experiences that are talked about outside the classroom.

De Corte's (1995, 2013) research showed learning needs to be situated if it is to be effective. The problem is that most school learning is situated in the same classrooms every day for years. Even so, experiential learning is most effective when there is preparation and then debriefing to show and share what has been learned and how it was learned. When opportunities are limited for outside of school experience, teachers and pupils bring in 'found objects' or use materials, experiments, film, original resources and so on to provide some direct experience. Books supply secondary resources and experiences.

Motivation, interest, creativity and curiosity

A teacher with a year 3 class brought in an old coat that she had 'found' by the dustbins. The children were asked to suggest to whom the coat might have belonged and what might be found in the pockets and so on.

There was a lot of pupil talk, and curiosity was generated. They were then set to write a story about how they thought the coat came to be left behind. They could discuss the idea with a partner or just begin. They discussed a 'scaffold' to help them with the story structure (e.g. to describe the person who owned the coat and explain what had happened to that person and then why the coat was left in that spot and where the person was now.

Lessons in all subject areas that posed problems rather than told answers were more highly motivational. In the next chapter, such motivational strategies will be discussed in more detail.

Looking, listening and learning

Particularly effective lessons were observed when the teacher brought in objects for study. On one occasion, some large shells were the example, and the class groups were to study them carefully and then draw them preparatory to developing an imaginative painting, incorporating a shell or shells. Pupils were later encouraged to bring in their own found objects as a basis for their artwork.

A new fence put up round the school was used to develop poems about imprisonment. A building site in the school grounds was the subject for more poetry and artwork.

 ## Oracy foundations and pupil voice

What is essential as can be seen in the preceding examples is the talk that is engaged in not just by the teacher but also by the pupils. This is the most essential foundation for learning and achievement of underachieving and disadvantaged children. The inspectorate over decades has emphasised the need for more pupil talk in classrooms.

The problem has been that handing talk and elements of learning over to the pupils can make teachers feel they are not teaching enough and should instead be doing more and dominating the work. But teaching is not talking. Pupils learn best when they can construct their own meaning, and this is initially done through talk and explaining things to other people. Often, we do not know what we think until we try to explain it to someone else, so it is essential that pupils have experiences that permit this. Techniques for making more opportunities for hearing the 'pupil voice' will be detailed in a later section.

 ## Five examples of typical projects

1 **Gary Wilson** is an inspirational speaker, former teacher and educational consultant and has been a trainer over the last 15 years.
   garywilsonraisingboysachievement.com
   He offered the four following suggestions for promoting boys' writing:

   1 'In a recent project, part-sponsored by Oxford University Press, we created twenty small groups of peer police cadets. We gave them the name "THE TRANS-FORMERS" and gave them responsibility to help out younger boys with their reading and taking charge of eco projects around the school. Schools are full of adult role models! Or ask your local high school to send you down some young men on work experience or as Maths Ambassadors or Science Ambassadors'.

   2 'Make a stimulating writing corner in your classroom planned by the children. Instead of having a home corner, have a space research station or a superhero

base, where missions are planned and reports written for the government. Use the kinds of paraphernalia attached to their favourite superheroes or TV or film characters'.

3 'Seek the boys' help to design and stock an area of the library, giving it real boy appeal' (see www.oxfordowl.co.uk/).

4 'Hold a parents' workshop that looks at boys' achievement to help address the issues, highlight the importance of developing independence in boys. Parents need to know the significance of male role models in the family – fathers, grandfathers, uncles, older brothers – and the important role they have in supporting their boys' education'.

2 **Another web source gives 23 Top Tips** for the motivation of boy writers
motivatingboywriters.blogspot.com/2010/ . . .
It reports that 'the boys' writing improved during activities that were highly motivating'.

3 **The Primary National Strategy Boys' Writing examples (DCFS, 2011)**

Talk for writing: key principles:

- Children learning English as an additional language benefit from orally rehearsing writing.
- Children need to activate knowledge of what they are going to write about. This can be done in a first or additional language.
- Children need to experience language being used in order to be able to use it effectively themselves.
- Talk for writing can be used across the curriculum.
- Boys and girls may communicate in different ways. We can make the most of the differences by planning a variety of different groups, pairings and seating arrangements.
- The collaborative skills developed through talk for writing can be used in social as well as academic situations.
- Drama is a successful tool to stimulate writing at all ages.
- Talk for writing is most effective when it is a carefully planned, and thoroughly prepared, part of learning.
- The teacher/practitioner's own talk can be a powerful way of demonstrating for writing. Signing and alternative means of communication should be used where appropriate.

Purpose and audience: key principles

- Build on boys' enjoyment and motivation through ICT, film and visual texts.
- Make explicit links between visual texts and a written outcome.

- Teach understanding/vocabulary of media structures to support the writing sequence.
- Discuss images and pictures to generate wider vocabulary.
- Develop children's visual skills through games and role play.
- From the foundation stage onwards, ensure that 'real' writing activities are planned for.
- Plan that each literacy session/activity is part of a cohesive unit of work and is not just a 'one-off'.
- Make boys aware of the purpose of each task within the unit, in particular how a skill or concept can be applied to other learning or in another curriculum area.
- Demonstrate how skills learned in word-level and sentence-level teaching are applied in 'real' writing activities.
- Ensure that the audience for writing is made clear and that, wherever possible, the audience goes beyond the immediate classroom/setting environment.
- Facilitate 'partner peer-review' during writing sessions so that children are kept aware of the importance of revisiting their work to make changes and improvements.
- Create real opportunities for audiences, involving parents and carers.
- Learning objectives, success criteria and curricular targets provide a framework for feedback on learning.
- Involving boys in creating success criteria for writing provides them with clear expectations.
- Paired assessment and self-assessment are ways of engaging boys in understanding their progress in learning and identifying next steps.
- Boys need to be supported so that they learn how to give effective feedback to each other.
- Time needs to be built into literacy activities for giving oral and written feedback and for boys to reflect and act on feedback.
- One of the most effective forms of feedback is to focus on success and improvement.
- Whole-group shared marking allows for discussion and analysis in a secure environment.

4   **Julie Cigman Oxfordshire Boys Writing Project 2011–12**

Adults who understand how children learn to write can support children at all stages of their writing.

- Follow boys' interests
- Male role models
- Stimulating environments that children want to explore
- Celebrate all kinds of mark-making and writing
- Engage the parents
- Big paper!

- Exciting and accessible resources
- Real-life experiences
- Opportunities to talk first . . . then write
- Extended time for activities
- https://www2.oxfordshire.gov.uk/cms/sites/default/files/folders/documents/childreneducationandfamilies/informationforchildcareproviders/Oxfordshire BoysWritingProjectReport.pdf Accessed 03/04/2019

5 **'Writing in the Air'** *Nurturing young children's dispositions for writing,* Kent Co. Co. (2003)

Children's talk during free play was investigated, and it was found that boys used language to control but not as narrative as girls did. Girls used characters and set roles and engaged in fantasy play, whereas boys made noises for rockets and cars and so on. Boys were found to have as much as girls going on inside their heads, but it was not expressed. In mixed groups, girls would frequently support boys with story language.

The research encouraged oral story telling of personal experience and acting out familiar stories and their own tales before writing. Teachers learned to add incidents to resolve in the personal stories. Parents were involved in the project, and a newsletter was sent home to support the work. The result was that both boys' and girls' storytelling and writing was improved as they became fluent storytellers.

It was recommended that adults should scaffold story writing and make explicit links between play experiences and stories and to record the 'played stories' and put the publications in book corners. Sustained thinking and talking to compose stories should take place regularly.

Reading to learn – higher-order study and research skills

The previous chapter presented research and strategies for improving the acquisition of reading and writing skills. Once the basic skills of learning to read have been acquired, we begin to use them in reading to learn. What we learn from reading can be promoted by the application of higher-order study skills.

Higher-order study skills are a form of self-directed learning and are implemented whenever material is read or viewed in order to use it in a communication. In the Schools Council Project (1980) to promote literacy in the secondary school, reading was defined in two ways – receptive reading, a running read such as we use when reading a novel or newspaper and reflective reading, a more complex activity in which we use higher-order study skills to glean information and ideas from the text. In fact, it is equally possible to apply the same terms – receptive or reflective to viewing of video, artwork and screen data or real-life events. One of the major concerns of the project was that pupils did not distinguish between the two forms and tended to apply the same strategy, receptive reading, to all their study tasks.

The difference between **receptive reading and reflective reading** is important. In receptive reading, the text is transparent and easy to understand. When we read to learn, the text is often complex and compacted with many concepts contained or implied in a sentence. It may also have deep structures to penetrate. This means we need to learn to use different reading strategies and engage in reflective reading.

For example, some cognitive activities used in studying are surveying, locational and referencing skills. In reading for the main idea or to understand the logic of a piece, interpretative skills are needed to understand structure and sequence, to find meaning and to understand tables, graphs, illustrations and ideas. If it is necessary to understand the overall structure of something, then information has to be organised, summarised, outlined and perhaps labelled.

Critical comprehension will involve the use of thinking strategies at literal, logical, interpretative, critical and creative levels. In the process, we may reflect on ideas presented, tap into the writer's organisational plan and relate new ideas to old using mental imagery. All of these activities are potentially at work together, and as can be inferred, it is essentially a constructive learning activity in the sense of the learner or reader being actively engaged in making meaning.

Even though pupils might know how to survey text, there was no guarantee that they would use the skills and save themselves time (Neville and Pugh, 1977). They needed systematic teaching in primary and then again in secondary school. They also found little correlation between reading ability and the ability to use a range of study skills effectively.

Because of the information revolution and more particularly because of a concern to ensure that students at all levels really learn how to learn and can become self-organised learners, the conception of study skills has been significantly developed beyond a consideration of the narrow confines of information skills (Weinstein et al., 1988). Different types and levels of study skills are needed for different tasks, from simple note-taking to writing a report or doing research. The first thing that should be done is to survey the information by scanning the title and subtitles, looking at the pictures, reading the summaries, flipping through each page and using the index to locate specific information.

Most pupils are unaware of these skills and need to be specifically taught. They may even feel they are cheating if they do not start at the beginning and read steadily through. In addition to scanning a text, Anderson (1980) found that there were other activities going on. He found that nearly all his students were trying to answer three additional 'how' questions. These were

* How much do I already know about this topic and text? If anything is already known, it can act as 'advance organisers' (Ausubel, 1968) to make later acquisition more effective.

- How interested am I in it?
- How difficult or time-consuming will it be for me to learn what I need to know from it?

If by scanning they could not answer all these questions, they went on to read sections in more detail or the surveying would break down, and they turned to another book or another activity.

These learning strategies are often called DARTs (directed activities related to texts). They may also be referred to as higher-order reading or learning strategies. The important aspect is the process in which the learner is engaged that causes him or her to engage with the material at deep cognitive levels so that what is already known is linked to the new or is changed by it. The learner in the process learns the relevance of the content and how it may be applied perhaps in a modified form to another situation.

Reading to Learn Project Using a Reading Event Recorder, the researchers identified five different types of reading strategies (Harri-Augstein et al., 1982). They found that first-year students on several degree programmes who were ineffective readers engaged in several rapid read-throughs of text. They were later unable to summarise what they had read or complete satisfactorily a short-answer factual recall test on it. Successful readers engaged in reading through the text but rolling forwards and backwards in order to check up on points, and they also paused for thinking and reflection time as well as to organise their notes.

Partially effective readers engaged in slow runs through the text, stopping to make notes as they did so. These students were only successful on the objective test and not the summary. It is typical of the strategy that many students learn to collect information for an essay. They do not do a survey read to get an overview but just do a note-taking run, expecting by this means to understand what is written. The result is that the essay looks like a neatly written version of the original note-taking exercise and is not organised to answer the question.

Examples of higher-order study and research skills

DARTs were devised in order to encourage pupils to slow down and engage with the text in more reflective reading. The activities illustrated different ways in which pupils could be obliged to give detailed attention to the text, and the results could be discussed with them to show the value of adopting different study strategies. Reflection helped them gain metacognitive control over their mental processes, but then they were able to promote and control them better in subsequent activities.

Watson (1996) showed the value of such reflection to her groups with moderate learning difficulties, and they were also successful with slower learners in mainstream (Montgomery, 1990).

The following examples, or DARTs, can apply to textual, visual, auditory and performance material.

- Locating the main points and subordinate ones
- Flow-charting
- Completion activities
- Prediction activities
- Sequencing
- Comparing and contrasting
- Drafting and editing
- Organising – tabulating, classifying, ordering, diagramming, categorising
- Drawing inferences and abstractions
- Recognising intent, bias and propaganda
- Planning
- Managing one's learning and keeping it on task and on schedule

These sorts of study skills are different from those that involve lower-order activities, such as using a dictionary or an index and finding one's way about a book and what its main contents are or recovering factual information from a text and making notes to write a summary or an essay.

Study skills are a form of self-directed learning, and although reading skills are taught in primary school, it is not usual to teach higher-order reading and cognitive skills there or in secondary school, although they are considered to be essential to the educated person and a requirement for success in higher education. Even able children do not automatically develop them, although Freeman (1991) noted that the characteristics of her able learners were that they probed text to seek deeper meaning and did not learn by rote.

In the following sections, some of the methods of teaching the higher-order strategies are illustrated.

A concept completion exercise

1   UNDER GROUND by James Reeves
    In the deep kingdom under ground
    There is no light and little ____
    Down below the earth's green ____
    The rabbit and the mole explore.

The quarrying ants run to and fro
To make their populous empires _____
Do they, as I pass _____
Stop in their work to hear my tread? Etc.

In pairs, the pupils should fill in the gaps, trying to reconstruct the author's meaning. On completion, they can be asked for *three* reasons why they produced words that rhymed. Those who finish quickly can try the exercise again but try to find another word to put in the gap that may or may not rhyme but preserves the sense.

A similar activity called Cloze procedure is used in comprehension tests. Gaps are introduced every seven words or so, and the pupil must complete the sentence. In concept completion, the gaps are not at regular intervals but defined by the concepts the teacher wishes the pupils to focus upon.

2   A more difficult example of a concept completion activity for pairs of pupils might be to read the poem by Stephen Spender and try to reconstruct the author's original intent.
Ultima Ratio Regum (first verse only here)
The guns spell money's ultimate reason
In letters of _____ on the Spring hillside.
But the boy lying _____ under the olive trees
Was too young and too _____
To have been notable to their important eye.
He was a better target for a _____.

Asking pupils to work in pairs is to promote talking and listening and social interaction. It is also an aid to poorer readers.

Reading or listening for the main point

For example, instead of taking a poem or a piece of prose and asking the pupils to read it silently in sections and then questioning them about the content, trying to get at their factual and inferential comprehension, the teacher might ask them to read it and then in pairs identify the *main point* or main idea. The strategy is *read – think – pair – share*. After their deliberations, they then can present their main ideas to the rest of the class for evaluation. Similarly, the rest of the structure can be explored in like fashion.

Pictures can be examined and ideas about them discussed using this procedure. Identifying main and subordinate ideas can lead on to producing flow charts and chronologies or time lines, whatever method of recording and representing might be appropriate. The pairing and sharing ensures that all the pupils have an opportunity to express their own ideas in complete sentences, not just one-word responses to the teacher. There is also opportunity for pupils to question each other and where necessary engage in teaching the other how they arrived at their main ideas. Some training examples follow.

1   Ask individuals to talk for thirty seconds about 'noses', for example, and then discuss with them the apparent targets in the speaker's thinking. These can then be expanded upon and used as the basis for an introduction to a project on the sense of smell. Targets that might be expanded are nose structure, functions and physiognomy; historical noses; animal 'noses'; anthropological noses; illness and noses; and so on.

2   Read the poem written by Sir Walter Raleigh, and find its main point. Identify the type of structure he uses. Decide on a similar structure, and write some lines of your own using his technique.

> What is our life? a play of passion;
> Our mirth, the music of division;
> Our mother's wombs the tiring houses be
> Where we are dressed for this short comedy
> Heaven the judicious sharp spectator,
> That sits and marks still doth act amiss
> Our graves that hide us from the searing sun
> Are the drawn curtains when the play is done.
> Thus march we playing to our latest rest;
> Only we die in earnest – that's no jest.

(It shows the use of metaphor.)
Give the pupils the following simile to try:

> 'Life is like an apple.'

Two Dundee head teachers on CPD wrote their response:

> Life is like an apple.
> From seed to core
> And nothing more,
> Naught but rot in store.

3   The following extract and main point exercise was taken from Royce-Adams (1977).

> With a food surplus, the Pueblos were able to turn their attention to other activities besides locating or growing food. In one particular area – pottery making – the Pueblos developed a high degree of artistry. Potters became artists and developed individualised techniques, painting fine-lined geometric designs as well as reproductions or life forms on their vessels. Paints were improved, and pottery has been found that contains three or four different colours.

(From *Columbus to Aquarius*, Dryden Press 1975)

Identify the main point of this extract: _____
and then decide which of the following writing patterns is exemplified in it.

a   illustration – example   e   cause and effect
b   definition   f   description
c   comparison – contrast   g   a mixture – state which
d   sequence of events

Pupils can then practice rewriting the Pueblo passage in each of the different patterns to get the feel of the different options available in writing any passage. This can be done individually or in collaborative pairs.

Questioning text

The type of questions will vary, but to reflect on text, these are possibilities.

What is the author trying to say?
What is the point that the data makes – does it match up to the claims?
Does the text really explain what it sets out to?
What do I still need to know?
Do I understand all the words used?
Does it make sense to me? Why not?
What other explanation is there?
What is fact, and what is an opinion?

Concept mapping comparisons

Concept mapping is related to the notion of identifying main points. Now the mapping links them and also includes related ideas in the net attached to each main idea. The essence of the map is that it represents one's own ideas about a subject, and by representing these on paper, one can inspect them, compare them with those of others and discuss them. As new knowledge is accumulated, it can be incorporated into the map, and a new map may need to be drawn showing a complete change in the whole structure so that developments in learning can be seen.

It is a useful strategy for finding out what pupils bring to a topic and getting this recorded. Subjects might be castles, settlements, rivers, weather, homes, animals, fish or towns. Any topic can begin with such a personal map or a group 'brainstorm'.

After several teaching inputs, readings and so on, the pupils can be asked to draw another concept map to show their current thinking. From this, the teacher can see conceptual developments without having to read large volumes of notes that may or may not reflect knowledge or understanding. To help the pupils reflect upon what they know and have learned, five differences between the pre- and post-teaching maps may be asked for and discussed in dyads. Then in a plenary, they share their reflections upon these. Again, the pairs-work helps focus the attention as each discusses the work with the other and tries to explain it. They can also do an analysis of levels of the different concept maps using the SOLO taxonomy (Biggs and Collis, 1982).

Brainstorming and drawing the concept maps enables the pupils to bring to the forefront of the mind the previous knowledge and experience and inspect it to try to establish connecting links. Having heightened awareness in this way, there is a better chance that the information in the new learning will be integrated into the past structures.

In Chapter 7, there is an example of how the SOLO (structure of observed learning outcomes) taxonomy was used for evaluation in teacher education programmes. It can be used in the same way with pupils as was shown in CPD training programmes by NACE (2019).

Assessment

If learners take on an assessment role, then their learning of the material is likely to be as high as 95 per cent (Race, 1992) and is able to reach deep levels so that it is available for transforming and using in various creative ways. ITT students were asked to evaluate one of the tests of reading set out in a workshop and to use the criteria set out in a lecture on 'What makes a good test'. In-service students on a distance programme were asked to write (not answer) a short answer paper on dyslexia worth 100 marks. It had to consist of true or false, multiple choice and sentence completion items. The main bulk of the questions had to be based upon three recent research papers and their own knowledge of the subject.

In general science and biology teaching, pupils were asked to work in small groups to produce an end-of-year exam paper. They then had to draw up answer plans and assign marks to model answers to each question. Young pupils in reception then did similar activities but in relation to four tabloid newspapers' front-page news. They had to identify the papers' two or three main news stories on a particular day and produce a list of the themes; then they had to design their own newspaper front page. Older pupils in teams analysed and then designed their own school newspapers.

When looking at paintings on a wall-gallery, pupils in pairs were asked to draw up a list of five criteria for judging the merits of the paintings. These were then shared with the rest of the class, discussed, condensed and then applied to a major artwork.

Editing and marking Pupils' essays from previous years can be used as edit material. Good and poor anonymous examples can be used for comparison to discuss what makes quality writing. The subject can be a story or a narrative, such as about the Wars of the Roses. The original can be used as a scaffold for producing a good account, and pupils can learn from assigning grades based upon agreed subject criteria from A to E. They can use these scaffolds to build their own accounts for homework.

Older pupils and students in ITT working for exams can be given the task in pairs to mark an exam essay using the institution's criterion referenced grading system. They then have to justify the mark they have given and write some constructive points of guidance on how the writer could have improved the essay. Again, content is learned incidentally in this process as well as exam technique.

Summarising

There are many summarising strategies that can be used as part of study skills to enhance learning. Most study material contains information of various kinds, such as facts, opinions, methods, steps, ideas and so on. A quick assessment by the teacher can enable such questions to be asked as

1   **List the three (five, ten and so on) main points** in the chapter about, for example, the role of the church/monarchy/peasantry. Extra marks and special praise can always be given for finding more points. Write the points in order of importance from the most to the least important.
2   **Ask the pupils to write a summary** of a book/chapter they have just read in exactly 50 words, a minisaga. This really causes them to focus on the essentials of the text and to consider each word of their sentences carefully.
3   **A book or a section of work** can be recorded in a summary. Pupils often do not know how to summarise something and so the introductory techniques of stating how many main points there might be or how many words they are to use can be helpful training exercises. They have to stop copying out sections verbatim and think over the sections of the content. Discussing how they approached their task will give helpful clues on how to develop their techniques further. Many careers, such as in police investigation work, travel agencies, travel guiding, advertising, teaching, research, journalism, medical practice and so on require summarising skills. The value of the technique should be made explicit, emphasised and practiced.
4   **Writing summaries for different audiences** can help pupils understand the deeper structure of learning contents. For example, a section of historical information might be written up in the style of a modern-day newspaper, such as the

Sun. Pupils can have a lot of fun with this as well as secure their knowledge of an historical topic.

5 **Newspapers and broadcasts** Pupils might be encouraged to put all their work together as an historical newspaper or present it as a version of the *Today* programme on radio or a news broadcast on TV. The National Curriculum is still so full that much of the development work on such projects would need to be done independently outside lessons, but the enthusiasm that can be generated is usually sufficient for this to happen. Writing the same information for different audiences can also help it to be learned in a pleasurable way rather than by rote. The audiences may be real, imaginary or historical, and presented in different registers or for different cultures and sub-cultures.

Critical reviews of topics or a play will include a brief description of the key aspects with some appropriate evaluation. Examples of the structure of such reviews can be used as models for the pupils to follow. They have to gain more than knowledge of the content in order to do any summarising task such as this. It is also important to identify the overall structure of the ideas and their relations to each other.

Different review perspectives can also be adopted, such as in relation to gender, ethnicity and class not only in English classes but also in technology, science, art, geography, mathematics and history. Children's storybooks can provide an easy training exercise.

Comparing and contrasting information is another approach to identifying main points and summarising the key issues in many subjects. Sometimes it can be helpful to tabulate such data. At other times, the differences can be represented diagrammatically.

Organising, tabulating, classifying, ordering, diagramming and categorising are all strategies for reducing information into smaller, more manageable and more meaningful chunks. The process of doing so is also very useful for assisting learning at deeper levels to take place, especially where the learners have done the work for themselves.

Time lines, lists, critical incident analyses and chronologies in their own ways are summaries that can be useful processes to aid learning.

The hook and eye technique This consists of drawing a ring round key concepts or themes in a text and linking them with lines to their next point of emergence. It makes a mess of the paper but helps focus the mind.

Underlining and highlighting These techniques are widely used when reading a text in preparation for note-taking to identify important ideas. They allow immediate access to these key issues on the occasion of note-taking or re-reading. It is similar to 'Search in Document' using a computer. The tendency is that too much is underlined, circled or highlighted when receptive reading strategies are used.

Teaching by pupils, micro-teaching In order to help pupils learn, it is sometimes helpful and interesting to provide them with learning materials and set them to design a short teaching session on some aspect. This can be prepared in small groups and then the mini-teaching session can be given to the group. Some might be encouraged to give their presentation to the class. Nothing concentrates the mind more on getting down to the essentials of a subject than when it has to be taught to someone else, as every teacher knows. After assessment, it is one of the best methods for ensuring something is learned. Teaching sessions need careful structuring so that the same material is not repeated and the class do not have to listen for long periods to topics that the teacher could present better.

This is where group work is an important sub-stage and all presentations must have a time limit. An alternative may be for the presentations on what they have learned to be offered at parents' evenings as a change from wall displays and neat books. Both parents and pupils gain an enormous amount from these teaching sessions, and this was a regular feature of our science work.

Exhibitions and posters also summarise achievements and can be accompanied by pupils giving mini presentations on their work and what they were trying to achieve. Even the youngest of pupils can do this.

Other types of summary might be to make two PowerPoint slides to illustrate the main points of a topic. Only seven words to a line are permitted and only ten lines to be used so that it is large enough for all the class to see easily and compare summaries.

They can learn from this that the best method is to put as little on the slides as possible and then speak to them – the presenter uses these key points to elaborate upon. On another occasion, they might be asked to produce their summary notes as an A5 four-page leaflet for visitors or as a cartoon sequence. Pin men drawing needs to be taught for those who would rather not exercise or exhibit their artistic repertoire. Personal computers can be used to support this if pupils prefer.

Sequencing and flow charts Pupils can read a research paper/story/chapter or piece of poetry or prose to identify its main and subordinate points, separate these out and then put them in an order that reflects the meaning of the text. They can then be asked to make this into a flow chart. Alternatively, the teacher can take a flow chart designed by another class, empty it of its contents and give it to the new class to puzzle out what goes in the empty boxes. In each case, a puzzle or problem is given for the pupils to resolve. In the process, they will have to give the content their most detailed attention, and they learn it very well without any apparent effort, enjoying themselves in the process, especially if they are allowed to work in pairs and are not made to feel it is some kind of test.

Any process or procedure in a subject area can be made into a sequencing activity. For example, there is a set sequence or procedure to lighting a Bunsen burner in science or following a routine or recipe in food technology, even making a cup of tea or boiling an egg.

Once a procedure has been demonstrated and practised, it can be useful to say, instead of 'Now write down that procedure',

> Now look at this work sheet with your partner and you will see that someone does not know how to do it at all. Write down the number of the sentences showing the order in which they should be.

This means that the poorer writers are not handicapped and can focus on the real issues. Scissors can be provided if they need to cut the text up and move it about physically. If there is a fear that scissors would be too big a distraction, then prepared cut slips can be given out in envelopes, which adds to the little bit of mystery.

The same technique can be applied to paragraphs or short stories. What sometimes results is that the pupils may produce a better order than the original author. Very young pupils enjoy being given puzzle envelopes in which the lines of a nursery rhyme have been cut up and jumbled. In pairs, they can then practice their reading skills whilst they try to reconstruct the nursery rhyme correctly. Self-correction can be built into the task by having a picture on the reverse of the card that is only complete when all the lines are in the correct order- a self-checking device.

After exams, it was a very popular demonstration of science exam technique when a pupil would read out an answer such as on 'How to make a barometer'. The reader would instruct, and the teacher would follow the instruction, e.g., 'You get an evaporating dish . . . and stand in it!'

Schools Council Project (1980) sequencing example

The example is an extract from a school text that pupils were asked to learn about. To facilitate their learning, the text was cut into eight sections and the author's order was altered. 'Read through all the sections and decide which order makes the best sense to you. It is easiest if you do cut up the sections'.

(A) Just as the Neolithic Revolution happened in the Stone Age, so the Industrial Revolution produced the machine age. From it sprang large towns.
(B) Although the craft of weaving had been practised as early as 5000 BC, it only became mechanised in the middle of the 18th century. This is what marked the beginning of the Industrial Revolution.
(C) This meant that still more machines and factories were needed to make more goods. Towns grew where there were materials for the machines and suitable conditions for working them.

(D) Indeed, some argue that the Industrial Revolution has not yet ended. Their opinion is that it cannot end until the problems that came from it have been solved. There is something to be said for this point of view.

(E) Man has started depending for his living more upon trade than upon his farm animals or on the crops he himself could grow.

(F) It was 5000 years before the next step change – the Industrial Revolution of 1760–1840. This is so recent that elderly men today can still remember speaking to people who were still alive at the end of that period.

(G) They had begun as the villages man built when he settled down to farm, but they were not necessarily near his farms any longer.

(H) One thing is certain, there could have been no Industrial Revolution had not the Neolithic Revolution come first. Changes carried out by factory owners two centuries ago were based on the ideas and methods of their Stone Age ancestors.

From Darlington, F. 1974 *Neolithic Revolution, Pollution and Life*. Dorset: Blandford Press (p. 7).

Flow chart completion example

Laurie Thomas and Sheila Harri-Augstein (1975) undertook a long-term research project on Reading to Learn using materials such as this. They charted the eye movements of undergraduates reading complex text extracts. They found that those who engaged only in the note-taking runs were the least effective learners and had not grasped the overall structure of the text. Those who paused for thinking time and moved backwards and forwards through the extract were the effective readers and could complete both objective tests and summaries very well.

Example task: Reading for the Main Point, to Summarise and to Produce a Flow Diagram of the Logical Structure of the Paragraph

Darwin's *On the Origin of Species*

1) Again, it may be asked, how is it that varieties which I have called incipient species, become ultimately converted into good and distinct species, which in most cases obviously differ from each other far more than do the varieties of the same species?

2) How do those groups of species, which constitute what are called distinct genera and which differ from each other more than do the same genus, arise?

3) All these results, as we shall more fully see in the next chapter follow from the struggle for life.

4) Owing to this struggle, variations, however slight, and from whatever cause proceeding, if they be in any degree profitable to the individuals or a species, or in

their infinitely complex relations to organic beings and to their physical conditions of life, will tend to the preservation of such individuals, and will generally
be inherited by the offspring.

5) The offspring also, will thus have a better chance of surviving, for, of the many
individuals of any species which are periodically born, but a small number can
survive.

6) I have called this principle by which each slight variation, if useful, is preserved, by
the term Natural Selection, in order to mark its relation to man's power of selection.

7) But the expression often used by Mr Herbert Spencer of the Survival of the Fittest
is more accurate, and is sometimes equally convenient.

8) We have seen that man by selection can certainly produce great results, and can
adapt organic beings to his own uses, through the accumulation of slight but
useful variations, given to him by the hand of Nature.

9) But Natural Selection, as we shall hereafter see, is as immeasurably superior to
man's feeble efforts, as the works of nature are to the works of Art.

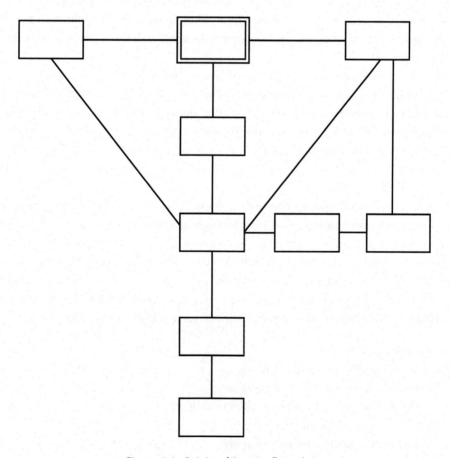

Figure 6.1 Origin of Species flow chart

Deep and surface-learning strategies

Marton and Säljo (1976) defined deep and surface learning, showing that an over-filled curriculum and lack of appropriate strategies led to superficial learning. Surface learning is prominent when we read a newspaper or a novel and simply do a 'run-through' read without pause and pick up bits of information as described in receptive reading earlier. It is implicit in didactic methods of teaching and learning.

Surface strategies are usually seen in post-study activities. The pupil reads the material or listens to the teacher's exposition, and then at a later date, even though practice exercises have been undertaken, a number of post-study activities are used to help reinforce the strength of the learning and aid later recall. Examples are rereading the text and note-taking.

Creating a mnemonic such as "Richard Of York Gave Battles In Vain" to remember the colours of the rainbow is a device known as clustering. The sentence is mildly more memorable than the separate colours, a semi-cognitive activity, but the end product involves rote learning and of course is wrong, as there are only six colours in the rainbow (red, orange, yellow, green, blue, violet); the 'scientists' of the day were much influenced by magical notions associated with the number seven and its universality.

The typical content of such a study skills programmes was illustrated by Pascal (1998) in his one-day courses for NASEN. The programme covered active classroom revision; examination skills such as question analysis, answer planning and proof-reading; specific skills – organisation of notes and study time, note-taking, note-making, essay planning; and finally learning techniques. These activities are all directed to organising memory for better recall and are useful end strategies, but there are better methods.

Most revision strategies involve rote learning activities after the event, whereas if the initial learning task was involving and constructive, directed to some real purpose the learner wanted to achieve, then there would be little chance of forgetting. It would be better if we did not start from there. If we can make the original learning more effective, detailed and extensive, much revision would not be required. Revision is required in inverse proportion to the effectiveness of the original learning.

Gibbs (1990) defined the characteristics of surface learning as follows:

- A heavy workload
- Relatively high class contact hours
- An excessive amount of course material
- Lack of opportunity to pursue subjects in depth
- Lack of choice over subjects
- Lack of choice over methods of study
- Threatening and anxiety-provoking assessment systems

All these surface characteristics are implicit in high stakes education systems, such as the English National Curriculum. Fostering a deep learning approach rests in the obverse of surface approaches:

- Relatively low class contact hours
- Intrinsic interest in the subject
- Freedom in learning in content and method or scope for intellectual independence
- Experience perceived as 'good' teaching
- A positive and supportive assessment system

Although some HE programmes in the humanities have low contact hours, students may not have sufficient self-regulation to use the time wisely; others may have to engage in part-time work to pay fees. Students frequently come from secondary and public schools where they have not been allowed free curriculum time nor been helped to develop the self-regulatory skills that would have supported their independent learning.

In 'the Information Age', when data is so readily available that key words can summon it up on *Wikipedia*, search skills are not necessary. What is becoming increasingly important is to know how and where to find information when it is needed and then how to understand, manage, organise, use and communicate it effectively to meet specific purposes such as in decision-making and problem solving. Reading to learn becomes especially important.

The National Literacy Trust on World Book Day, 12 March 2019, released new research that showed the need to celebrate books and reading was greater than ever. It showed that the number of eight- to 18-year-olds reading for pleasure had dropped to 52.5 per cent, from 58.8 per cent in 2016, and only a quarter (25.7 per cent) now read daily, compared with 43 per cent in 2015.

Reading for meaning needs practice and is especially important as a study skill. Instead of reading to learn, it is easy now to find relevant texts on the Internet, locate key words and patch extracts together to answer questions and 'write' essays.

In the present period, students in lectures tend to take photos of the PowerPoints on screens or make the notes on their laptops, and this has been shown to be less effective for their deep learning outcomes when compared with making their own notes. It was investigated in *The Pen Is Mightier Than the Keyboard: Advantages of Longhand Over Laptop Note-Taking* by Mueller and Oppenheimer (2014).

Strategic approaches to teaching and learning

After ten years and more of the national curriculum, the weaknesses in its design became more and more obvious, especially from results being attained at the older age ranges. Intervention was planned at Key Stage 3 to produce more cognitive challenge in foundation subjects (Higgins, 2002).

It had been obvious to those involved with professional training that the new curriculum was not and would not be meeting the stated needs of the new millennium. Government's and employers' needs to compete in world markets were a workforce with the following skills:

- Good communication skills
- Problem-solving skills
- Creative thinking abilities
- Flexibility
- Good listening skills
- Ability to learn from experience
- Ability to learn from others
- Cooperative abilities to work in teams

Although these skills and abilities might be implicit in some teaching programmes, it was concluded that there must be some deliberate teaching of the skills if widespread competence was to be achieved. None of them were being explicitly taught in most schools or university programmes, except perhaps in business education. The list of millennium skills is intimately related to lifelong and self-regulated learning, and this indicates that methods of effective training are not achieved in product-based, content-dense education, didactics. The model on which the 1989 general national curriculum practice was based was Ausubel's (1968) reception learning. Moving backwards!

Reception learning, didactic teaching and the NC

The term 'advance organisers' was coined by Ausubel (1968) to describe the short outline of the whole material introduced before the lesson or lecture begins, now called 'objectives' or targets. He believed that learners learn more effectively by 'reception'. In this method, the teacher (or lecturer) presents the whole content of what has to be learned in its final form. It places a great emphasis on the teacher's skill in structuring the content to be learned. The learning is meaningful if it allows reproduction with understanding at a future date.

The NC government model involved a statement of objectives followed by an 'ice-breaker' activity to generate interest, challenging and open questioning and a lively presentation by the teacher of the main content of the lesson followed by practice/

individual desk work by the pupils. Group work was frowned upon. The teacher must be seen to be in control and dominate the proceedings. Ofsted inspection criteria reinforced this procedure as 'good' teaching, and teachers were failed if they did not engage with them. It was, and still is, difficult for many pupils, especially the disadvantaged, to sustain motivation to learn in this kind of passive learning environment, and the overt signs of their distress are disaffection and misbehaviour.

Reception learning does not even meet the effective learning criteria established by De Corte (1995, 2013). It is a highly structured form of didactics, and the methods are likely to lead to superficial or 'surface learning' and memorising. This means that the material needs frequent revision to make it available for use. It will also have a low degree of transfer to new and different situations and remain relatively inert. The question it raises is that if we have to keep revising knowledge, can it have been effectively taught and learned in the first place? It reflects Blagg et al.'s (1993) 'Bo Peep theory' of transfer (leave them alone, and they'll come home by themselves) – in this case the millennium needs will not be transferred from reception learning classrooms to the needed workplace skills.

The system put in place was the old grammar school style of secondary education that was itself a watered-down version of what took place in the universities. We were even regularly told 'The good man knows his subject'. It did not seem to occur to them that he might not be able to teach it. My criterion was that a good teacher can teach the same topic to an infant or an A-level student equally effectively. It was not surprising that problems began to emerge.

Discovery learning

In the same period as Ausubel, Jerome Bruner described the activities that he thought were essential to make teaching and learning realistic and constructive for pupils. He termed it *discovery learning*, and it was an inquiry training that enabled pupils to gain a fundamental understanding of the underlying principles of the subject they were studying. In this process, they also learned the concepts and relationships. When pupils worked in these ways, he found that they grew in intellectual potency, were intrinsically motivated, had mastery of principles that enabled them to apply their learning and showed gains in memory as a result of the organisation of their knowledge (Bruner, 19668).

Taba (1962) identified four steps in discovery learning that can also be used as a teaching-learning protocol:

* The problem creates bafflement.
* The learners explore the problem.

- The learners are prompted to generalise and use prior knowledge to understand a new problem or pattern.
- There is a need for opportunities to apply the principles learned to new situations.

Bruner illustrated his ideas in *Man a Course of Study* (MACOS, Chapter 4, 1968). Discovery learning, however, was misunderstood and regarded as a method in which children were taught nothing but had to discover knowledge for themselves and 'reinvent the wheel' every time. In the NC development period, it was classed as another version of 'child minding', the criticism made of the whole of primary education. This is a classic case of misunderstanding and misinformation by those who had never trained a teacher or taught an infant.

Teaching thinking skills strategies

At the same time as the advisory group on teaching the gifted and talented had been established and the findings included in DfEE (1999), a report that had been commissioned by the Department for Education and Employment (McGuinness, 1999) provided a review and evaluation of thinking skills research. It appears that the NC was seen to be failing in its remit, and thinking skills were viewed by many policy makers and educators as the answer. They were important elements in raising standards of academic achievement.

McGuinness identified several 'core concepts' with regard to thinking skills and learning.

> Although it may seem self-evident, focusing on thinking skills in the classroom is important because it *supports active cognitive processing which makes for better learning*. Thus, pupils are equipped to search out meaning and impose structure; to deal systemically, yet flexibly, with novel problems and situations; to adopt a critical attitude to information and argument, and to communicate effectively . . . *Standards* can only be raised when attention is directed not only on what is to be learned but on *how children learn and how teachers intervene to achieve this*.
>
> (McGuinness, 1999, 5)

The key conclusion of her report was that a framework for developing thinking skills was needed that included

- The need to make thinking skills explicit in a curriculum
- Teaching thinking through a form of coaching
- Taking a metacognitive perspective

- Collaborative learning (including computer-mediated learning)
- Creating dispositions and habits of good thinking
- Generalising the framework beyond a narrow focus on skills to include thinking curricula, thinking classrooms and thinking schools

Three models for delivering thinking skills were identified:

1   Enhancing general thinking skills through structured programmes that were additional to the normal curriculum, for example, Instrumental Enrichment (Feuerstein, 1980), Somerset Thinking Skills Course (Blagg et al., 1993) and CoRT (de Bono, 1983) – these are 'bolt on' provisions and can lack transferability except in the hands of experts.
2   Targeting subject-specific learning, such as science, mathematics, geography, for example, CASE (Cognitive Acceleration Through Science Education) (Shayer and Adey, 2002), and later through Technology Education (CATE) – these involved reflective periods for thinking about the thinking engaged in, metacognition.
3   Infusing thinking skills across the curriculum by systematically identifying opportunities within the normal curriculum for thinking skills development (Swartz and Parks, 1994) and ACTS – Activating Children's Thinking Skills, McGuinness, 1999).

The review found that several classroom evaluation studies had successfully linked teaching thinking methodologies with learning outcomes both in the short and the longer term, such as CASE, though not all interventions were equally successful. The more successful approaches tended to have a strong theoretical underpinning, well-designed and contextualised materials, explicit pedagogy and good teacher support.

McGuiness also found that information and communication technologies could be linked to the thinking skills framework in several ways and provided a tool for enhancing children's understanding and powers of reasoning through exploratory environments/microworlds, multi-media and hypermedia. Networked communication (local and wide area) provided special opportunities for collaborative learning.

Much of the research on the efficacy of teaching thinking had been conducted under optimal learning conditions. Problems with scaling up and transferring the effects to everyday classrooms were identified. In particular, it was noted that the more successful were characterised by explicit models of teacher development and teacher support.

What McGuinness did not identify in her survey was thinking skills and problem-solving activities that were **intrinsic** to the subjects under study, making them an inclusive way of life in classrooms. These are the methods that will be detailed in Chapter 7 under the heading of CPS (cognitive process strategies or 'engage brain' strategies).

The revised National Curriculum (DfEE, 1999) incorporated six key skills (communication, application of number, information technology, working with others, improving own learning and performance, problem solving and thinking skills. These thinking skills were exemplified and extended for pupils with more significant learning difficulties in 'Developing Skills' (QCA, 2001). Here, it states,

> Thinking combines the related structures and processes of perception, memory, forming ideas, language and use of symbols – the basic cognitive skills which underlie the ability to reason, to learn and to solve problems. . . . For pupils with learning difficulties, the development of thinking skills also involves working on sensory awareness, perception and early cognitive skills.
>
> (QCA, 2001, 11)

The National Curriculum now stresses that when pupils use thinking skills, they focus on 'knowing how' to learn as well as 'knowing what' to learn.

In 2002, DfES introduced the initiative Teaching and Learning in Foundation subjects at Key Stage 3 that sought to improve the teaching and learning methods. Its main focus was to emphasise the teaching of thinking skills, offering challenging questioning and making assessment serve learning. They were beginning to catch up with what had been going on in a wide range of schools prior to the Education Reform Act (ERA, 1988).

A word or two of warning is relevant here.

> Thinking skills' programmes enjoy a periodic popularity and seem to provide an antidote for teachers to the instrumentalism of prescribed curricula as they address more general aims of education. However, along with most other curriculum innovations, they usually fail to make a lasting impact or become established within school systems.
>
> (Leat, 1999)

TASC strategy training

Belle Wallace was an LEA adviser in Essex in the 1980s and then a consultant educator in Kwa Zulu Natal. She set about dealing with similar issues, and the work led her to establish the TASC project – 'Thinking Actively in a Social Context' – using the TASC problem-solving wheel. The wheel was used to give pupils strategy training in how to approach tasks and problems and is now used in thousands of schools worldwide. Belle with colleagues has produced a wide range of books containing examples of TASC that can be used in many different classrooms across the age ranges, for example Wallace (2002).

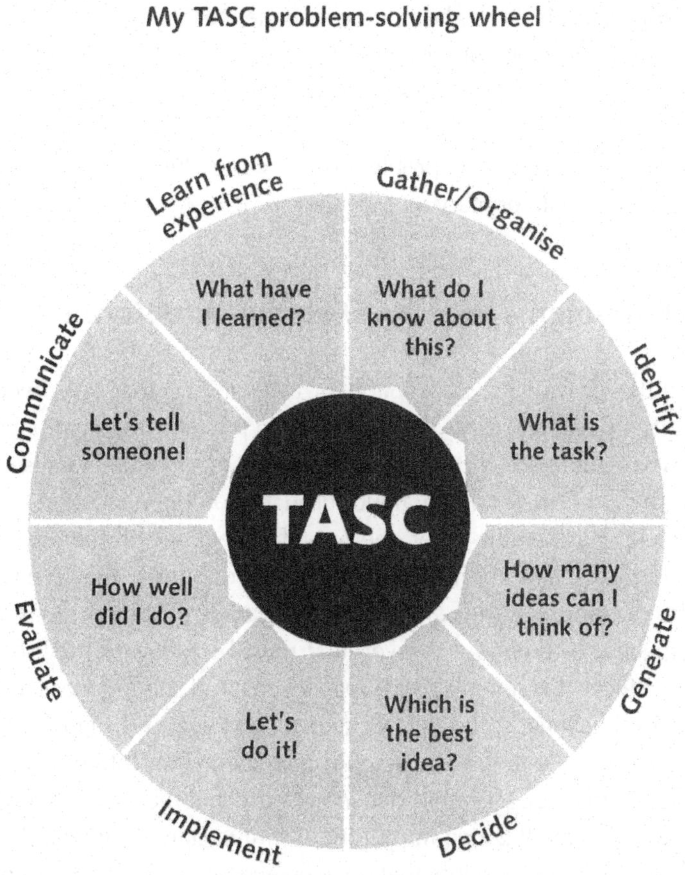

My TASC problem-solving wheel

Figure 6.2 The TASC Wheel. www.nace.co.uk

Infusion strategy

Wrestling with similar issues, Swartz and Parks (1994) in the United States also developed a strategic approach with primary and secondary pupils. They called these 'graphic organisers' to aid problem finding, decision making and problem solving. The pupils are given an example problem, and they work through the steps in resolving it with the teacher and then are given a blank organiser and a curriculum-based problem to practice the strategy – the infusion aspect. They do this part in pairs or groups as appropriate.

The linked boxes (graphic organiser) have such headings as

Decision-making – Choosing an energy source

- Why is this decision necessary?
- What are the options?

- What information is there about the consequences?
- How important are the consequences?
- What option is best in the light of the consequences?

The authors list dozens of typical problem-based curriculum topics across the subject areas and age ranges both primary and secondary.

Thinkback strategy – peer questioning and tutoring

Lockhead (2001) provided a description of a technique that had been shown to improve pupils' intellectual skills. It is based upon pupils working in pairs collaboratively. Even when adults solve complex problems, they often talk themselves through the process. This process of talking aloud through a problem solution is encouraged in one of the pupils whilst the other one provides feedback on the performance and questions the process. He calls it 'Thinkback'. It is economic in that it requires no special apparatus or resources and can be used in a variety of subject areas and settings. It is a very specific technique, however, that must be followed precisely to get the improvement effects. It is not just two pupils talking and sharing ideas about a task.

The book by Lockhead (2001) is written for college and high school teachers 'who would like their students to be more intelligent'. An interesting claim in the light of evidence that suggests that our inherited capability is relatively stable and if born with average intelligence in propitious circumstances, we tend to remain in that category. Could it be possible that an average student might, with the aid of the strategies in this book, gain a higher IQ rating and become a 'high average' or even a 'more able' student? Lockhead claims that his studies of thousands of students using 'Thinkback' show that they do grow more intelligent and perform better on tests and in graduate studies confirmed other evidence that intelligence is not fixed at birth.

However, is the book about using the intelligence we have more effectively and efficiently in the undertaking of college assignments exploiting our capacity to the full? If so, does this suggest that the social environment and the education process up to that point have not enabled students to learn to cope with work in the higher levels of education? If this question were raised in the context of education in the UK, experience in teaching in schools and universities would result in the answer being in the affirmative. Could this also be the case in the USA or at least in Conway, Massachusetts, where Jack Lockhead works? From the statements he makes about education, it would appear so.

The author states,

> Thinkback spans the wide gap between unstructured constructivist style instruction and lock-step memorisation drills. Using Thinkback can convert a

teacher-centred rote mastery lesson into an intellectually challenging student-centred exploration, whilst at the same time maintaining specific content mastery objectives.

(Lockhead, 2001, 8)

Thinkback itself is a modification of talking aloud, a metacognitive strategy based upon his earlier work with Arthur Whimbey. It can be used in a range of subjects in the mastery of basic facts and vocabulary as in thinking about complex relationships amongst abstract concepts. It also can be used to enhance creative problem solving, and even though the teacher leads the process, by determining the content, the students have autonomy in their learning. Thus they are developing the higher-order cognitive skills of planning, regulating and evaluating their own learning (SRL).

Although the work has been going on since the 1970s, it is a strategy that has found its time. It was an attempt to break down the formal, didactic and doctrinaire approach to education undertaken in 90 per cent of classrooms. The book is divided into eight chapters. The first two introduce the strategy, and then the rest illustrate how it may be applied in subjects such as science, mathematics, language arts and social sciences. Some powerful evidence in support of the approach is quoted from Xavier University and Morningside Academy. For example, at Morningside, three months of instruction in Thinking Aloud Pair Problem Solving (TAPPS) followed by five months of mathematics instruction produced substantial gains on the Iowa Tests of Basic Skills, and some students improved by four grade levels.

Xavier is a small, historically Black university in New Orleans. The Xavier program does not use Thinkback but rather its main ingredient, TAPPS. In the early 1970s, Xavier's record in training students for the sciences was solidly second-rate. Only a handful of students, four or five a year, were making the leap to medical school. Xavier's president decided things had to change. He turned to J.S. Carmichael, an energetic young chemistry professor, and named him the pre-med adviser.

Carmichael and his colleague attacked the problem energetically, picking up information and teaching hints wherever they could find them. They tested a range of methods in the classroom, searching for the special combination of elements that would work and found Arthur Whimbey's book, *Intelligence Can Be Taught* (1975), and he soon became involved with the Xavier effort.

Whimbey defined intelligence as a skill at interpreting materials accurately and mentally reconstructing the relationships. This can be taught much like skiing or playing the piano. Forcing students to think about every step in the problem-solving process and providing feedback as they go along can be used to correct their bad reasoning habits. One method was to pair students up and have one solve a mathematics problem aloud as the partner critiqued the analysis.

In 1977, Xavier launched a summer programme called SOAR (Stress On Analytical Reasoning). It was aimed at students who had not yet started college. The programme immediately became the foundation of Xavier's educational uplift efforts. The heart of the programme was intense work on reading skills, mathematics, vocabulary building and exercises in abstract reasoning.

The approach worked. In 1993, forty-nine graduates of Xavier were accepted to medical schools. The following year, the number rose to fifty-five and the year after that, to seventy-seven. This put Xavier far out in front of any other university in America in the number of blacks placed in medical school. The number continued to rise. It was ninety-six in 1998 and over one hundred in 1999 (Lockhead, 2001).

Xavier's most impressive accomplishment, however, was not in the number of medical school slots it had won, but in its success in fostering an atmosphere of achievement; the typical SOAR student gained about three grade levels on the Nelson-Denny Reading Test and the equivalent of 120 points on the Scholastic Aptitude Test (Cose, 1997, 55–57).

As measured by medical school slots won, Xavier's improvement had been more than twenty-fold or 2,000 per cent. Yet, medical school acceptances are only a small part of the gains at Xavier. Many other majors made similar gains (www.xula.edu). The success shows what is possible. But it also shows us the level of effort required. Although an individual can raise reading and SAT scores in a month of hard work, an institution takes far longer to show progress. The Xavier story unfolded over 20 years.

The basic thesis is that humans learn much by the process of imitation. However, thinking is not an observable event and so is impossible to learn by imitation. The Thinkback strategy is based on the notion of video playback in sports training. The person doing the thinking – the problem solver – is paired with a listener and thinks aloud. Together, they work over the problem, making the thinking about it a slow and noisy process so that it is easy to observe and question.

The problem solver reads the problem aloud and begins the solution, for example, 'If the circle is taller than the square and the cross is shorter than the square . . . I'll put my finger on the circle . . . then I'll read the problem again'.

The listener might say, 'Why did you decide to put your finger on the circle?" This identifies a hidden reason or thought process that should have been made explicit – a stealth thought.

In this special pairs work, the listener's role is crucial in continually checking for accuracy and in demanding constant vocalisation. It is an extension of the 'think – pair – share' strategy, which is becoming widely used in schools because pupils frequently do not know what they think until they try to explain themselves to someone else. Feuerstein (1995) demonstrated a similar technique in his mediated learning exposition.

- The Problem Solver strives to avoid stealth thinking
- The Listener tries to determine how the problem solver is thinking.

(Lockhead, 2001, 21)

The result of Thinkback practice is to improve critical analysis and reasoning and the ability to explain the logic of an argument. The difference is that it is the students who do the mediation. The general advice to teachers is that the strategy should be part of their teaching practice, not all of it. It needs to be used judiciously by the skilled teacher to supplement other methods, including direct transmission of information and explanations.

Listening strategies. Skills practice examples

1   Each group of five pupils is asked to appoint an explainer. The explainer is given a simple diagram suitable for the age group. The rest of the group have sheets of paper on which they draw the diagram according to the explainer's instructions, but they are not allowed to see the diagram. On completion, they show and discuss what they have drawn. Each member can have a chance to be the explainer, and each time, a different diagram is given out. Plenary to discuss the results and what improves them.

2   Pairs of pupils sit opposite each other knee to knee. One of them describes to the other a little bit of their life story or a holiday or event they enjoyed. The other listens carefully, and then some of them offer to tell the class 'the story'. The tellers report on the success of their reporter. This is often used in settings where pupils do not know each other well to help them become acquainted.

3   The pupils sit in a semicircle, and the teacher starts the session at one side and whispers a message into the ear of the first listener. L1 whispers this to L2 and so on. The final member of the group then tells the rest what the 'message' was. This is compared with what was originally said and a discussion of listening and rumour can usefully follow.

Active listening means, focusing attention on what the other person has to say in words, actions, and feelings. It is more than listening to just the content of the message. It is also trying to understand what is behind the content.

These are some of the blocks to good listening:

* Feeling that you must answer or come to a decision about what is being presented to you
* Evaluating what is being presented to you
* Being hurried and listening on the run
* Hearing what you want to hear – selecting what stands out for you
* Having something to say – and wanting to take time away from the speaker

- Other things on your mind – those things fill all available space so there is no room for what the speaker has to say
- Disagreeing with the other person's point of view
- Looking away from the speaker or staring at the speaker

Accelerated learning (AL) strategy

The original concept emerged from the work of Philip Adey and Michael Shayer on science education in schools during the 1980s. They ran projects in which one lesson per fortnight was reserved for talking with the pupils about what had been learnt and how it had been learnt. The idea was to develop language and metacognitive skills in science. It was found that in Cognitive Acceleration through Science Education (CASE) projects, not only did the pupils learn more than controls, but they retained it better and understood it more. The effects were not however limited to science; they spread to better results for the CASE pupils in English and maths GCSEs (Shayer and Adey, 2002).

The principle underlying AL is that the methods develop the thinking ability of the pupils. This includes knowledge acquisition, concept change and the development of processing power. AL is intended to encourage the concept of lifelong learners. There are three main principles:

Cognitive conflict involves stimulating thinking and motivation to learn by offering cognitive or intellectual challenges of moderate difficulty. This is accompanied by support in the form of leading questions and invitations to discuss problems and ideas, looking at them from different angles and so on. This work could be in the form of class discussion, group or pairs work.

In order to promote discussion, the learning environment is supportive so that pupils are not discouraged from putting forward their ideas. The teachers model fairness, consistency and a problem-solving approach.

Social construction of knowledge and understanding the work is based on Vygotsky's (1978) principles – understanding develops during social communication and then becomes internalised by individuals; this is promoted by the discussion and 'group think'.

Bridging involves developing new thought processes, where a range of associated ideas is taught and solutions generated which apply to new contexts.

AL in popular use is said to be structured on 'learning cycles'.

- At the beginning of the task, the pupils are introduced to the 'big picture'.
- The learning outcomes are then described; sometimes these are written on cards.
- The learning input follows and may involve visual, auditory and kinaesthetic activities. The student is then asked, 'What are the most important things for you?'

- Take five key words and sing them to a tune. (!)
- Next the pupils demonstrate what they have learned to the rest of the class.
- They review together what they have done and learnt, and finally, it is all linked back to the 'big picture'.

As can be seen, many influences, such as Brain Gym, collaborative learning, reflection, active learning and cognitive challenge, have all been bound into AL. The research on its more general effectiveness is still awaited, but pupils and staff enjoy the collaborative enterprise, and it should have some long-term gains in promotion of language skills. The main criticism is that AL in this form has been adapted to fit in with the transmission model of teaching.

CoRT thinking skills strategies de Bono (1974, 1983)

Edward de Bono (1983) developed the CoRT training programme (Cognitive Research Trust) for developing ways of thinking and problem solving using a wide range of strategies such as

CAF – Consider All Factors
Yes, No and PO
PMI – Plus Minus and Interesting
C and S – Consequences and Sequels
AGO – Aims, Goals and Objectives
FIP – First Important Priorities
APC – Alternatives, Possibilities and Choices
OPV – Other Point of View

The programme was published as a series of pamphlets with teachers' notes and examples of some initial results. The results across a range of schools showed that those trained on the programme were able to produce twice as many reasons, answers and solutions to general problems as those without CoRT training. They were more effective thinkers and decision makers.

Even after one CoRT session with a class of 12–13-year-olds, the difference was marked. For example, an essay was set – *Do you think there should be special weekend prisons for minor offenders?*

Result: Arguments put forward for and against the proposal:

Class 1 (CoRT training session) total: 200
Class 2 Control class (no CoRT training session) total: 109

The materials were originally designed for secondary age pupils and were used in 350 schools. However, primary schools (8–11-year-olds) also wanted to try them, and their results were very successful, as the pupils were more flexible and responsive to the methods and enjoyed them much more than some of the older pupils.

The whole CoRT programme consists of 60 training lessons with teachers' notes and pupils' notes in A5 double-fold pages. It is also possible to use the materials selectively as one-off lessons.

Example of yes – no – po pupils' notes

1 Say 'yes' or 'no' to the following seven questions:
   Five plus six equals twelve
   Ice floats in water and so on.
2 Judgment
   When you judge something to be true or right, you say, 'Yes'.
   When you judge something to be untrue or wrong, you say, 'No'.
   When you are unsure, you can say, 'Maybe', 'Perhaps' or 'Don't know'.

You may not want to judge something or want to treat it creatively, in which case, 'Po' can be used. 'Po' comes from 'poetry', 'suppose', 'hypothesis'.

3 A list of statements is given to apply Yes, No Po to.
4 To apply po, use a two-step operation – Do I want to judge this? Do I want to treat it creatively?
5 More statement examples are given to judge.
6 Make up a deliberate po statement about
   cars, school, food, hair

Learning styles and strategies

What we observe in schools is a tendency for the learning mode or style to be through the spoken and written word, and different attempts have been made to extend these, including through notions of learning style. These other modes of learning and responding are particularly important for pupils who have literacy difficulties.

In a review and meta-analysis of research on cognitive and learning styles, Riding and Rayner (1998) found that we do not really have multiple cognitive styles but a preference for or bias towards the ways in which we deal with situations. These apparently all boil down to an orthogonal model in which sequential processing (verbal) is linked to simultaneous processing (visual). We all need to use both as and when appropriate, so it would be damaging to learning potential to assert that a particular learner is a kinaesthetic or a visual learner, as some have done, and then restrict their inputs and outputs through one of these. In these circumstances, it is the disadvantaged learner who will be doubly disadvantaged.

Conclusion

The changes in literacy teaching suggested in this chapter are easy for teachers to try in their different subject areas so they can evaluate the results for themselves.

At the older age ranges, higher-order literacy teaching still needs to be undertaken with a wide range of pupils to overcome the early methods that have failed them. The three decades of an overfilled curriculum requiring transmission or content ramming methods have left few opportunities for deep learning. It needs to be changed. The designers ignored the principles of effective learning and teaching. This is not to deny that some teachers have been trying hard to modify the approaches.

There is a need to test the DfE guidelines, not just follow them. Many of the guidelines are drawn up from adults' ideas about steps towards good literacy from the point of view of capable learners and what children should be able to do. Unfortunately, these techniques do not meet the wide range of needs that many children, such as the disadvantaged, have and can actually cause them to underachieve more and fail.

In addition, as was shown in Chapter 5, it is unreasonable to expect pupils to write fluent, thoughtful narrative and creative compositions when their basic handwriting and spelling skills are not fit for purpose. But they can be improved, as shown in Chapter 5, and then it will be found that their compositional skills need improving because they have missed so many opportunities for deep and thoughtful learning. A key constituent in compositional development is formal talk, not chat. The higher-order reading strategies detailed provide opportunities for this as well as for deep learning.

The final section details strategic approaches to teaching and learning and the resources that the different authors offer.

Inclusion, differentiation, personalisation, challenge and enrichment are the hopes and claims for all pupils. It is the English model, but in practice, it is not being achieved. The reason seems to me to be that there is a conflict between the pedagogy that would promote it and the pedagogy that has been forced upon schools. Pedagogy is the subject of Chapter 7.

Pedagogy

Practical teaching strategies across the curriculum and age ranges

 Introduction

This research began in the 1970s when there was widespread concern about behaviour problems in schools (DES, 1979). Experienced teachers as well as students in training were looking for help and the Learning Difficulties Research Project was set up in 1981 with some pump-priming funding from a School's Council project run by Ralph Callow. The purpose was to promote and publish teacher research in classrooms. Many of the teachers were on B.Ed in-service programmes that had started in 1973 or had followed 'Custom Courses' from 1975 specifically designed to meet a local need defined by a school, a teachers' centre leader or an LEA advisor/inspector in the five surrounding LEAs. The first publication was *Learning and Teaching Strategies – Study Skills* (1981, 1991). Then an appraisal project results were published *Evaluation and Enhancement of Teaching Performance* (1983). These were followed by *Managing Behaviour Problems* (1984), a dyslexia series (TRTS 1983–87) and *The Special Needs of More Able Pupils* (1985). These booklets became coursework materials and guidance for ITE students, and publishers also became interested.

The findings on behaviour problems for example showed the behaviour could be improved through positive management techniques some of which are described in Chapter 3. It also became clear that motivation and interest in subject learning was an equal contributor to gaining attention and maintaining a quiet, disciplined environment. Motivation thus became a key construct for investigation, and it was the concept of 'cognitive dissonance' (Festinger, 1957) that was relevant. Festinger had found that when learning was open-ended and the learner did not know the answer, then the human mind sought to make closure and find a resolution of the unknown. According to Kelly (1955), the human was a scientific problem solver from birth. In schools, however, the model was that the teacher would present a summary of what was to be known about a topic with advance organisers and the pupil's task was to write it down, memorise it, and recall it for tests. Little was open ended and left for the pupil to discover, and many pupils with other concerns seldom saw the relevance in what they were supposed to be learning (SED, 1978). They express similar concerns today.

In this early period, there was a major change from the tripartite system of the 1944 Education Act to the introduction of comprehensive education (1970) in the majority of the state sector. No specific training had been offered to support teachers through these changes, and so it was not surprising that so many needs were becoming exposed. Mixed-ability classes were set up in many of these new settings, but not every teacher was able to cope. In the UK, there was a dearth of research to fall back on to help them and so it was a period when researching practice became essential. Teacher educators were in a good position to help do this. They assessed practice competence by visiting students in schools to observe them teach. They taught about teaching, however not necessarily *how* to teach. They needed to build a pedagogy. Was it an art or a science? Opinions differed.

Practice supervisors would discuss the student teacher's progress with the class or subject teacher and agree on a grade – pass or fail. Later, this became distinction, pass or fail. The extraordinary thing observed in Practice Examination Boards in several different colleges was that many tutors and supervisory teachers could not define the criteria for the grade they had given – they just 'knew'. Some claimed to 'know' the standard in the first ten minutes of a lesson, but there were no agreed criteria that defined 'good' or effective teaching and so the colleges began to research and develop them. Even Edgar Stones's (1979) *Psychopedagogy*, Dennis Childs's popular book on the *Psychology of Teaching* (1991) and *Good Teaching Observed* (DES, 1985), all fell short.

When teachers were asked for their definitions, they would say good teaching was to 'cover the syllabus' or 'develop the child to his or her full potential' and 'meet the needs of society'. These are typical aims, but the role of pedagogy is to show how these may be achieved.

Pedagogical theory and practice

A history of teaching in England and Wales showed that over two centuries and especially since mass education in 1897, it had changed and developed not only in content but also in methods that teachers used. They had moved from rote training and the 19th-century monitorial system to state education for all. It was a period when memorising techniques were the priority. Rote learning of basic skills was used to develop literacy. Rote learning of the scriptures was deemed to imbue children with moral standards, and rote learning of poetry developed culture.

Colleges for primary teacher training were established and best practice began to be disseminated along with influences from abroad. The curriculum was broadened from basic skills tuition and some useful craft skills for boys (gardening) and girls (sewing) and so on to include history and literature. Private schools still existed, and they tended to lead the curriculum expansion to attract customers. Methods changed, and more time was devoted to developing understanding in subject learning and the acquisition of facts. Teachers presented a digest of the content to be learned, and reading to learn also became a main method. Over the 20th century, teachers developed more interesting strategies and techniques to improve pupils' fact learning of subjects.

The primary school ethos developed differently, as already discussed in Chapter 5, but graduated towards the secondary school 'content ramming' method. Initially, secondary school teachers were untrained. They merely had to have a subject degree from a university, but it became evident they also needed training to teach children more effectively. This was especially the case when the tripartite system was introduced and when, after the war, emergency training courses were set up for returning soldiers wanting to enter the profession.

As teaching skills improved, attention was turned to pupils' needs and how these were not always being met by the methods then in use. This shortfall increased as the comprehensive system was introduced. At this period, the 1970s, motivation and intellectual challenge began to be the focus of a range of exploratory programmes to find even more effective teaching and learning strategies. Organisations to support the programmes and their pupils were also established, including NACE, and more problem-based learning was investigated initially to meet the needs of the more able.

These changes in teaching method over the century were by analogy likened to changes in the stages of intellectual development of children defined by Piaget (1952). These were from pre-operational intuitive thinking (rote era) to concrete operations (content/product learning era) to abstract operations (investigative problem-based learning). This enabled the two central objectives in teaching (Montgomery, 1981) in the 'new era' to be defined as

- To enable students to think efficiently
- To express those thoughts succinctly

These were to be the core theme in every subject and skills area of the school curriculum and at each of the age levels beginning in pre-school. The methods and problems would take account of the children's level of intellectual development and provide a curriculum of strategies that could be used to train teachers. These were termed 'Cognitive Process Strategies' (CPS) or 'brain engage' techniques (see Figure 7.1).

The developmental context referred to development in perception, emotion, personality; physical, intellectual and language, motivation; and social skills. It was evident

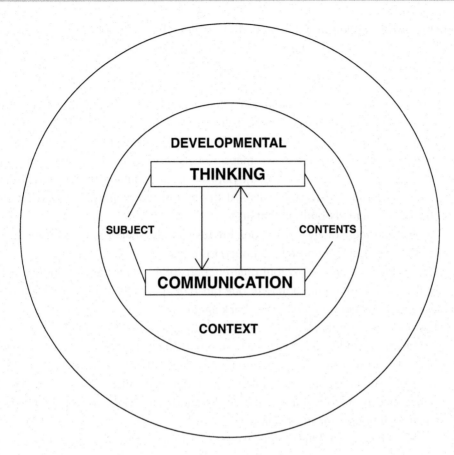

Figure 7.1 A model of modern teaching

for example that many individuals entered the adult world without having developed beyond Piaget's concrete operational level of thinking and still do.

Boiling theory down to bare essentials in this way was necessary because teachers in their daily decision-making do not have time to riffle through a series of research abstracts in the mind; they need some overarching principles or key constructs to guide their daily teaching activities. Critics of the 'traditional versus progressive' debate in this period argued that process methods advocated by the progressives were empty of content and therefore useless. There is a whole range of methods that are content free, but these have specific purposes for dealing with behaviour, mediation and problem issues, such as in *Ways and Means Problem Solving* (Bowers and Wells, 1988), *Circle Time* (Moseley, 1991) and *Let's Cooperate* (Masheder, 1988).

CPS was content-dense as befitted the needs of a teaching curriculum and designed to be inclusive. The problem was that the examples had to be invented to help teachers understand the general principles. The initial ideas were set out in *Teaching Thinking Skills in the School Curriculum* (Montgomery, 1983b) as in the following examples.

- Environmental and social studies – project Homes. In a study of homes, it is usual to consider homes on stilts. Instead of showing pictures and drawings of them and talking and writing about them, the following was suggested. Show pictures of the landscape / give maps, details of vegetation, monsoon periods and tools available, and then set the pupils in small groups to discuss and design a suitable home (boats and stilts). At the end of the plenary, reveal what the inhabitants actually build in that area.
- Design and technology – using one broadsheet newspaper and half a metre of sticky tape, design a house big enough to sit in.
- Physical education – using four different parts of the body, move from one side of the room to the other and over one piece of apparatus. Then, with a partner, use four parts between you to get back again.
- History – you are the master builder in an area in mediaeval England. A local merchant would like a new house built on the main street to be consistent with her wealth and status. Examine the pictures and records of the period and the ways in which the people lived then and design her house. Research and compare the costs of the building materials then and now. (Visit a local town that has mediaeval houses for study purposes.)
- English – pairs of children produce a holiday brochure for their town or suburb. They begin with an analysis of the style, content and format of typical holiday brochures. Their brief includes developing costed, all-inclusive 'packages' bringing people to the area for a range of seasonal breaks based upon actual prices 'at the time of going to press'.
- Science – in the context of the study of solvents and solutions, the children were given an envelope whose contents they must investigate. It is clearly a mixture, but of what? (Sand and salt.) Could it be harmful? They had to design apparatus that could be used to separate the mixture and then use it to see if it would work. An hour is usually necessary to complete the task and needs to be followed by a good 20-minute debriefing. Even after this, a lot of the pupils like to return in a lunch hour to just work through the experiment again, especially if the problem of how to get clean sand and salt is left open.
- Maths – triangles. Instead of explaining that there are three types of triangles, naming them and then giving examples to measure, draw and verify, pairs of pupils are given a page of 20 small triangles unlabelled to work out their similarities and differences, record results and suggest names. Reveal/confirm formal names and differences at the end of the session.

The methods were designed to be used with mixed ability classes to include all the children (Montgomery, 1990) and represent the 'English model'.

Another feature that had to be considered was the different teaching methods and contents required for concept development and concept attainment. In the early years of schooling, much of teaching is concerned with concept development so that play and experiential learning are key methods. Concept attainment is when we use the concepts we already know to help form higher-order, often more abstract concepts (justice, peace and so on). The concept of apples, pears, bananas and strawberries enable us to attain the category concept of 'fruit'. Over time, we build up hierarchies of concepts from banana to fruits to the whole class of plants. A lot of later teaching is about concept attainment, hierarchies of concepts (constructs) and protocols (schema). Teachers can explain the higher-order concepts (didactics), or children can deduce them for themselves, given the right sort of grounding. Constructing meaning for oneself makes learning more secure and interesting and fits better into what we already know or helps adjust it to take in the new ideas.

Whilst these developments were taking place, other adventurers were developing their own strategies and schemes. Two of the most significant were the 'Maidenhead Group' of teachers led by Johanna Raffan and including Deborah Eyre and the Essex LEA curriculum project led by Belle Wallace. Both projects were developed because of concerns that more able children were not being sufficiently stretched by the methods then in use. These new methods were problem-based learning projects that were used to stimulate and interest groups withdrawn from the main classroom. From these experiences, Belle Wallace went on to develop her inclusive and strategic TASC learning approach (Teaching Actively in a Social Context). Raffan, Eyre and Wallace later all became leaders of NACE.

Didactics

Didactics in most countries means pedagogy or teaching methods, and there is as yet little distinction made between types of pedagogy. The traditional transmission mode is the accepted norm. In an OECD study, Skilbeck (1989) found that 90 per cent of education worldwide took place in a didactic format; Wallace and Eriksson (2006) confirmed it. This was termed a 19th-century model of the educated person (Paul, 1990), who is to be taught more or less *what* to think not *how* to think; it is important to focus on significant details, definitions, explanations, rules and guidelines. Thus educated, literate people are fundamentally repositories of content analogous to an encyclopaedia or a data bank, directly comparing situations in the world with facts in storage. This is the true believer, and discussions are detail-orientated and factual. This also described the 'content ramming' or product-based curriculum and methods in operation in the UK.

Paul described the 21st-century model as critical theory mode in which students are taught *how*, not *what* to think. An educated literate person is thus fundamentally a repository of strategies, principles, concepts and insights embedded in processes of thought. Much of what is known is constructed as needed. This describes in part the model of modern teaching proposed earlier in which the methods are also developmental and help the pre-operational and concrete operational thinker to move towards being a creative thinker, problem solver and lifelong learner. Students' becoming critical thinkers is just one of its goals.

> Critical thinking is reasonable reflective thinking that is focused on deciding what to believe or do.
>
> (Ennis and Norris, 1990, 1)

Critical thinking theory has been widely adopted in more progressive programmes in higher education institutions since the 1990s (Gibbs, 1994; Fry et al., 2015) and is based in an informal thinking approach rather than formal logic and reasoning originally only taught at university. Coles and Robinson (1991) described related developments in education for teaching in the UK. These were Feuerstein's (1980) *Instrumental Enrichment* and Blagg et al.'s (1993) *Somerset Thinking Skills Course*, which was based on it, the *Oxford Schools Project*, de Bono's (1983) CoRT programme and Lipman's (1990) *Philosophy for Children*.

They were all to a degree inclusive and based in informal thinking, especially in English lessons. All suffered from the same disadvantage in that they were 'bolt-on' provisions that needed significant skill and experience in making the skills transferable. They have all faded except *Philosophy for Children* with more able pupils because it is embedded in everyday stories, issues and events. Another reason for their disappearance has of course been the implementation of the national curriculum that gobbled up the time.

Another element of these initiatives was that they were in a sense 'top down'; they were handed down from the university professors and were not arising from the teaching profession itself. The theory became more a technique to be applied rather than an implicit theory of teaching and learning that guided everything that teachers would plan and do in whatever subject they taught and at every age level.

Learning

Hirst (1975) maintained that we are our concepts and that if we teach it assumes that the learners have learned or are in the process of doing so. The problem is that it cannot exactly be observed; the only evidence is to be inferred from behaviour, a performance, verbal recall or graphic and written responses. What is often missed is that in the teaching and learning process, attitudes and emotions are also learned because running alongside the school curriculum is this 'hidden' curriculum and the transference of ideas, emotions, attitudes and skills.

Autocratic teachers and parents 'teach' children how to become autocratic too. A coercive system of high stakes education encourages teachers to become coercive in order to meet the league table targets and Ofsted requirements so that children are put under pressure and the vulnerable with no escape can become ill. This is in the presence of cyberbullying and may even be teaching bullies to do it.

Emphasis in school improvement is often laid upon pupils having respect for others and for difference. But it is teachers who need to model this in the way they treat pupils on a daily basis and in how they treat each other. Fairness is also highly valued by pupils (Kerry, 1983; Pomerantz and Pomerantz, 2003), and they must experience it in the daily classroom as they learn.

Disadvantaged learners

An early study by Weber (1982) addressed the teaching needs of underachievers and those with learning disabilities in Toronto schools. He found they showed the following difficulties, but they could be taught strategies for dealing with them.

* Identifying starting points
* Attending to detail
* Forward planning
* Systematic exploratory behaviour
* Reasoning and deciding
* Establishing and testing hypotheses
* Divergent thinking

In the Learning Difficulties Research Project studies over several decades, similar learning difficulties were found amongst disadvantaged and underachieving pupils. The teachers would describe the random behaviours that pupils used in approaching curriculum topics and problems in general and their trial-and-error responses. They needed to be specifically taught strategies and protocols in context that would help them learn and solve problems.

At the extreme end of these 'shotgun' behaviours are those with ADHD, and their treatment involves 'pause, think, act' strategy training, visual cueing with yellow and red card systems and so on (Montgomery, 2015). However, there is a continuum on which pupils are to be found and disadvantage places many pupils lower on this scale than the average learner. Because they have been very poor, confined perhaps to a single room with others, hungry and left to their own devices, there will have been little opportunity to explore and gain task mastery at even simple levels. They will have had little opportunity to develop coordination skills preparatory for writing or to learn to control their behaviour at a command from the teacher. They are disorganised in the complex environment of schools and lack the required attentional skills and so miss much of what is going on. The behaviour and social skills are more typical of a much younger child. Temper tantrums are typical of two-year-olds, not ten-year-olds, but may be the only way they have learned to gain attention or get their own way.

An extract from a year 10 science lesson observed,

> 11.25 a.m. 15 pupils (half classes) enter the room at random intervals, throwing bags down, shouting at each other. Boys spread themselves out and make sneering comments at some of the girls who swear at them. Others are checking their phones or fiddling with the gas taps. The teacher arrives late from another lesson, shouts for quiet and asks the question, 'Now, do you remember what we were doing last lesson?'. Several shout him an answer and the rest mainly ignore him. He demands that they must put up their hands to answer questions. Some hands go up but he takes a called out answer. Squabbles begin.

Chaos of varying intensity reigned throughout the lesson, and little or no learning took place. The pupils' behaviour was reminiscent of a class of very large reception-year children from disorganised families. (The 5 Star Coaching system put this situation to rights in two sessions.)

This type of disorganised behaviour was typical of many young children on entering school from disadvantaged backgrounds in the Inner London Education Authority (ILEA) in the 1980s. They were placed in nurture groups with two adults to about eight children for a term to settle them and teach them the basic school and social learning skills. The nurture groups were disbanded when 'secondary school trained leaders and inspectors took over and did not agree with the project' (Bannathan, 1998, personal communication). However, ten years later, Marion Boxall found all her old records and followed up the nurture group children to see what had happened to them. Not surprisingly, in comparison to those who had not been in the projects, they were well integrated and achieving (Bannathan and Boxall, 1998), rather like in Weikart's Perry Pre-school project. Since then, some more nurture groups have been set up not only in primary but also in secondary schools. In the long term, nurture groups save the education and social system money. It is this long-term perspective for education that is needed in the political sphere.

Criteria for effective learning (De Corte, 1995, 2013)

For over a decade, Eric de Corte had been researching the psychology of what he called 'Instruction' and shared these findings at an ECHA (European Council for High Ability) conference in 1994 in Nijmegen. It was an important contribution to constructivist theory and so useful for teachers to know. His findings were that in order to be effective, learning experiences needed to be

- **Constructive** – and obey the constructivist principles that learners must be given opportunities to construct their own learning. Students are not passive recipients of information; in order to learn, they have to participate in the construction of their own knowledge and skills.
- **Situated** – be connected in time and place and have relevance to other meaningful learning events. It means that learning essentially takes place in interaction with the social and cultural environment.
- **Cumulative** – it is on the basis of what they already know that pupils construct new knowledge and derive new meanings and skills.
- **Self-organised** – learning is best when self-organised. This is related to the metacognitive nature of effective learning, especially the managing and monitoring of learning activities (self-regulation).
- **Goal-oriented** – Learning is generally goal oriented, although a small amount of learning is incidental. An explicit awareness of and orientation towards a goal facilitates effective and meaningful learning, especially when the learners can choose the goal and define their own objectives.
- **Individual** – Finally, learning is individually different. Individual differences in ability, skills, needs, interests, learning style and so on mean that we each construct our learning of the same experience in different ways.

It was found that when applied to many lessons observed in schools at the time and since (Montgomery, 2002, 2017c) they did not meet most of these criteria. In addition, many pupils were still complaining that they could not see the relevance of what they were doing and often said, 'It's boring, Miss', 'Do we have to do this?'

Cognitive process pedagogy

These are a set of teaching activities that constructivist teachers engage in and were developed with and taught to teachers in training over two decades and since then by distance learning on master's programmes. These are now published as Study Guides (Montgomery, 2019 at www.ldrp.org.uk).

Initially four then six and now ten CPS have been identified and adapted for use in classrooms by all teachers to promote inclusion and personalisation. They are essentially developmental 'brain engage' strategies. Metacognition in which we think about our thinking is also closely involved. Flavell (1979) found that this was a key to improving intelligence, and it is an important 'tool' for reflective teaching and learning in constructivism.

The cognitive curriculum

- Challenging questioning – to provoke thought and reasoning, it involves more open questions
- Cognitive process study and research skills in all subject areas
- Teaching thinking skills and encouraging investigative learning
- Reflective teaching and learning
- Real-world problem-based learning
- Developing creativity
- Games and simulations
- Experiential learning
- Language experience methods
- Self-regulated learning strategies and opportunities

In the model in Figure 7.1, the other central objective was to communicate thoughts succinctly. This means that pupil talk and its development is an essential part of the educative process. Schools however are continually falling short in this dimension, according to successive Ofsted reports and chief inspectors. It has become evident however that private schools and the well-known public schools are much better at preparing their pupils to engage with confidence and self-esteem in debate, communication and social skills. Seven per cent of the population attend private schools, but 47 per cent of those students attain the highest positions in business, the professions, politics and the arts (Sutton Trust, 2018). These figures have not substantially changed over the decades and are raising concerns about social mobility once again.

The talking curriculum

This is a curriculum that emphasises and embeds talking and reflection about learning before writing and recording in a variety of response modes:

- TPS, think – pair – share
- Show and tell
- Explainer time
- Hot seating
- Pupil teaching
- Circle time
- Small group work
- Group problem solving
- Collaborative learning

- Reciprocal teaching
- Peer tutoring
- Thinkback (Lockhead, 2001)
- Role-play, games and drama
- Debates and 'book clubs'
- Presentations and 'teach-ins'
- Poster presentations and discussion
- Exhibitions and demonstrations
- Organised meetings

All these strategies are intimately related to the cognitive curriculum. It is not only the slower learners, underachievers, disadvantaged and twice exceptional with writing difficulties who need to talk things through before they are set to writing them down; all young learners need such opportunities. In solving complex problems, we often talk ourselves through the difficult aspects to keep our thinking on track. Pupils need talk-time not for social chat – they can usually do this well enough – but for formal talk about the subject in hand or a range of topics, and they must have much more practice than they currently enjoy.

When children come from disadvantaged cultural and linguistic environments, the talking approaches are essential. This not only helps vocabulary learning and comprehension but also helps develop presentational skills and abilities and the ability to engage in rational argument. This can help pupils avoid difficult and confrontational episodes with peers and teachers.

Talking approaches can help build skills in composition and organisational abilities. They can be supported by the technique of scaffolding. Direct teaching of **'scaffolds'** can be especially helpful because those from disadvantaged linguistic backgrounds will have had fewer opportunities to learn strategic approaches to assist their learning and understanding. The scaffold provides the inner speech or substance of the metacognitive processes. An example of one type of scaffold is the TASC wheel (see later example).

> Scaffolding thinking consists of supporting student application of a cognitive operation by structuring the execution of that operation with verbal and/or visual prompts . . . they . . . benefit immensely from having their initial attempts to practice a procedure scaffolded until they have internalised the procedure and can execute it on their own.
>
> (Beyer, 1997, 171)

A simple story scaffold that teachers use is 'beginnings – middles – and ends'. Unfortunately, they do not always develop the strategy to the next level and simply say, 'You must use adjectives or some describing words'. The result is the children stuff in an adjective and often the same one each time (e.g., 'It was a dark night.' 'It was a cold, dark night'). A next-phase strategy would instead be to copy some first pages from a range of storybooks, ask pairs to discuss them and suggest what kind of opening or beginning they reveal. Examples are time, place, area, historical period, genre and atmosphere. There are many famous examples at all levels of literacy. The same techniques can be used to define the characters in the story, the main events and finally the endings.

These are many forms of scaffold. In science, we use introduction, method, results, conclusions. Writing a critical review of a book can also reflect the knowledge pupils have gained and can be supported by scaffolding. Teaching how to construct a review for a particular age range can help support their discussions and individual writing. The important feature is for them to understand the audience need. This means that the first task is to present a brief summary of what is being reviewed, as many reading the review may not have read the article or story; then aspects of genre and style may need to be outlined before some positive aspects and then the critical points are presented. A final summary sentence or paragraph is then needed. The aim should be to offer constructive criticism supported by evidence or example, not a diatribe.

In school projects and research dissertations, students need to think not only about the overall structure but also about the structure/scaffold for each chapter. The chapter/section structures will vary, but the side headings should indicate the underlying theme (e.g. issues basis, chronological order, themes). All need a logical sequential structure.

The recording curriculum

Using CPS involves all the learning codes (Munro, 1996) and many different modes of input and output other than writing. These can include mind maps, diagramming, cartooning, PowerPoints, drawing, painting, construction, role-play, videos, film, performances, games, exhibitions and so on.

Examples of the cognitive process strategies

CPS. Challenging questioning

To provoke thought and reasoning, more open questions are necessary. In the ORACLE classroom observation project, Galton et al. (1980) found that less than 1 per cent of teachers' questioning in classrooms required any kind of cognitive challenge. The majority were factual recall questions ('When was the Battle of Hastings?') and pseudo questions such as 'Will you sit down?' meaning, 'Sit down, please'. When challenging questioning was explored in some early appraisal research and

CPD, Montgomery (1983) found that open and challenging questioning was difficult for teachers to manage. This was because when a pupil gave an extended and thoughtful answer, the rest of the class could become restless, as they wanted to give their extended answers. The lone teacher could provoke 30 pupils to want to respond but could not give the time to hear them all and often could not manage the response, so methods needed to be devised to enable those answers to be heard. It was easy to see why recall questions were the most popular. This was how and why the think – pair – share strategy was evolved.

Students in ITT did not always know how to construct cognitively challenging questioning. They had often only experienced it in examination questions that required written answers, so they also needed some help and examples, especially for developing them 'on the hoof'. It was the 'why' questions that most frequently elicited a thoughtful response. Open questions that may ask for a personal response pose a particular problem. Even 'when' and 'where' questions can be modified to elicit more than recall, for example, 'What do you think?' or 'When do you think . . .?' 'What would happen if . . .?'

Questions that require causal reasoning are particularly important to learn, and in English, an example might be

> Study the text, and with your partner, decide who if anyone was responsible for the deaths of Romeo and Juliet
> a) Feuding parents?
> b) The Prince?
> c) Friar Lawrence?
> d) The lovers?

Develop an argument for each one in turn. Select the best case, and draw a causal chain.

> Are there any analogies between the play and real life today?
> Do you have any experiences of similar issues?

The ability to ask the right questions of ourselves and make good judgments are essential to daily life – from deciding on a hairstyle to buying a car or working in a company and planning a career.

In history,

> Read the two-page extract from **Hitler: A Study in Tyranny** by Alan Bullock, and answer the following questions.

> What reasons does the author give for the crisis in 1934?
> To what extent do you think that Rhoem was a genuine threat to Hitler's leadership?

Attempt to predict what might have happened if Hitler had not moved against Rhoem. In geography,

> Study the modern physical features map you have been given, and explain why the town of Maldon was built on its present site. Try to find at least three reasons. What further data might be useful?

CPS. Higher-order study and research skills

These were detailed in Chapter 6.

CPS. Reflective teaching and learning

The reflective teacher is one who is able to develop teaching and learning for critical thinking. Developing reflective thinking and the metacognition of learners is the key objective.

Pollard (1997) identified the aim of reflective teaching as a move from routine action to reflective action. While routine action is the type of practice that is relatively static, reflective action embraces the idea that teacher competence and professional development is a career-long process guided by self-appraisal and empirical evidence. Through making the unconscious explicit, the teacher is in a better position to decide whether what is believed in fits the purpose of what she or he is trying to achieve.

Pollard (1997, 11) describes reflective teaching as having six key characteristics.

1   *Reflective teaching implies an active concern with aims and consequences, as well as a means of technical efficiency.*

This means that teachers are not only concerned with what goes on in their class-rooms but with the whole school and with national policy. There is a commitment to be actively involved in all aspects of school development and to be constructively critical in order to be able to justify effective practices.

2   *Reflective teaching is applied in a cyclical or spiralling process, in which teach-ers monitor, evaluate and revise their own practice.*

(Pollard, 1997, 13)

This process involves teachers reflecting, planning, making provision, acting, col-lecting data, analysing the data and evaluating the data. While this process is similar to action-research, the fundamental difference is that reflective teaching involves examining all practices from national policy to curriculum planning and the hidden curriculum. It is in this way that reflective teaching leads to professional competence and development.

3   *Reflective teaching requires competence in methods of classroom enquiry, to support the development of teacher competence.*

(Pollard, 1997, 14)

In order to be able to complete the reflective process described earlier, it is necessary for teachers to develop competences in collecting data in many different ways, to be able to make sense of the evidence and to be able to see how the results from the evidence can be applied to future decision-making about policy and practice.

4   *Reflective teaching requires attitudes of open-mindedness, responsibility and wholeheartedness.*

(Pollard, 1997, 15)

Open-mindedness is necessary to make the step from routine action to reflective action. A certain degree of responsibility to students and to their professionalism is necessary for teachers to embark on reflective teaching, and an enthusiasm or wholeheartedness allows the process to continue.

5   *Reflective teaching is based on teacher judgment, which is informed partly by self-reflection and partly by insights from educational disciplines.*

(Pollard, 1997, 16)

This involves a recognition that while reflective action involves constant self-appraisal, which helps teacher-judgement, all answers cannot be found by teachers alone. Educational research is a valuable resource.

6   *Reflective teaching, professional learning and personal fulfillment are enhanced through collaboration and dialogue with colleagues.*

(Pollard, 1997, 18)

Lastly, reflective action should be shared action in order to clarify and hone ideas. In order for change to come about, reflective action should take place on many different levels – looking at ourselves as teachers, our strengths and weaknesses; at the students and their relationships to make the environment more conducive to learning and to plan for their needs; at the learning environment, communication skills, assessment and the importance of the hidden curriculum and ethos of the school; and at the school policies and finally national policy.

In summary, through reflective teaching, teachers are being asked to examine their personal values and aims carefully. Reflective teaching is flexible and learner-oriented so that learners also can become reflective and learn in ways best for them. Their contribution and collaboration is important in the intimate relationship between teaching and learning.

As can be inferred, there are close links between reflective teaching and learning and personalised learning. It is probably safe to say that we cannot achieve the goals of personalised learning if we are not reflective teachers and learners. Unfortunately, whilst we would all claim to be reflective teachers, it may be that we need to engage in Thinkback TAPPS (as in Lockhead 1991, in chapter 6) in order to achieve it and make our stealth ideas and strategies explicit.

CPS. Real problem solving and investigative learning

Human nature is such that if you present a person with an open-ended situation in which the answer to a problem is not given, it sets up cognitive dissonance, and the mind automatically tries to solve the problem and make closure unless it is ill. Although not everything can be converted into a problem, there is considerable scope for doing so across the curriculum. Some examples follow:

In didactics, a study of 'homes' usually consists of showing the children pictures of different types of buildings in which people have lived and getting the children to describe them (e.g. homes on stilts). The cognitive process strategy is to show them pictures of the terrain, probably show the same film clip or video of a monsoon, and describe the flora and fauna of the region and the tools available to the locals. The pupils, in small collaborative groups, are set to design the most appropriate form of home for those conditions. They present their designs after 10 to 15 minutes – houseboats, homes on stilts or tree houses – with a justification and discuss the best-fit solution before researching what the locals actually do. This form of learning is more memorable and meaningful to the pupils, as well as encouraging argument, teamwork, organising and planning skills.

Characteristic of the approach is that there needs to be plenty of content material around to research to help develop ideas and strategies or verify solutions. Because the activities start from the children's own ideas and knowledge, each is building up his or her own cognitive structures and knowledge hierarchies and can interrogate the various sources. The teacher in this setting is not the only interactive resource but the manager and facilitator of learning.

An example of the approach from the Essex LEA Extension and Enrichment materials promoted by Belle Wallace, their adviser for the gifted in the 1980s, was as follows:

It is 1280. You are King Edward I's master mason. You have been told to design and organise the building of a new castle at David in North Wales. Draw up a castle design and cost it within budget for King Edward.

(It is suggested that the pupils work in pairs or threes.)

Information given to pupils:

- Labour force details and costs
- Materials and equipment
- Purposes of the build – defence
- Site of the gatehouse
- Bursary for reconnaissance visit
- Budget for the whole project

Additional costs to be built in:

- Round versus square towers
- Price per crenellation
- Windows and doors versus slits
- Overhangs
- Accommodation, storage and armoury

The resources available include the ground plans of parts of some actual castles, pictures of a range of castles, video clips of castles in lieu of site visits and maps to illustrate the terrain. Alternatively, the teacher may decide to work in a more open way in approaching the subject with the class and start first with a different strategy, such as a simulation or game as in the later section.

Another excellent example from the Essex Project was Julian Whybra's (1980) problem booklet *The Battle of Isandlwhana: Essex Curriculum Extension Project* (Chelmsford: Essex County Council) to be used with more able 12- to 16-year-olds.

The aims were to develop the pupils' powers of reasoning, investigation and research when confronted with primary historical sources; to achieve a greater understanding of the meaning of responsibility and the consequences of one's actions; to promote a deeper understanding of and interest in history; and to elicit an emotional response from the child to an emotive study to produce an empathetic reaction.

The outline content was as follows:

The pupil is put in charge of a Court of Inquiry to look at a British military disaster at Isandlwhana, Zululand, from which only a handful of Europeans escaped with their lives. The pupil is given the following documents: the army commander's order-book, the camp commander's order-book, several maps of the area and seven survivors' accounts in addition to several other sources. The pupil must then write a report with explanatory maps, finding a scapegoat or scapegoats on whom the disaster can be explained and showing clearly how the disaster occurred. It must also vindicate the blameless. Once the report is finished the pupil is given two further documents 'new' evidence on which the report may be amended, or take an alternative course of action.

(p. 2)

The objectives were to discover why the disaster occurred, how 1,900 troops were annihilated and who was responsible for it.

As can be imagined, this is a prodigious task even for an individual more able child, but it can work well for mixed-ability groups and even be presented as a courtroom drama.

CPS. Real-world problem-based learning

The Maidenhead Group of Teachers (1987) set up and chaired by Johanna Raffan developed the Motorway Project enrichment materials for more able learners from eight to 11 years during the period when the M4 was being constructed nearby. They later developed Townscapes and the Village of Edensfield based on the same principles.

The Motorway pack consists of six worksheets and gives pupils instructions, materials and guidance for their use.

Worksheet 1, 'The Speedy Construction Company', requires the pupils to study the materials and statistics and then imagine they are the site foremen of a construction company building part of the motorway. They have to write a memo to the civil engineer explaining why the workforce has fallen behind schedule in certain weeks.

The second worksheet, 'A Motorway to Portheigh', asks the pupils to imagine they are the minister of the environment and must draw up plans for a motorway for the island within a certain budget, plot the route, overcome certain obstacles and so on.

The third sheet, 'Albert Biggins', asks the pupils to write a conversation between a workman building the M1 in the 20th century and a construction worker building the first railway in the 19th century.

The fourth sheet, 'Ockwells Manor and Home Farm', has two suggested routes, and the pupils have to consider the effect of choosing whether the motorway should run through one estate or the other. Details are given of the estates and the owners and their opinions, and the pupils take sides and have to present a case to the rest of the class on which should be the preferred route and the reasons why and why not. Teachers are encouraged to discuss persuasion, argument and manipulation with the pupils.

Worksheet five, 'Build a Bridge', concerns the role of a civil engineer, and the pupils build a model bridge on sand subsoil with straws, card, pins and so on to support a can of Coke representing a tractor driving over the motorway.

Worksheet six involves collecting, collating and writing a factual report; constructing a graph to identify the traffic trends that emerge; and discussing the problems identified.

Other teachers have used similar designs to motivate pupils to study local problems in building a new hospital adjacent to a local city or the introduction of two garden suburbs inside the boundaries of a historic town. Recent projects have centred on local flood prevention measures, HS2 and rewilding issues.

PBL is now widely used and researched in higher education programmes, having been initially developed in master's programmes in business education and in gifted education enrichment programmes.

> PBL is characterised by an enquiry process where problems – mostly from real and complex situations – are formulated and drive the whole learning process. Learning through PBL promotes critical thinking, self-learning skills, lifelong learning, self-achievement, self-regulation, self-efficacy, communication skills, and interpersonal skills for students.
>
> (Guerra and Kolmos, 2011, 4)

CPS. Games, simulations and role play

Over the last 30 years, there has been a growing acceptance of games as a teaching technique particularly in high school and in business studies and management programmes at universities. They are however equally valuable in primary and secondary education, although they are mostly used in remedial education for literacy difficulties. Recently, however, computer program games have been developed that encourage and develop thinking skills through the pursuit of a game.

In the non-simulation game, students work in groups and have to know certain facts, perform certain skills or demonstrate mastery of specific concepts to win or be successful. The participants agree on objectives, and there are sets of rules to obey. Typical of this form is the card game that can be adapted to educational purposes, such as 'Phonic Rummy', 'Alphabet Snap' and so on.

Role play in English and drama role play is frequently used as part of the lesson development. Role play is an important activity that helps pupils develop their personal speaking and listening skills as well as presentational and dramatic techniques. It can be used in PSHE to examine and resolve problems as in Bowers and Wells

(1988) *Ways and Means Handbook, Problem Solving* and Rawlings (1996), as well as Circle Time activities.

The liver transplant list (Ways and Means)

There are a set of role cards that vary the text according to the ability and interests of the groups. Each card describes a person's role – for example. pop singer (age 19), unemployed man with wife and three children (age 45), one of two children of a single parent (age 13). The groups are asked to imagine they are patients waiting for a liver transplant. A donor has become available, and the liver is suitable for any of them. They are asked to put forward the case for the role they have been given and then agree among themselves who is to be selected for the operation.

* Emphasise there are no right answers.
* Ask them to repeat the process, but this time argue the case for themselves.
* Next, argue the case for the person on your left (or right).
* New roles can be developed by groups who complete these stages.

Pairs can discuss their card, then form in groups to present their case to the rest of the transplant group, and try to decide who will get the operation. In a plenary, the teacher can hear the groups' decisions and their reasons and open the discussion up to the whole group.

It is less common to use role-play in science, but it can be a lot of fun with young pupils. It was used with them to liven up revision sessions. They formed groups of three to five, and each group chose an experiment from the programme, planned what they would do and then mimed the whole event. They mimed molecules of water in three different states, sausages exploding in a pan when they had not been pricked to release air and telephone wires and train tracks expanding and causing trouble. It was fascinating to see their imaginations at work and how it could inspire the interest and show new skills of many of the underachievers.

Simulation games contain the elements of real situations, and students individually or in groups interact with and become part of the reality. Role playing is often an important feature of the game. For example, in working with a class of children on the problems of bullying or stealing, it is often very useful to organise small group work role play so that individuals can practice expressing their own and others' feelings about the subject, as well as analyse the issues and suggest solutions or resolutions of the problem. Characteristic of all games is that they must be followed by a discussion-debriefing session to discuss what transpired so that educational and metacognitive objectives can be achieved.

The balloon debate is a typical example of such a role-play when someone has to be 'thrown out' and pupils have to discuss the criteria.

Place the castle simulation game

The class is shown an outline map (see Figure 7.2) with six proposed castle sites, a plateau, hills, a lake island, a village, land surrounded by marsh and land on a low peninsula between rivers. The class is divided into six groups with about five students in each group.

Place the castle can be played with young pupils through to adults. It is intended to be a starter lesson in a series about the mediaeval period. The purpose is to draw together from the pupils what they personally know about castles and can deduce from the picture. It is also intended to be creative fun and language developing for mixed-ability groups.

Each group is given a ground plan of the whole area, or it is on the whiteboard with the six potential castle sites. Each site is randomly assigned to a group; two groups might even have the same site. Their task is to prepare a marketing brief to persuade

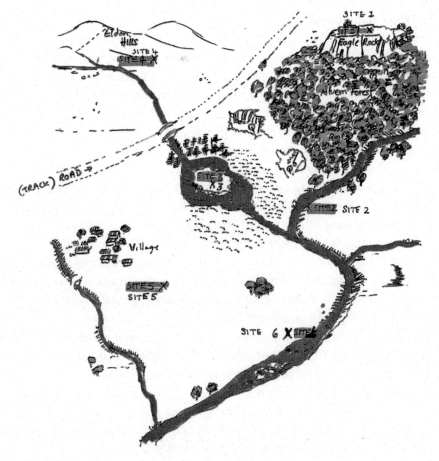

Figure 7.2 **Place the castle** Q = Quarry V = Village

the noble lord or lady (teacher) to decide to build the new castle on their site, pointing out the advantages of their own site over the disadvantages of the others.

After about ten minutes, they should have had time to discuss and note down their main ideas, and then one member from each group gives the marketing presentation with help from the group. This can be a lot of fun, and in the concluding session, the teacher can use this experience to help the children reflect upon which would be the best site overall and the reasons for this. It brings them to a deeper realisation of the purposes and needs of mediaeval castles and castle builders. At the same time, the children are developing discussion and negotiation skills and their communication and presentation skills. It has been a continuing concern of HMI in that the children do not have sufficient opportunities for practising oral communication, and these techniques can provide them.

In collaborative learning activities such as these, slower learners are able to ask questions for clarification in their groups, and able learners can learn to explain their thinking more clearly and even teach. Teaching is the one method that can ensure 90 per cent understanding on the part of the 'teacher' (Race, 1992).

The Whole Book Game is another useful strategy. In primary education, where it is common to read children stories and get them to predict what is going to happen next, it is also possible to turn the whole story into a game with a game board, dice and counters or pieces based on the story characters. A pathway or track is made round the board with hazards and leaps forward. Each part of the pathway represents a section of the story. By the shake of a dice, the players move forward, and at each stop, they also have to pick up a study skills question card. The cards ask them about events or potential events in the story. If they answer correctly, they keep on track; if they do not, they lose places and have to backtrack or go to other sections and so on.

The questions are based upon factual and cognitive skills and so not only encourage reading and rereading of the text to check the answers but also help promote thinking and reasoning by the nature of the questions. Non-readers can have an adult to read the cards for them but still can participate in the learning and thinking activities. It also encourages them to reflect upon what they hear and read. The book is kept to hand so that the children can check the facts. This is a powerful way of making children want to read, and they particularly enjoy making improvements to the game or adapting it for younger children and reading with them.

Older pupils can be set to design such games for younger children as language, ICT or design projects. The teacher can also design games that feature events and characters in key texts and chapters, or pairs and groups can make a game for other groups to play. Imagine Romeo and Juliet as an electronic game and the amount of deep text study and learning that would be involved.

The following is an example of the question cards in a whole book game based upon the children's story *Shakoor Is Born* (Jones, 1987), a game for two or three players. There is a game board with a circle track of squares, illustrations from the story,

MIME what Grandfather did in the hospital	WHO is Ammi?	HOW old is Shakoor?	WAS the baby a boy or a girl?
MIME what ABBI did to the baby when Grandfather whispered in his ear	WHO is Abbi?	DID Ammi come home in an ambulance?	WHAT does father say about the baby?
RETELL two events in the story in a sequence	WHO is Amma?	HOW many people are there in the story?	WHAT is the baby's name?
RETELL three events in the story in a sequence	WHO made the children's breakfast on hospital day?	NAME all the people in the story	
WHY did Ammi put honey on the baby's tongue?	WHO took Ammi to hospital?	WHY do you think Kausar said the baby had a funny face?	WHAT is the name of the hospital room Ammi was in?
JOKER	WHO chose the baby's name?	HOW many children are there in the family?	HOW long did Granny think it would be before the baby came home?
WHO seems to take most of the decisions?	TELL one further piece of factual information about the Muslim way of faith	GIVE one main point from the story	WHAT might have happened if the car had broken down on the way to the hospital?
TELL one piece of the story but introduce a new person (character) into it	ADD another piece to the story before the baby is born	GIVE another piece of the story after they came home	Ammi put ------- on the baby's tongue

Figure 7.3 Some examples of study skills questions cards in a whole book game

a pack of question cards, dice and shaker and coloured counters to move along. The squares are as follows: orange squares (pick up another card, answer it correctly and treble the score you have thrown), white squares (pick up another card, answer correctly, move two places forward; if incorrect, move back two places), joker (make up a question for another player – move one square forward if correct; if wrong, move three squares back), red squares (move five places back) and so on.

Rules

Must throw a six to start. Player takes the top card each time and reads it to the rest. They must agree the answer is correct. The number on the die is the number of squares to be moved. After the game, pupils are allowed to make suggestions to improve it.

CPS. Experiential learning

Experiential learning involves learning by doing or *action learning*. It is surprising how much students in schools and colleges remain passive in the learning process and yet how much more effective their learning could be if they were direct participants. This has long been recognised in early years education and primary education in Britain.

Kolb (1984) showed that experience dictated that unless the learner reflected upon the learning during and after the event, it was not so effective and meaningful; it would not result in 'deep' learning.

Although learners may often learn without direct experience by observing and modelling others, and some learners can be particularly adept at this, it does not mean that direct experience is not useful. The experience does however have to be cognitively challenging; otherwise, it is no more than other mundane activities.

Some examples can involve museum, concert and theatre visits; local studies; and school outings. Other techniques involve drawing and painting from life – the building site, the taxi rank, the store front, the beach, the weeds in the pavement, a flower head and so on. These experiences can lead pupils to write poetry about them in more fulfilling and interesting detail and at a deeper level. Comparative writing can be explored.

CPS. Language experience methods

Whole book games are a language experience technique. In the main, language experience methods initially involved getting pupils to tell their own stories and then with the help of a scribe making them into a book with photographs, drawings and magazine cut-outs. In technology, they make PowerPoint presentations to illustrate a favourite or topical theme to present to peers and parents or younger children.

Language experience methods are where the teacher uses the child's own language and stories to construct reading material. The children write their own storybooks and may usefully work in pairs to construct a story on the word processor. Photographs, cut-out pictures or clip art can be used to illustrate the work and give it a professional look. This method also involves genuine **co-operative learning** that can prove a very powerful learning technique for language development.

Learning experiences in this sequence are best understood and internalised when the children **discuss as they experience** and put their ideas into words. The discussions do not have to be channelled through the teacher but are between children and structured by the task. The teacher listens and draws the whole together. The children then are in a better position to express their ideas more formally in writing, through drama or in pictures

Older pupils can be involved in programmes in which they write stories to read to young pupils or hear them read. This helps them develop planning and writing skills and gives them a real audience for their work.

Concept formation and development The disadvantaged and children with learning difficulties can show an inability to generalise from their observations. Not only do they fail to notice key features but they also often need to be taught what other children learn incidentally by being in contact with the environment. For example, without necessarily being taught, most of us infer that the numbers on a bus indicate it travels a particular route and that the same letters can be used to make up different

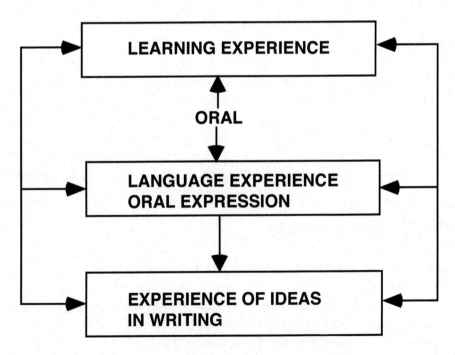

Figure 7.4 A language experience / oracy model

words. Slower and inexpert disadvantaged learners take longer to grasp these essentials than other children and may need a great deal of experiential learning incorporating these concepts. Once established, they are able to use them as well as others.

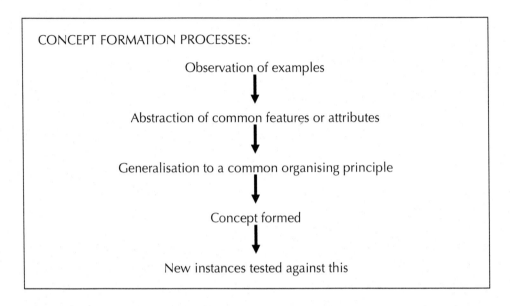

CONCEPT FORMATION PROCESSES:

Observation of examples

↓

Abstraction of common features or attributes

↓

Generalisation to a common organising principle

↓

Concept formed

↓

New instances tested against this

For example, a two-and-a-half-year-old was very fond of the family's half-Siamese female cat called 'Percy' and was leafing through a storybook (Fleur Cowles's *Tiny Tiger in the Grass*) and was being told the story in the pictures. Immediately, with great excitement, the striped tiger was identified as 'Percy!' Tiger and domestic cat in one conceptual leap both became the cat family. At an early and less discriminating stage, cat, tiger and dog might all be distinguished as 'Percy-type' as distinct from humans.

This ability to generalise from observations, to deduce simple and more complex rules, applies to concept formation in general. Inexpert learners need more instances and more practice. Daily reading and telling of stories with very young children builds these experiences, and this is something that many disadvantaged children do not have and so they are conceptually and culturally deprived on starting school.

CPS. Developing creativity

Young learners are said to be more creative than older students, and this is likely to be because they have not been over-trained in the education system to be convergent thinkers. It is here that some creativity training may be helpful, and over time, a number of strategies have been recommended.

One of the important features of creativity is that it needs time and space to develop, and these are not readily available in an overfilled curriculum time in school. Experts distinguish between creative potential and productive creativity. In both, chance plays a role because if for example there is no clay to work on, it can be impossible to show a talent or begin an early career in sculpture. The same is true for a talent in playing a particular musical instrument.

There are other considerations about creative development that are not so clear. For example, creativity in science may require an openness of mind and a willingness to master a large amount of material before the questions at the frontiers of that knowledge can lead to new and creative insights. But the ability to raise those relevant questions is a talent in itself. What facilitates this kind of talent seems to be multifactorial. It seems to depend upon not only an openness of outlook that will consider alternatives to previously adhered to beliefs but also the ability to consider the negative instances and their value in problem solving.

For example, a mathematician tells us that she has in mind a simple rule. The rule is exemplified by the numbers 2, 4 and 6. The task is to define the rule by posing more instances. The mathematician will only tell us, 'Yes, that is an example of the rule,' or 'No, it is not'. How many instances do we take to find the rule? (four or five). One post-graduate mathematician took 45 minutes proposing dozens of instances and 'rules' and still did not have the correct rule.

Another aspect that was found to be relevant to creative thinking was in the concept of divergent thinking in which many solutions and examples are proposed as in 'How many uses can you think of for a brick?' as opposed to convergent thinking in which we narrow down on to one solution, a strategy much taught in schools. The problem with divergent thinking, also termed 'synectics' and 'brainstorming', is that the divergent answers need to be gathered, organised and used or applied in some way. This is more difficult and may even lead nowhere. A schizophrenic may be able to propose many extraordinary uses for a brick but not necessarily in a structured or purposeful way.

Synectics – Brainstorming

1) First, state the purpose
2) Second, generate the possibilities
3) Third, reclassify the possibilities into types
4) Fourth, review the possibilities to pick out unusual ones and feed them into (2). Use (3) to generate more possibilities.

SCAMPER Osborn (1963)

Osborn provided the SCAMPER checklist for developing creative ideas as follows:

Substitute – change elements in the problem: Who else? What else?
Combine – bring it together with other ideas, purposes.

Adapt – what else is like this? Create metaphors.

Modify – magnify, minify, multiply (what to add, alter, change).

Put to other uses new ways to use, other uses if modified.

Eliminate – remove irrelevancies, parts, wholes.

Reorganise – try different patterns, layouts, schemes; turn upside down, inside out, round; and try opposites.

To try this as a training for a creativity project, start with simple objects, such as a toy, a tool, a picture or an object to work through the SCAMPER checklist. Osborn emphasised the need to keep in mind the principle of deferred judgment.

Lateral thinking Edward de Bono (1970, 1974) placed great emphasis on lateral thinking and offered many examples of our tendencies to be stuck in a particular frame or mode of thinking when we needed to 'think outside the box'.

An example of this would be Scheerer (1963) nine-dot insight problem:

```
*       *       *


*       *       *


*       *       *
```

The task is for the problem solver to join all the dots with only four straight lines without removing the pencil from the paper.

de Bono claimed to be able to train people to become more lateral thinkers, but this did not prove that they became more creative; creativity for him was an element within lateral thinking. He distinguished between vertical thinking, which is rather like convergent thinking, drilling down into a subject with an emphasis on logic, and lateral thinking, which he considered under the following but not exclusive four headings:

- Recognition of dominant, polarising ideas
- Search for different ways of looking at things
- Reversal of the rigid control of vertical thinking
- The use of chance

Infusion for creative thinking (Swartz and Park, 1994)

Swartz and Parks (1994) divided creative thinking into two main strategies:

1) Alternative possibilities
2) Composition

First, they described the process of generating different possibilities and then of creating metaphors (288–336). In generating possibilities, they suggested a number of strategies beginning with the following:

1 Decide what you want to describe about something.
2 Describe the key characteristics of it.
3 Think what other objects and so on share these characteristics.
4 Select which of these key characteristics might make a good metaphor.
5 Think what details of the metaphor fit the characteristics you are describing.
6 Consider whether there are differences that make the metaphor misleading.
7 Is the metaphor a good fit? Why?

They then created a series of boxes (graphic organisers) to fill in to go through these steps from topic to metaphor with a series of detailed examples.

Creative thinking through questioning (Sousa, 2003)

Open-ended questions are effective for encouraging creative thinking because they rarely have one answer and they stimulate further inquiry. They ask for clarification, probe for assumptions, search for reasons and evidence, and look for implications and consequences. Here are a few examples:

> What would you have done? Why do you think this is the best choice?
> Could this ever really happen? What might happen next?
> What do you think might happen if . . . ? What do you think caused this?
> Is what you are saying now consistent with what you said before?
> How is it different from . . . ? Can you give an example?
> Where do we go next? Where could we go for help on this?
> What do you mean by that expression?
> Can we trust the source of this material?
> In what other ways could this be done? How can you test this theory?
> What might be the consequences of behaving like that?
> Do you agree with this author/speaker? Why or why not?
> How could you modify this? How would changing the sequence affect the outcome?
> (p. 94)

Leroux and McMillan (1993, 53) offered the following creative problem-solving model for use with pupils and students of all ages; it was originally developed in business and industry training.

Fact finding   Pupils gather all possible information on the question or 'MESS' they have raised.

Problem finding	Pupils look at their information to identify the core of the problem; they must rephrase the question to an open-ended one. For example, 'How can we earn the money to pay for our trip to the zoo?'
Idea finding	Pupils brainstorm all possible ideas to make money. The rules include no criticism, acceptance of all ideas, quantity of ideas is desirable and combination of ideas is encouraged.
Solution finding	Ideas are evaluated against criteria that students establish, such as time involved in earning money, organisation of the project, feasibility and so on.
Acceptance finding	Pupils have to present the plan in a way that will convince the teacher and the principal to agree.

CPS. Co-operative learning

Dansereau (1988) gave student dyads scientific content to master. He broke the co-operative learning strategy down into six stages, which he found facilitated co-operation and learning, and labelled them MURDER (i.e., establishing the positive *mood* for studying, *understanding* while studying, *recall* – summarising what is read, *detecting* errors and omissions, *elaborating* to facilitate learning and *reviewing*).

The think – pair – share collaborative strategy is a much less formal procedure than Dansereau's but none-the-less valuable for most learners and very helpful to teachers with large classes because every child can be heard and practice some extended language.

The main problem in classrooms at present is that the desks are often arranged in groups, but the pupils are engaged in individual work whilst at them. Their talk then tends to be social chat not problem solving or collaboration. It is therefore the teachers' responsibility to set the task in such a way that the pupils do share their knowledge and that they do this in a purposeful manner that has an appropriate out-come. Teachers need to legitimise the talk that goes on in classrooms by defining it as purposeful activity leading to more productive solutions and learning outcomes, such as in TPS. It is these sorts of experiences that can prepare pupils for teamwork in their careers.

CPS. Self-regulated learning

The construct of self-regulation refers to the degree to which students can regulate aspects of their thinking, motivation and behaviour during learning.

Self-regulated learning is an active constructive process whereby learners set goals for their learning and monitor, regulate, and control their cognition, motivation, and behaviour, guided and constrained by their goals and the contextual features of the environment.

Pintrich and Zusho (2002, 64)

As may be inferred, very little SRL can take place in didactic environments where the teaching model is transmission. It can and does take place in constructivist teaching environments. In the preceding examples of CPS and other techniques, the potential for training pupils towards SRL is extensive. An important aspect is for the teacher gradually to extend more autonomy to the pupils and take the opportunities that it gives to observe them in their interactions and problem solving so that programmes can be more personalised.

Evaluation of curriculum challenge

The Taxonomy of Educational Objectives constructed by Bloom (1956) was used to help assess the levels of operation that the materials were able to achieve without teacher intervention in the form of judicious questioning. Success was counted as operations at the higher levels of analysis, synthesis and evaluation. Most so-called enrichment activities were just achieving applications level because they only offered content or product enrichment and were really more oriented towards content acceleration. Most of our CPS tasks commanded operations at all Bloom's levels and could enable even average-ability five-year-olds to operate at abstract or formal operational levels in the right context (Montgomery, 1985).

Curriculum evaluation using Bloom's (1956) taxonomy

Bloom's (1956) taxonomy is often used in curriculum design and evaluation for gifted groups. However, the taxonomy is also helpful in any curriculum evaluation and assessment for learners.

1   Knowledge is defined as the remembering/recall of previously learned material from specific facts to complete theories. Knowledge represents the lowest level of learning outcomes in the cognitive domain.
2   Comprehension is the ability to grasp the meaning of material and represents the lowest level of understanding.
3   Application is the ability to use learned material in new and concrete situations; it includes the application of rules, methods, concepts, principles, laws and theories.

4   Analysis is the ability to break down material into its component parts so that its organisational structure can be understood. This may include the identification of the parts, analysis of the relations between parts and recognition of the organisational principles involved.

5   Synthesis is the ability to put parts together to form a new whole. This may involve the production of a unique communication (theme or speech), a plan of operations (research proposal) or set of abstract relations (scheme for classifying information). Learning outcomes in this area stress creative behaviours with major emphasis on the formulation of new patterns or structures.

6   Evaluation is the ability to judge the value of material (statement, novel, poem, research report) for a given purpose. The judgments are based on definite criteria. These may be internal criteria (organisation) or external criteria (relevance for the purpose), and the student may determine the criteria or be given them. Learning outcomes in this area are highest in the cognitive hierarchy because they contain elements of all of the other categories, plus conscious value judgments based on clearly defined criteria.

When it was initially introduced in the US, it was argued that none of the school programmes should operate at levels higher than applications and the higher levels were for students on advanced academic programmes, such as in colleges and universities. This did not fit with the ethos in the UK, and it was found that with significant support, many children in infant schools (Key Stage 1) were capable of working at the higher levels even in mixed-ability groups in reception (Montgomery, 1985, 1996).

Although it is expected that the materials and methods for the students in higher education will involve the three higher levels of Bloom's taxonomy, it is to be expected that with suitable preparation and development, all the learners will be enabled to work at these higher levels, not just at low-level memorisation. This was an important development because at that period, it had been discovered that few pupils leaving school at 16 were capable of engaging in abstract operational thinking, and a number of projects were established to engage with this problem. This research needs to be undertaken again.

The SOLO taxonomy (Structure of Observed Learning Outcomes) by Biggs and Collis (1982) was used as an evaluation tool in the master's programmes so that teachers could introduce the ideas into their work with pupil self-evaluation strategies using the concept mapping technique. It is now being recommended for use with more able pupils in schools in NACE training days. Why not use it with all pupils?

For example – Formative and Diagnostic – MA SEN Module one: Draw a concept map of your knowledge and understanding about SEN before and again a week

Table 7.1 SOLO taxonomy (Biggs and Collis, 1982)

Taxonomy Level	Description
Prestructural	There is no evidence of any knowledge of the processes or content.
Unistructural	One relevant aspect is understood and focused upon.
Multi-structural	Several relevant and independent aspects are given but are not integrated into an overall structure.
Relational	Relevant aspects are integrated into an overall structure. Main issues and ideas are incorporated into this.
Extended abstract	The integrated knowledge is generalised to a new domain.

later after reading the rest of the unit and doing the short tasks specified (diagnostic). (Examples of concept maps or mind maps and their uses are given).

Write down ten differences between your first and second concept maps, and give your reflections on each one (formative and diagnostic).

Assess the level of your concept maps using Bigg's SOLO taxonomy (Table 7.1), and compare this to the assessment system used by the university at master's level detailed in your student handbook (formative).

The concept map drawn initially represents the 'flipped learning' technique that helps front-loaded learning. The tutor, when marking the differences, could evaluate the development and quality of the thinking at surface and deep levels and suggest further areas for analysis and reflection.

Testing for creativity, Torrance (1963)

Creativity is difficult to analyse, and so testing for creative potential is a problem not yet resolved. The Torrance Tests of Creativity (1999) are probably the most well-known attempts. One of the easiest to undertake with a class is the figural circles subtest. The test consists of about 30 circles on a page, and the testee has to 'Draw as many interesting and unusual objects as possible involving the circle in 10 minutes, and give each a novel label.'

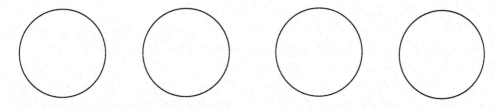

Figure 7.5 Part of Torrance's figural circles test

The scoring procedure

Torrance suggested 4 ways of marking this subtest.

1   Fluency: the number of circles used or incorporated into other pictures. Count the total number of different things drawn. Exclude nonsensical figures.
2   Flexibility: the number of different category changes (e.g., face, clown, ball, sphere) would count as a score of *one*, as the categories changed from face types to spheres.
3   Originality: the scores range from 2, 1, 0. Everybody draws faces so this scores 0. Only a few draw screws, so this scores 1. Objects which only one person in the group or sample draws score 2 (e.g. underside of Tilley lamp).
4   Elaboration: this is the amount of detail given in the picture. It is extremely difficult to mark objectively.

One pupil did not draw anything at all but gave every circle a different and valid label. Another connected all the circles and drew a honeybee in the top left-hand corner. Both were very creative and unusual responses, but how to score them? Eventually, Torrance found that the elaboration score was the most predictive of creativity!

It is a useful task as a talking point for developing critical thinking about tests!

NACE, the National Association for Able Children in Education, 2019

Whilst current ITT provision may be too limited to produce the most effective teachers on the widest scale, there are important innovations taking place in some schools. Within them, we find innovative heads and curriculum leaders. In the background, we find organisations such as NACE. It was established in 1974 by a group of innovative teachers, and despite the take-over of the curriculum by government in the 1980s, NACE continued as an independent organisation developing ideas on teaching and learning methods for the more able and highly able. These methods were those that would also support and improve the learning of all pupils (HMI, 1992) and promote differentiation and inclusion.

Their early successes were the Motorway Project described earlier, Today, NACE has developed the Challenge Award System in which school provision is audited by a trained external assessor against the NACE criteria for effectiveness and offers a wide range of training through accredited tutors. It holds regular conferences, seminars, webinars and meet-ups. As an example, the following outline is from a meet-up of a range of teachers from schools giving details of their work on SRL (independent learning skills) in preference order.

'At its spring term meeting NACE (2019) members from all phases and sectors of education joined to discuss and share approaches to developing independent learning skills. The top 8 ways to develop independent learning in order of priority were:'

1   Extended research projects: in years 8 to 10 and Extended Project Qualifications
2   Flipped learning: resources and readings provided ahead of lessons so knowledge can be applied, analysed and evaluated during the lesson.
3   Presenting to peers: taking the role of experts and presenting and clarifying an aspect of a topic.
4   TIF tasks: each lesson and home-learning task includes a 'take it further' task. TIFs are more fun and quirky and pupils can devise their own TIFs.
5   Student-run revision quizzes: they are devised by pairs and small groups; they create PowerPoint presentations and decide how points will be awarded.
6   Super-curricular activities: pupils in years 3 to 6 can join a problem-solving club; other schools had Art Scholars Club linked to local museums and galleries; Sixth-form Feminist Society; and discussion suppers, where selected small groups of staff and pupils discuss a prepared topic over supper.
7   Building blocks for discussion: in small groups pupils take turns to contribute to a discussion adding a Lego or Duplo brick to a construction each time they speak – red for agreement, yellow to build and blue to challenge.
8   Access to other students' solutions: pupils learn from others beyond their own school engaged with the same University of Cambridge NRICH maths resources.

All these projects could be adapted and beneficial for use with disadvantaged and underachieving pupils at all levels of ability and ages.

As can be seen, if teachers are allowed and encouraged to be creative, significant improvements and advances can be made to help children learn. But they do need a forum such as provided by NACE in which to share their ideas. Their strategies promoted pupils' motivation and interest and enabled them to operate at the higher levels of Bloom's taxonomy. Earlier in the year, the NACE newsletter included an article showing how the SOLO taxonomy could be used with pupils at all ages to promote critical analysis and reflection when used to assess their own learning.

It is important that there is such an organisation as NACE to gather and spread 'good curriculum practice' and to develop its own experts. It is a particularly important feature of English education at present to have other than government-endorsed 'experts'.

Autonomous learning – Self-Regulated Learning (SRL)

The strategies and pedagogy detailed in this chapter and Chapter 6 have been designed to promote inclusivity, challenge and interest among disaffected and disadvantaged learners. What they also do is provide training for pupils to work both independently and collaboratively.

In 1972, the international committee, the Organisation for Economic and Co-operative Development (OECD), noted that the changing role of the teacher in modern society emphasised the importance of the transfer of responsibility for learning to the learner while the teacher became less of a transmitter of knowledge and more a manager of the learning environment and the central organiser of supports for the learner. The goal was that schools should be producing lifelong learners with the capacity and motivation to learn for themselves throughout life. Changing the role of the teacher from lecturer to facilitator was seen as the way of accomplishing this.

Over the decades, self-regulated learning appears under many different headings. Frequent titles have been autonomous learning (AL), self-managed learning (SML), learner managed learning (LML), self-organised learning (SOL), independent learning (IL), self-directed learning (SDL), independent research strategies (IRS) and independent study skills (ISS).

Self-regulatory activities were defined by Brown et al. (1983) as including

*   Planning – predicting outcomes and scheduling time and resources
*   Monitoring – including testing, revising and rescheduling
*   Evaluating outcomes – using criteria developed by the individual and also those that were externally defined

Self-monitoring and self-regulatory activities not only contributed to improved acquisition of subject content but also to improved generalisation and transfer of knowledge and skills. They also gave students a sense of personal agency, a feeling of being in control of their own learning. These experiences are crucial for disadvantaged learners to profit from their education, and they are more likely to need training in the necessary sub-skills. Some however are more naturally autonomous leaners and also do not fit well into some coercive school environments. They often only 'blossom' and thrive after leaving school.

Self-regulated or autonomous learners, according to Niehart (2011), have the following characteristics: they

*   Do well at school but may not be in the top 10 per cent
*   Handle stress well
*   Are good self-advocates
*   Persistent
*   Are self-directed and self-regulated
*   Are self-motivated
*   Are risk takers

She was working with the gifted end of the spectrum, but the same criteria, apart from 'do well at school', can apply throughout the ability range. It can mean that those with the most limited ability can maintain an independent lifestyle and run a household. The seemingly average can become high-earning entrepreneurs or develop some unique talent. In a nurturing, therapeutic educational environment that recognises and celebrates difference, many more such individuals can become lifelong learners and achieve their full potential. But school must be interesting and enjoyable to fulfill these needs.

Conclusion

This chapter has been concerned with the analysis of effective teaching and learning first from a theoretical standpoint and then for its practical implications in class-rooms. In the process, the transmission model of the 19th and 20th centuries has been contrasted with methods suitable for 21st-century needs.

In general terms the examples in both Chapters 6 and 7 have exemplified the ways in which pupils can be encouraged to think and problem solve when tasks are set in an appropriate manner. The purpose is to get them in the process to think about their thinking. This is termed 'metacognition'. Between finding the problem and determining its solution, the scaffolds, strategies and 'learning conversations' in their heads provide the means. It is these that disadvantaged pupils lack because of their limited experience and limiting environments and can benefit from learning.

Schools have to be preparing pupils to become self-regulated and lifelong learners, but what Gibbs (2015) has found is that it is what learners do not what their teachers do that leads to academic success at university. The ratio needed is about 10 hours student time on task to one hour of tuition time. At school level, it is the Finnish, Chinese and Hong Kong pupils who engage in extensive independent study time and achieve the highest PISA scores so we have something to learn and something to share. The second factor is that the students should receive constructive, formative, regular feedback on learning.

It is evident that higher education for teaching also needs to undergo some major pedagogical changes. Telling teacher education students about how to change the teaching that they have experienced for nearly 15 years does not promote long-term behavioural change. Higher education must also 'walk the talk' if it is to be effective. In an experiment in ITE when students were taught their SEN curriculum using CPS methodology for a 108-hour programme, examination first grade results rose from the usual 1 to 2 per cent to over 27 per cent (N=72).

In this chapter, techniques for developing thinking and communication skills in classrooms have been exemplified for teachers who want to change their methods. Selecting pupils on the G and T register for special and intellectually challenging experiences is unequal and discriminatory treatment for those not on the register. The underachievers and the disadvantaged are unlikely to be placed on such registers and so face double discrimination. This must be changed because all pupils need interesting and challenging curriculum experiences. The examples of how these changes in teaching can be achieved have been developed and tested in diverse classrooms with success. The techniques enhance inclusion and personalised learning, and promote problem solving, critical thinking, SRL and lifelong learning.

Postscript

In this book, I have tried to show how a well-trained teacher can be the key to the success of all pupils and develop inclusive learning experiences. The teacher is both the resource and the key to the resources that are human and humane. Money spent on the appropriate training of teachers will bring this success. Disadvantaged pupils will become integrated and contributing members of the society and will earn the same rewards as others.

Unfortunately, the theory of education and practice developed in the NCC was not fit for these purposes. It was a watered-down version of a university curriculum designed to feed that system. It was particularly inappropriate as a model for primary education and not that much better at secondary level. The model handed down was a transmission model treating pupils, whatever their levels of development, as jugs to be filled. No proper account was taken of the need of all learners to construct meaning for themselves or the fact that different methods were appropriate for children in the early years who were developing concepts and constructs or for disadvantaged older pupils with delayed development. Teachers became technicians and manual readers.

Teaching wisdom needs to be built on systematic exploration and analysis of experience by teachers trained essentially in the teacher-researcher role. The current situation, which separates researchers in 'hubs' from teachers in classrooms, is not leading to the promotion of effective teaching and learning, especially for the disadvantaged.

Teachers find themselves in a sea of documents and regulations, and although most spend 50 hours a week on work, they spend less time in the classroom than they once did. This only depletes their time and energy as the key resource, the creative learning experience maker.

Another feature of our education system that needs to be addressed is its structure. An option could be to change secondary education in schools from 11/12 to end at 16 so that from 16 all pupils would leave school and go to colleges. It was tried successfully in some local authorities before the NC. It would aggregate numbers and advanced resources. It would not be favoured by some teachers who cherish their A-level work but would help focus their minds on creative teaching and learning rather than subjects. It would help promote identity and achievement amongst younger pupils, who can lose these in large factory schools. It would also give them more opportunities to be seen as leaders and responsible members of the school community. It takes account of the current trend for pupils to be more mature in terms of attitude and life experiences.

Differences between private and public sector school achievements need addressing. Rather than closing private systems of education that gain most of the higher-paid jobs for their pupils, the aim was to improve the state system to make it as good. The issue was the lack of state funds or intention to make them available. Thus whilst the private sector could take in almost anyone and make the 'silk purse', the state system has not done so. Once in the higher status positions, the routes in are closed to those 'others' who are not in the network despite the efforts being made in 'high places' to open access.

In identifying a register of the most able and giving them specialist enrichment experiences, streaming, setting and acceleration, the state sector has sought to compete. This has failed because once again, as in the old grammar school system in which 80 per cent were excluded, it has now failed the 90 per cent who were not included. The complaint from the pupils is that after the enrichment day, they have to go back to the same boring old lessons as before. The aim of the English model is to raise the basic quality of education for all pupils with the ultimate goal of developing them to their full potential and producing lifelong learners.

This aim was set out by the OECD and taken up by educators and politicians for schools to produce these lifelong learners. But our current system has clearly failed to do this if even the more advantaged are turning away.

Developing children to their full potential is a widely held aim among teachers, but full potential is seldom defined and for what? It is not just the following of school rules and learning subjects; it is wider in personal and social terms, and it is often in the hidden curriculum that values, beliefs and attitudes are transmitted. Employers need creative problem solvers and people capable of working in teams and listening and learning from experience. Ten good GCSEs and 3 or 4 A levels are no indication of any of these, although a portfolio of wider experiences and achievements might be of some help.

If we can close the excellence gaps for disadvantaged learners, we could raise the standards in education of all learners – tackling the problem from the other way around. Perhaps, schools need an 'excellence gap' advisor. Research in higher education (Gibbs, 2015) showed that the most successful students were self-regulated learners. To foster achievement and self-regulation, there were some key attributes:

- a motivational problem-based curriculum and problem-solver approach,
- opportunities for autonomy, creativity and goal setting,

- regular and supportive formative and summative assessment,
- a ratio of 10 hours student time on task to one of tuition.

These attributes might also be considered to be the components of any attempt to have a successful career in work or self-employment.

Lifelong learners have characteristics in common. They are grounded and have a well-founded sense of self-esteem and self-efficacy. They are, in Maslow's terms, 'self-actualised'. This means they are not self-centred but have a mission in life that serves the larger good, they respect all persons, and they have a sense of kinship with all human beings and an existential sense of humour and detest laughing at the expense of others.

Bibliography

Allcock, P. 2001 'The importance of handwriting skills in key stage 3 and GCSE examinations of more able pupils' *Educating Able Children* 5 (1) 23–25.

Anderson, J.R. 1980 *Cognitive Psychology and Its Implications* San Francisco: Freeman.

APA 2006 *DSM V Internet Gaming Disorder* New York: American Psychiatric Association (APA).

APA 2013 *IDSM V Internet Gaming Disorder Update* New York: American Psychiatric Association (APA).

Arnold, R. 2004 *Gleams from the Beacon: Good Practice in Transition in Education* Slough: NFER.

Arnot, M. and Gubb, J. 2001 *Adding Value to Boys' and Girls' Education: A Gender and Achievement Project* West Sussex: West Sussex County Council.

Askew, M., Bibby, T. and Brown, M. 1997 *Raising Attainment in Primary Numeracy* London: Kings College.

Augur, J. and Briggs, S. (eds.) 1991 *The Hickey Multisensory Language Course* (2nd edition) London: Whurr.

Ausubel, D.P. 1968 *Educational Psychology: A Cognitive View* New York: Holt, Rinehart and Winston.

Bannathan, M. and Boxall, M. 1998 *Nurture Groups* London: David Fulton.

Barnard, H.C. 1961 *A History of English Education* (2nd edition) London: University of London Press.

Basildon Headteacher 2009 'Lifting underachievement in transition year 7' Optimus London Conference, Essex (Personal Communication).

Baum, S.M., Renzulli, J.S. and Hebert, T.P 1995 'Reversing underachievement: Creative productivity as a systematic intervention' *Gifted Child Quarterly* 39 (4) 224–235.

BDA 2019a *British Dyslexia Association* home page www.bda-dyslexia.org.uk.

BDA 2019b 'The human cost of dyslexia' report of the *All-Parliamentary Group for Dyslexia and other SpLDs Westminster*, House of Commons.

Berninger, V.W. 2004 'The role of mechanics in composing of elementary students: A review of research and interventions' keynote *Annual DCD Conference* April Oxford.

Berninger, V.W. 2008 'Writing problems in developmental dyslexia: Under-recognised and under-treated' *Journal of School Psychology* 46 1–21.

Berninger article Retrieved November 25, 2015 from http://online.wsj.com/articles/SB10001424052748704631504575531932754922518.

Berninger, V.W. and Graham, S. 1998 'Language by hand: A synthesis of a decade of research on handwriting' *Handwriting Review* 12 11–25.

Bernstein, B. 1970 'Education cannot compensate for society' in A. Cashdan and E. Grugeon (eds.) *Language and Social Context* London: Kegan Paul.

Beyer, B.K. 1997 *Improving Student Thinking: A Comprehensive Approach* London: Allyn and Bacon.

Biggs, J.B. and Collis, K.F. 1982 *Evaluating the Quality of Learning: The SOLO Taxonomy* New York: Academic Press.

Blaas, S. 2014 'The relationship between social-emotional difficulties and under-achievement of gifted students' *Australian Journal of Guidance and Counselling* 24 (2) 243–255.

Blackwell, F. 1991 *A Model for Curriculum Development: A Study of Curriculum Design in the USA* MA dissertation, School of Independent Study. Stratford, London: East London Polytechnic.

Blagg, N.R., Ballinger, M.P. and Lewis, R.E. 1993 *Development of Transferable Skills in Learners: Research Series* Sheffield: The UK Government Employment Department.

Blank, M. and Solomon, M. 1969 'How shall the disadvantaged child be taught?' *Child Development* 40 47–61.

Bloom, B.S. 1956 *Taxonomy of Educational Objectives* (Volume 1) London: Longmans.

Board of Education 1923 *Report on the Differences between Boys and Girls Achievements* London: Board of Education.

Bond, G.L. and Tinker, M.A. 1967 *Reading Difficulties* (2nd edition) New York: Appleton Century Crofts.

Bowers, S. and Wells, L. 1988 *Ways and Means: A Problems Solving Approach* Kingston upon Thames: The Friends Workshop Publication/LDRP.

Brookes, J. and Brookes, M 1993 *In Search of Understanding: The Case for Constructivist Classrooms* Alexandria, Virginia, USA Association for the Supervision and Curriculum Development.

Brown, A.L., Brandsford, J.D., Ferrara, R.A. and Campione, J.C. 1983 'Learning, remembering and understanding' in J.H. Flavell and E. Markham (eds.) *Carmichael's Manual of Child Psychology* (Volume 1) New York: Wiley.

Bruner, J.S. 1968 *Toward a Theory of Instruction* New York: W.W. Norton.

Bryant, P.E. and Bradley, L. 1985 *Children's Reading Difficulties* Oxford: Blackwell.

Butler-Por, N. 1987 *Underachievers in Schools: Issues and Interventions* London: Wiley.

Butler-Por, N. 1993 'Underachieving and gifted students' in K.A. Heller, F.J. Monks and A.H. Passow (eds.) *International Handbook of Research and Development of Giftedness and Talent* Oxford: Pergamon 648–668.

Cefai, C. and Camilleri, L. 2015 'A healthy start: Promoting mental health and well-being in the early primary school years' *Emotional and Behavioural Difficulties* 30 (2) 133–152.

Child, D. 1987 *Psychology and the Teacher* London: Holt Educational

Chomsky, C. 1971 'Write first, read later' *Childhood Education* 47 (6) 296–299.

Christensen, C.A. and Jones, D. 2000 'Handwriting: An underestimated skill in the development of written language' *Handwriting Today* 2 56–69.

Clay, M.M. 1975 *What Did I Write? The Beginnings of Reading Development* London: Heinemann.

Cole, T., Visser, J. and Upton, G. 1998 *Effective Schooling for Pupils with Emotional, and Behaviour Difficulties* London: David Fulton.

Coles, M.J. and Robinson, W.D. (eds.) 1991 *Teaching Thinking a Survey of Programmes in Education* Bristol: Classical Press.

Coltheart, M. 1984 'Writing systems and reading disorders' in L. Henderson (ed.) *Orthographies and Reading* Hove: Lawrence Erlbaum 67–79.

Connelly, V., Dockrell, J. and Barnett, A. 2005 'The slow handwriting of undergraduate students constrains their overall performance in exam essays' *Educational Psychology* 25 (1) 99–109.

Cooper, P. (ed.) 1999 *Understanding & Supporting Children with EBD* London: Jessica Kingsley.

Cose, E. 1997 *Colour Blind* New York: Harper Collins.

Cowdery, L.L., McMahon, J., Montgomery, D., Morse, P. and Prince-Bruce, M. 1994 *TRTS: Teaching Reading Through Spelling* Wexford: TRTS Publishing.

Croll, P. and Moses, D. 1985 *One in Five* London: Routledge and Kegan Paul.

Cropley, A.J. 1994 'Creative intelligence: A concept of true giftedness' *European Journal of High Ability* 5 16–23.

Cullen, S M., Cullen, M-A., Dytham, S. and Hayden, N. 2018 *Research to Understand Successful Approaches to Supporting the Most Academically Able Disadvantaged Pupils* London: DfE.

Daly, C. 2015 *Literature Search on Improving Boy's Writing* London: Ofsted.

Dansereau, D.F. 1988 'Co-operative learning strategies' in C.E. Weinstein, E.T. Goetz and P.A. Alexander (eds.) *Learning and Study Strategies* New York: Academic Press 103–120.

Darwin, C.R. 1859 *On the Origin of Species by Means of Natural Selection or Preservation of Favourite Races in the Struggle for Life.* London: John Murray.

DES 1975 *The Bullock Report: A Language for Life* London: HMSO.

DES 1979 *Aspects of Secondary Education: A Survey by HMI* London: HMSO.

DES 1985 *Good Teaching Observed* London: HMSO.

DfEE 1994 *The Education of Children with Emotional and Behavioural Difficulties* Circular 9/94 DH LAC 9(94) London: DfEE.

DfEE 1999 *Excellence in Cities* London: DfEE.

DfES 2002 *Key Stage 3: Teaching and Learning in Foundation Subjects* London: DfES.

DfES 2005 *Higher Standards, Better Schools for All* London: DfES.

DfES 2006 *Primary National Strategy: Framework for Literacy and Mathematics* London: DfES.

DCSF 2007a *Getting There – Able Pupils Who Lose Momentum in English and Maths in Years 4 to 6* London: DCSF.

DCSF 2007b *Gifted and Talented Education – Guidance on Preventing Under-achievement: A Focus on Dual and Multiple Exceptionalities* London: DCSF.

DCFS 2009a *Statistics in Education 2007–2008* London: DCFS.

DCFS 2009b *The Steer Report* London: DCFS.

DCFS 2009c *Personalised Learning – A Practical Guide* London: DfES.

DCFS 2010 *Gypsy, Roma and Traveller Pupils: Improving Educational Outcomes* London: DfE.

DCFS 2011 Retrieved March 3, 2011 from www.standards.dcsf.gov.uk/NationalStrategies (Accessed 03/04/2019).

DfE 2014a *Gypsy, Roma and Traveller Pupils: Supporting Access to Education: Successful Practice* London: DfE.

DfE 2014b *National Curriculum, Key Stages 1 and 2: Framework for English and Mathematics* London: DfE.

DfE 2019 *SATs: Writing Boys* London: DfE.

de Bono, E. 1970 *Lateral Thinking* London: Ward Lock.

de Bono, E. 1974 *CoRT Thinking Notes* Blandford, Dorset: Direct Education Services Ltd.

de Bono, E. 1983 *Cognitive Research Trust (CoRT) Thinking Programme* Oxford: Pergamon.

De Corte, E. 1995 'Learning and high ability: A perspective from research in instructional psychology' in M.W. Katzko and F.J. Monks (eds.) *Nurturing Talent: Individual Needs and Social Ability Proceedings of the 4th ECHA Conference* Assen, The Netherlands: Van Gorcum.

De Corte, E. 2013 'Giftedness considered from the perspective of research on learning and instruction' *High Ability Studies* 24 (1) 5–20.

Delisle, J.R. and Berger, S.L. 2009 'Underachieving gifted students' www.kidsource.com (Accessed 17/07/2009) from ERIC EC Digest 1990 #E478.

Dept. for Employment 2001 *Further Education* London: HMSO.Desforges, C. 1998 'Learning and teaching: Current views and perspectives' in D. Shorrocks-Taylor (ed.) *Directions in Educational Psychology* London: Whurr 5–18.

Dewey, J. 1909 *How We Think* New York: D.C. Heath and Co.

Dewey, J. 1938 *Experience and Education* Kappa Delta, NY: Collier Books reprint (1967).

Dowker, A.D. 2001 'Numeracy recovery: A pilot scheme for early intervention with young children with numeracy difficulties' *Support for Learning* 16 (1) 6–10.

Dunn, J. and Dunn, M. 1997 *The British Picture Vocabulary Test* London: GL Assessment.

Dutton, K. 1992 'Writing under examination conditions: Establishing a baseline' *Handwriting Review* 80–93.

Dweck, C. 1999. Self-Theories: Their Role in Motivation, Personality and Development Philadelphia, PA: Psychology Press.

Dweck, C. 2011 'Mindsets and academic achievement' Keynote address. WCGTC Biennial Conference, Vancouver.

Ehri, L.C. 1980 'The development of orthographic images' in U. Frith (ed.) *Cognitive Processes in Spelling* London: Academic Press 313–336.

Ehri, L.C. 2018 'Acquisition of sight-word reading, spelling memory and vocabulary learning: The role of orthographic mapping' keynote lecture *11th International Conference of the BDA* April 12–14 Telford, UK.

Elton, L. 1989 *The Elton Report on Discipline in Schools* London: HMSO.

Ennis, R.H. and Norris, S. 1990 *Evaluating Critical Thinking* Midwest, CA: Midwest Publishing Company.

ERA 1988 *The Education Reform Act* London: HMSO.

Falvey, M.A., Forest, M., Pearpoint, J. and Rosenberg, R. 1994 *All My Life's A Circle: Using the Tools: Circles, MAP's and PATH* Toronto: Canada Inclusion Press.

Farnham-Diggory, S. 1978 *Learning Disabilities* Harmondsworth: Penguin.

Farrington, D. 1994 'Early developmental prevention of juvenile delinquency' *Royal Society of Arts Journal* 22–31.

Farrington, D.F. 2000 'Psychosocial predictors of adult antisocial personality and adult convictions' *Behavioural Science and the Law* 68 605–622.

Fawcett Society 2019 *Membership Email* March 8 International Women's Day, London.

Feller, M. 1994 'Open book testing and education for the future' *Studies in Educational Evaluation* 20 (2) 225–238.

Festinger, L. 1957 *A Theory of Cognitive Dissonance* Stanford, CA: Stanford University Press.

Feuerstein, R. 1980 *Instrumental Enrichment* Baltimore, MD: University Park Press.

Feuerstein, R. 1995 *Mediated Learning Experience* London: Regents College Conference July.

Fisher, R. 1995 *Teaching Children to Think* Cheltenham: Stanley Thornes.

Flavell, J.H. 1979 'Metacognition and cognitive monitoring' *American Psychologist* 34 906–911.

Freeman, J. 1991 *Gifted Growing Up* London: Cassell.

Freeman, J. 2010 *Gifted Grown Up* London: Metric.

Freeman, J. 2014 'Case studies in giftedness' invited paper presented at the *ECHA Biennial Conference* Paris.

Fry, H., Ketteridge, S. and Marshall, S. (eds.) 2015 *A Handbook for Teaching and Learning in Higher Education* (4th edition) London: Routledge.

Gagne, R.L. 1973 *The Essentials of Learning* London: Holt, Rinehart and Winston.

Gagné, F. 1995 'Learning about gifts and talent through peer and teacher nominations' In *Nurturing Talent* K.M. Katzko and F.J. Monks (eds) Assen: Van Gorcum (20–30).

Gallagher, J. 1997 'PBL: Where did it come from? What does it do and where is it going?' *Journal for the Education of the Gifted* 21 (1) 3–18.

Galloway, D. and Goodwin, C. 1987 *The Education of Disturbing Children* London: Longman.

Galton, M., Simon, B. and Croll, P. 1980 *Inside the Primary Classroom* London: Routledge and Kegan Paul.

Gibbs, G. 1990 *Learning through Action* London: Further Education Unit.

Gibbs, G. (ed.) 1994 *Improving Student Learning: Theory & Research* Oxford: Oxford Brookes University Press.

Gibbs, G. 2015 'Maximising student learning gain' in H. Fry, S. Ketteridge and S. Marshall (eds.) *A Handbook for Teaching and Learning in Higher Education* (4th edition) London: Routledge 193–208.

Glueck, S. and Glueck, E. 1968 *Delinquents and Non-Delinquents in Perspective* Cambridge, MA: Harvard University Press.

Good, T.L. and Brophy, J.E. 1986 *Educational Psychology: A Realistic Approach* London: Holt Rinehart and Winston.

Gregory, K. and Clarke, M. 2003 'High stakes assessment in England and Singapore' *Theory and Practice* 42 66–78.

Griffin, N.S., Curtiss, J. and McKenzie, L. 1995 'Authentic assessment of able children using a regular classroom observation protocol' *Flying High* (2) Spring 34–42.

Gross, J. 2019 'Why can't our children talk?' *BBC Radio 4* News Interview February 5.

Grossnickle, F.S 1935 'Reliability of certain types of errors in long division with a one-figure divisor' *Journal of Experimental Education* 4 7–14.

Guerra, A. and Kolmos, A. 2011 'Comparing problem-based learning models: Suggestions for their implementation' in J.W. Davies, E. de Graaf and A. Kolmos (eds.) *PBL Across the Disciplines: Research into Best Practice* Aalborg: Aalborg University Press 3–16.

Hackman, S. 2005 'Secondary national strategy: Educating the most able: The challenges we face, the challenges we bring' NACE London Conference April. London Conference.

Hallam, S. 2002 *Ability Grouping in Schools* London: Institute of Education Publications.

Hargreaves, D. 1984 *Improving Secondary Schools* London: ILEA.

Harri-Augstein, S., Smith, M. and Thomas, L. 1982 *Reading to Learn* London: Methuen.

Hattie, J. 2018 *Know Thy Impact: Visible Learning in Theory and Practice* London: Routledge.

Head of Year 2007 'Overcoming underachievement' NACE London Conference, Essex (Personal Communication).

Heng, M.A. and Tam, K.Y.B. 2006 'Reclaiming soul in gifted education: The academic caste system in Asian schools' in B. Wallace and G. Erikson (eds.) *Diversity in Gifted Education: International Perspectives on Global Issues* London: Routledge 178–186.

Higgins, P. 2002 'Teaching and learning in foundation subjects at key stage 3' *Curriculum Briefing* 1 (1) 3–6.

Hillman, P. 2014 'Internet gaming disorder and resilience building' paper given at the *Biennial ECHA Conference* September Ljubljana, Slovenia.

Hirst, P. 1975 *Visiting Professorial Lecture* Kingston upon Thames: Kingston Polytechnic.

HMCI 2007 *The Annual Report of Her Majesty's Chief Inspector for English Schools 2006–2007* London: Ofsted.

HMI 1992 *Provision for Highly Able Pupils in Maintained Schools* London: HMSO.

James, K. and Engelhardt, L. 2012 'The effects of handwriting experience on functional brain development' *Neuroscience and Education* 1 (1) 32–42.

Jeffery, J. 2016 *Teaching Reading Using Games* trugs www.readsuccessfully.com.

Jerrim, J. 2013 *The Reading Gap* Millbank, London: The Sutton Trust.

Jones, J. 1987 *Shakoor Is Born* London: Penguin Books.

Jordan, E. 2001 'Interrupted learning: The traveller paradigm' *Support for Learning* 16 (3) 128–134.

Kellmer-Pringle, M. 1983 *The Needs of Children* London: Longman.

Kelly, G.A. 1955 *The Psychology of Personal Constructs* (Volume 1) New York: Norton.

Kent County Council 2003 *Writing in the Air Project: Nurturing Young Children's Dispositions for Writing* Maidstone: Schools Advisory Service.

Kerry, T. 1983 *Finding and Helping the Able Child* London: Croom Helm.

Kibel, M. 2002 'Linking language to action' in T.R. Miles and E. Miles (eds.) *Dyslexia and Mathematics* (2nd edition) London: Routledge 42–57.

Klein, G. 1993 *Education Towards Race Equality* London: Continuum.

Kolb, D.A. 1984 *Experiential Learning: Experience as a Source of Learning and Development* New York: Prentice Hall.

Labon, D 1973 Assessment Chichester: West Sussex Psychological Services.

Labov, W. 1970 'The logic of non-standard English' in A. Cashdan and E. Grugeon (eds.) *Language and Social Context* London: Kegan Paul.

Lane, C.H. 1990 'Alleviating children's reading and spelling problems' in P.D. Pumfrey and C.D. Elliott (eds.) *Children's Difficulties in Reading, Spelling and Writing* London: Falmer Press, 237–254.

Leat, D. 1999 'Rolling the stone uphill teacher development and the implementation of thinking skills programmes' *Oxford Review of Education* 25 (3) 387–403.

Leroux, J.A. and McMillan, E. 1993 *Smart Teaching: Nurturing Talent in the Classroom and Beyond* Ontario: Pembroke Publishers.

Liberman, A.M., Shankweiler, D.P., Cooper, F.S. and Studdart-Kennedy, M. 1967 'Perception of the speech code' *Psychological Review* 74 (6) 431.

Liberman, I.Y. 1973 'Segmentation of the written word and reading acquisition' *Bulletin of the Orton Society* 23 365–377.

Lipman, M. 1991 *Thinking in Education* Cambridge: Cambridge University Press.

Lockhead, J. 2001 *Thinkback: A User's Guide to Minding the Mind* London: Lawrence Erlbaum.

Long, R. 2005 *Challenging Confrontation* London: David Fulton/NASEN.

Lyth, A. 2004 'Handwriting speed: An aid to communication success?' *Handwriting Today* 3 30–35.

Maidenhead Group of Teachers 1987 *The Motorway Project* Wisbech: LDA.

Maker, C.J. 2013 'Real Engagement in Active Problem Solving (REAPS): Practical ideas and research results' keynote paper presented at the *WCGTC 20th Biennial World Conference* August 10–14 Louisville, Kentucky.

Marton, F. and Säljo, R. 1984 'Approaches to learning' in F. Marton, D.J. Hounsell and N.J. Entwistle (eds.) *The Experience of Learning* Edinburgh: Scottish Academic Press 36–55.

Masheder, M. 1988 *Lets Cooperate* London: M. Masheder.

Maslow, A.H. 1970 *Motivation and Personality* (2nd edition) New York: Harper and Row.

McCluskey, K.W., Baker, P.A., Bergagaard, M. and McCluskey, A.L. 2003 'Interventions with talented at-risk populations with emotional and behavioural difficulties' in D. Montgomery (ed.) *Gifted and Talented Children with SEN; Double Exceptionality* London: David Fulton/NACE 168–186.

McCoach, D.B., Yu, H., Gottfried, A.W. and Gottfried, A.E. 2017 'Developing talent: A longitudinal examination of intellectual ability and academic achievement' *High Ability Studies* 28 (1) 7–28.

McGuinness, C. 1999 *From Thinking Schools to Thinking Classrooms* DfEE Research Report No 115 London: DfEE.

Meyer, E., Tilland-Stafford, A. and Airton, L. (2016) 'Transgender and gender-creative students in PK-12 schools: What can we learn from their teachers?' *Teachers College Record* 118 (8) 080308.

Miles, T.R. and Miles, E. (eds.) 1992 *Dyslexia and Mathematics* London: Routledge.

MISST 2019 'Music in Secondary Schools Project report' *BBC Radio 4* World at One, December 23.

Mongon, D. and Hart, S. 1989 *Improving Classroom Behaviour: New Directions for Teachers and Learners* London: Cassell.

Montgomery, D. 1977 'Teaching pre-reading through training in pattern recognition' *The Reading Teacher* 30 (6) 216–225.

Montgomery, D. 1979 *Visual Pattern Recognition Test and Training Materials for Early Reading* Windsor: NFER.

Montgomery, D. 1981 'Education comes of age' *School Psychology International* 1 1–3.

Montgomery, D. 1983 'Teaching thinking skills in the school curriculum' *School Psychology International* 3 108–112.

Montgomery, D. 1985 *The Special Educational Needs of More Able Children* Kingston upon Thames: Learning Difficulties Research Project.

Montgomery, D. 1989 *Managing Behaviour Problems* Sevenoaks: Hodder and Stoughton.

Montgomery, D. 1990 *Children with Learning Difficulties* London: Cassell.

Montgomery, D. 1993 'Fostering learner managed learning in teacher education' in N. Graves (ed.) *Learner Managed Learning* Leeds: Higher Education for Capability/World Education Fellowship 59–70.

Montgomery, D. 1994 'The role of metacognition and metalearning in teacher education' in G. Gibbs (ed.) *Improving Student Learning* Oxford: Oxford Brookes Centre for Staff Development 227–253.

Montgomery, D. 1995 'Subversive activity' *Education* 21 April 16–17.

Montgomery, D. 1996 *Educating the Able* London: Cassell.

Montgomery, D. 1997a *Spelling: Remedial Strategies* London: Cassell.

Montgomery, D. 1997b *Developmental Spelling Handbook* Maldon: Learning Difficulties Research Project www.ldrp.org.uk.

Montgomery, D. 1998 *Reversing Lower Attainment* London: David Fulton.

Montgomery, D. (ed.) 2000 *Able Underachievers* London: Whurr/Wiley.

Montgomery, D. 2002 *Helping Teachers Develop Through Classroom Observation* London: David Fulton.

Montgomery, D. (ed.) 2003 *Gifted and Talented Children with SEN: Double Exceptionality* London: NACE/David Fulton.

Montgomery, D. 2007 *Spelling, Handwriting and Dyslexia* London: Routledge.

Montgomery, D. 2008a 'Cohort analysis of writing in year 7 after 2, 4, and 7 years of the National Literacy Strategy' *Support for Learning* 22 (1) 3–11.

Montgomery, D. 2008b 'Effective teaching and learning strategies for the gifted and talented' in J. Fortikova (ed.) *Successful Teaching of the Exceptionally Gifted Child* Praha: Triton Press 93–138, 37–138.

Montgomery, D. (ed.) 2009 *Able, Gifted and Talented Underachievers* (2nd edition) Chichester: Wiley.

Montgomery, D. 2015 *Teaching Gifted Children with SEN: Supporting Dual and Multiple Exceptionality* London: Routledge.

Montgomery, D. 2017a *Dyslexia-Friendly Approaches to Reading, Spelling and Handwriting* London: Routledge.

Montgomery, D. 2017b 'Identifying and remediating dyslexia in the reception year: A new possibility?' *Support for Learning* 31 (1) 69–80.

Montgomery, D. 2017c 'Using classroom observation to improve teaching and prevent failure with the "five star plan" and audit system' in J.P. Bakken (ed.) *Classrooms: Assessment Practices for Teachers and Student Improvement Strategies* (Volume 1) New York: Nova Publications e-book 143–171.

Montgomery, D. 2019 *Dyslexia and Gender Bias: A Critical Review* London: Routledge.

Morton, J. 1980 'The logogen model and orthographic structure' in U. Frith (ed.) *Cognitive Processes in Spelling* London: Academic Press 117–134.

Moseley, J. 1991 'Setting up and running circles of support' *SEBDA News* (15) Spring 20–23.

Mueller, P.A. and Oppenheimer, D.M. 2014 'The pen is mightier than the keyboard: Advantages of longhand over laptop note taking' *Psychological Science* 1–10 DOI: 10.1177/0956797614524581 pss.sagepub.com.

Munro, J. 1996 *Gifted Students' Learning. Basing the Teaching of Gifted Students on a Model of Learning* Melbourne: Educational Assistance.

National Literacy Trust 2019 *Email Information Service*, London March 12.

NARA-III 1999 *Neale Analysis of Reading Abilities* (3rd edition) Dunn, J. and Dunn, M. London: MacMillan.

Neale, M.D. 1997 *Neale Analysis of Reading Ability* (2nd edition) Windsor: NFER-Nelson.

Neville, M. and Pugh, A. 1977 'Ability to use a book: the effect of teaching' *Reading* 11 (3) 13–18.

NFER 1983 *Study Skills* Windsor: NFER.

Niehart, M. 2011 'The revised profiles of the gifted: A research based approach' keynote address *WCGTC 19th Biennial World Conference* August 8–12 Prague.

Noguera, T. and Rawlings, A. 2019 'Envisioning the Helix learning model: A learning journey from theory to transdisciplinary pedagogy and practice' in press.

OECD 1972 *Note by the Secretariat* Paris: OECD.

Ofsted 1998 *The Annual Report of Her Majesty's Chief Inspector for English Schools 1996–1997* London: Ofsted.

Ofsted 2006 *The Annual Report of Her Majesty's Chief Inspector for English Schools 2005–2006* London: Ofsted.

Ofsted 2010 *The Annual Report of Her Majesty's Chief Inspector for English Schools 2009–2010* London: Ofsted.

Ofsted 2019 *The Annual Report of Her Majesty's Chief Inspector for English Schools 2018–2019* London: Ofsted.

ONS 2019 *Overview of the UK National Population Statistics* Estimate of non UK EU citizens 9th August 2018 London: Office for National Statistics.

Osborn, A.F. 1963 *Applied Imagination: Principles and Processes of Creative Problem Solving* New York: Scribner.

Pascal, L. 1998 'One day study skills programme' NASEN Conference Invitation Pamphlet. Tamworth.

Passow, H. 1990 'Needed research and development in educating of high ability children' *European Journal of High Ability* 1 (4) 15–24.

Paul, R.W 1990 'Critical thinking in North America' in A.J. Binker (ed.) *Critical Thinking: What Every Person Needs to Know in a Rapidly Changing World* Sonoma: Sonoma State University 18–42.

Peters, M.L. 1967 *Spelling: Caught or Taught?* London: Routledge and Kegan Paul.

Peters, M.L. 1985 *Spelling: Caught or Taught?* (2nd edition) London: Routledge and Kegan Paul.

Piaget, J. 1952 *Origins of Intelligence in Children* (2nd edition) New York: International Universities Press.

Pintrich, P.R. and Zusho, A. 2002 'Student motivation and self-regulated learning in the college classroom' in J.C. Smart and W.G. Tierney (eds.) *Higher Education: Handbook of Theory and Research,* Vol XVII, New York: Agathon Press.

Pizalski, J. 2012 'From cyberbullying to electronic aggression: typology of the phenomenon' *Emotional and Behavioural Difficulties* 17 (3–4) 305–318.

Plucker, J.A. and Peters, S.J. 2016 *Excellence Gaps in Education. Expanding opportunities for talented youth* Cambridge MA: Harvard Education Press.

Pollard, A. 1997 *Reflective Teaching in the Primary School* London: Cassell.

Pomerantz, M. and Pomerantz, K. 2003 *Listening to Able Underachievers* London: David Fulton.

QCA 2001 *Developing Skills* London: QCA.

Quinn, D.M., Desruisseaux, T.M. and Nkansah-Amankra, A. 2019 'Does 'the Achievement Gap' evoke a negative stereotype? What the research says' *Education Week* 39 (16) 24.

Race, P. 1992 'Developing competence' *Professorial Inaugural Lectures* Glamorgan: University of Glamorgan. Radio 4 2019 Today Programme London: BBC.

Raven, J. 2010 *Raven's Progressive Matrices* London: Pearson Assessment.

Rawlings, A. (ed.) 1996 *Ways and Means Today: Conflict Resolution Training and Resources* Kingston upon Thames: Kingston Friends Workshop Group, Eden Street.

Reis, S.M. and McCoach, D.B. 2000 'The underachievement of gifted students: What do we know and where do we go?' *Gifted Child Quarterly* 44 152–170.

Renzulli, J. and Reis, S.M. 2008 'What is this thing called giftedness and how to develop it? A 25 year perspective' in J. Fortikova (ed.) *Successful Teaching of the Exceptionally Gifted Child* Praha: Triton Press 8–92.

Rey, A. 1934 'A procedure for evaluating educability: Some applications in psychopathology' *Archives de Psychologie* 24 297–337.

Riding, K. and Rayner, R. 1998 *Cognitive Styles and Learning Strategies* London: David Fulton.

Rimm, S. 1986 *The Underachievement Syndrome: Causes and Cures* Watertown, WI: Apple Publishing Co.

Roaf, C. 1998 'Slow hand: A secondary school survey of handwriting speed and legibility' *Support for Learning* 13 (1) 39–42.

Robins, L. 1966 *Deviant Children Grow Up 1922–66* Baltimore: Williams and Williams.

Rogers, B. 2007 *Behaviour Management: A Whole School Approach* London: Sage.

Rose, J. 2006 *Rose Review: Independent Review of the Teaching of Early Reading: Final Report* London: DfES.

Rosencrans, G. 1998 *The Spelling Book: Teaching Children How to Spell* USA: International Reading/Literacy Association. Delaware, Newark.

Rosenthal, R and Jacobsen, L. 1968 *Pygmalion in the Classroom* New York: Holt, Rinehart and Winston.

Royce-Adams, W. 1977 *Developing Reading Versatility* New York: Rinehart and Winston.

Rutter, M.L. 1985 *Helping Troubled Children* Harmondsworth: Penguin.

Rutter, M.L., Caspi, A., Fergusson, D., Horwood, L.J., Goodman, R., Maughan, B., Moffatt, T.B., Meltzer, H.C. and Carroll, J. 2004 'Sex differences in developmental reading disability' *Journal of the American Medical Association* 291 (9/16) 2007–2012.

Rutter, M.L., Maughan, M., Mortimore, P. and Ouston, J. 1979 *Fifteen Thousand Hours* London: Open Books.

Rutter, M.L., Tizard, J. and Whitmore, K. (eds.) 1970 *Education, Health and Behaviour* London: Longman.

Ryan, R.M. and Deci, E.I 2000 'Intrinsic and extrinsic motivation: Classic definitions and new directions' *Contemporary Educational Psychology* 25 54–67.

Scheerer, M. 1963 'Problem-solving' *Scientific American* 208 (4) 118–128.

Schools Council 1980 *Study Skills in the Secondary School* (Pilot edition) London: Schools Council.

Scott MacDonald, W. 1972 *Battle in the Classroom* Brighton: Intext Publications.

SED Scottish Education Department 1978 *The Education of Pupils with Learning Difficulties in Primary and Secondary Schools: A Progress Report by HMI* Edinburgh: HMSO.

Sereny, G. 1999 Cries Unheard. The Story of Mary Bell London: Macmillan.

Sevcikova, A., Smahel, D. and Otavova, M. 2012 'The perception of cyberbullying in adolescent victims' *Emotional and Behavioural Difficulties* 17 (3–4) 319–328.

Sharp, R. and Green, A. 1975 *Education and Social Control: A Study in Progressive Primary Education* London: Routledge and Kegan Page.

Shayer, M. and Adey, P. (eds.) 2002 *Learning Intelligence: Cognitive Acceleration across the Curriculum from 3–25 Years* Buckingham: Open University Press.

Silverman, L.K. 1989 'Invisible gifts, invisible handicaps' *Roeper Review* 12 (1) 37–42.

Silverman, L.K. 2002 *Upside-Down Brilliance: The Visual-Spatial Learner* Denver: DeLeon Publishing.

Silverman, L.K. 2004 'Poor handwriting: A major cause of underachievement' www. gifteddevelopment.com/Articles/vsl/v37.pdf (Accessed 04/2007).

Sisk, D. 2000 'Overcoming underachievement of gifted and talented students' in D. Montgomery (ed.) *Able Underachievers* London: Whurr 111–126.

Sisk, D. 2003 'Marching to a different drummer' in D. Montgomery (ed.) *Gifted and Talented Children with SEN: Double Exceptionality* London: NACE/David Fulton.

Skilbeck, M. 1989 *School Development and New Approaches to Learning: Trends and Development* Paris: OECD.

Smith, D.J. 2017 *The Sleep of Reason: The Jamie Bulger Case* London: Faber and Faber.

Smith, D.J. and Tomlinson, S. 1989 *The School Effect: A Study of Multi-Racial Comprehensives* London: PSI Publications.

Snowling, M.J. 2004 'Language skills and learning to read' *The Psychologist* 17 (8) 439–440.

Snowling, M.J. 2019 'Interview about Dyslexia' *BBC Radio 4* February.

Solity, J. 2018 'Systematic synthetic phonics: A possible cause of pupils' literacy difficulties' lecture *11th International Conference of the BDA* April 12–14 Telford, UK.

Soriano de Alencar, E. 1995 'Developing creative abilities at university level' *European Journal for High Ability* 6 (1) 82–90.

Sousa, D.A. 2003 *How the Gifted Brain Learns* Thousand Oaks CA: Corwin Press.

Spender, D. 1983 *Invisible Women the Schooling Scandal* London: Writers and Readers.

Stamm, M. 2005 'Underachieving highly gifted students' *Gifted Education International* 20 (1) 7–11.

Stoeger, H. 2006 'First steps towards and epistemic learner model' *High Ability Studies* 17 (1) 17–41.

Stones, E. 1979 *Pychopedagogy* London: Methuen.

Sutton Trust 2010 'Childhood poverty and early cognitive development' by J. Waldfogel the Sutton Trust Millbank, London.

Sutton Trust 2019 'Summary of the report on the Trust research by Joanna Williams on BBC Radio 4' *Today Programme* February 2.

Swartz, R.J. and Parks, S. 1994 *Infusing Critical and Creative Thinking Into Elementary Instruction* Pacific Grove, CA: Critical Thinking Press and Software.

Taba, H. 1962 *Curriculum Development: Theory and Practice* New York: Harcourt Brace Jovanovitch.

Tannenbaum, A.J. 1993 'History of giftedness and gifted education in world perspective' in K.A. Heller, F.J. Monks and A.H. Passow (eds.) *International Handbook of Research and Development of Giftedness and Talent* Oxford: Pergamon 3–28.

Taylor, Sir W. 1986 'Education and the CATE criteria' *New Education Fellowship Conference* June Kingston Polytechnic, Kingston-upon-Thames.

Terman, L.M. 1925 *Genetic Studies of Genius: Vol. 1 Mental and Physical Traits of a Thousand Gifted Children* Stanford, CA: Stanford University Press.

Terman, L.M. 1954 'The discovery and encouragement of exceptional talent' *American Psychologist* 9 221–230.

Thomas, L. and Harri-Augstein, S. 1975 *Reading to Learn Project Report* London: Brunel University.

Timpson, E. 2019 *Timpson Review of Exclusions* London: DfE May.

Torrance, E.P. 1963 *Education and the Creative Potential* Minneapolis: University of Minnesota.

Torrance, E.P. 1999 *Torrance Test of Creative Thinking: Norms and Technical Manual* Bensenville, IL: Scholastic Testing Services.

Tymms, P. 2004 'Are standards rising in English primary school?' *British Educational Research Journal* 30 (4) 477–494.

van Daal, V. 2018 'A longitudinal study of self-teaching in learning to read and spell' keynote lecture *11th International Conference of the BDA* April 12–14 Telford, UK.

Van de Craen, P. 2016 'Fostering talent through multilingual education' EU Conference on the Development of Giftedness and Talent, Bratislava, Slovakia, September.

Vygotsky, L.S. 1978 *Mind in Society: The Development of Higher Mental Processes* Cambridge, MA: Harvard University Press.

Wallace, B. 2000 *Teaching the Very Able Child* London: David Fulton.

Wallace, B. 2002 *Teaching Thinking Skills across the Early Years: A Practical Approach for Children Ages 4–7* London: David Fulton/NACE.

Wallace, B. 2009 'What do we mean by an "enabling curriculum" that raises achievement for all learners? An examination of the TASC problem solving framework: Thinking actively in a social context' in D. Montgomery (ed.) *Able, Gifted and Talented Underachievers* (2nd edition) Chichester: Wiley 59–84.

Wallace, B. and Eriksson, G. (eds.) 2006 *Diversity in Gifted Education: International Perspectives on Global Issues* London: Routledge.

Wallace, B., Fitton, S., Leyden, S., Montgomery, D., Pomerantz, M. and Winstanley, C. 2008 *Raising the Achievement of Able Gifted and Talented Pupils within an Inclusive School Framework* London: G and T/NACE.

Wallace, B., Leyden, S., Montgomery, D., Pomerantz, M. and Winstanley, C. 2009 *Raising the Achievement of Able Gifted and Talented Pupils within an Inclusive School Framework* London: Routledge.

Warwick, I. 2009 'Overcoming class, race and cultural factors in underachievement' in D. Montgomery (ed.) *Gifted, Talented and Able Underachievers* Chichester: Wiley/Routledge 219–263.

Watson, J. 1996 *Reflection through Interaction: The Classroom Experience of Children with Learning Difficulties* London: Falmer Press.

Watson, J. 2001 'Social constructivism in the classroom' *Support for Learning* 16 (3) 140–147.

Watson, J. and Johnson, R. 2005 *Accelerating Reading Attainment: The Effectiveness of Synthetic Phonics* Edinburgh: The Scottish Office.

Weber, K. 1982 *The Teacher Is the Key* Toronto: Methuen.

Wedge, P. and Prosser, H. 1979 *Born to Fail?* London: Arrow Books.

Weikart, D. 1967 *Preschool Intervention: A Preliminary Report from the Perry Preschool Project* Ann Arbour: Michigan Campus Publishers.

Weikart, D. 1998 'Report of an international comparative study of pre-school education' *24 Hour World News* June 4 Strasbourg.

Weinstein, C.E., Goetz, E.T. and Alexander, P.A. (eds.) 1988 *Learning and Study Strategies* New York: Academic Press.

West, D.J. 1967 *The Young Offender* Harmondsworth: Penguin.

West, D.J. 1982 *Delinquency* London: Heinemann.

Whitehead, J. and Huxtable, M. 2009 'How can inclusive and inclusional understandings of gifts/talents be developed educationally?' in D. Montgomery (ed.) *Gifted, Talented and Able Underachievers* Chichester: Wiley/Routledge 85–110.

Whitehead, M.R. 2004 *Language and Literacy in the Early Years* (3rd edition) London: Sage.

Whitmore, J.R. 1982 *Giftedness, Conflict and Underachievement* Boston: Allyn and Bacon.

Whybra, J. 1980 *The Battle of Isandlwana Curriculum Project* Chelmsford: Essex County Council.

Williams, J. 2019 'Sutton Trust Research BBC Radio 4' *Today Programme* February 4.

Wilson, G. 2019 garywilsonraisingboysachievement.com www.oxfordowl.co.uk (Accessed 06/04/2019).

Wilson, J. 1994 'Phonological awareness training: A new approach to phonics' *PATOSS Bulletin* November 5–8.

Wilson, M. and Evans, M. 1980 *Education of Disturbed Pupils* Schools Council Working Paper 65 London: Methuen.

Woodhead, C. 1998 'The Radio 4' *Today Interview* 8.10 am September 6.

Wray, D. 2005 'Raising the achievement of boys in writing' NACE London Conference April. London Conference.

Index